TURKEY
A SHORT HISTORY

Roderic H. Davison

Second Edition

THE EOTHEN PRESS
HUNTINGDON
ENGLAND

To the memory of E.H.D. and W.S.D.
L.A.D. and S.D.

British Library CIP

Davison, Roderic H
  Turkey: a short history - 2nd enl.ed
  I. Turkey, history
  I. Title
  956-1

First published 1968 by Prentice Hall. Inc., New Jersey entitled
Turkey (The Modern Nations in Historical Perspective) and
reprinted by The Eothen Press, 1981

Second edition published by The Eothen Press, 1988

ISBN 0 906719 13 5 Hard covers
ISBN 0 906719 14 3 Paperback

Preface

to the First Edition

The Republic of Turkey was established in 1923. It emerged, after a bitter struggle for national independence, from the ruins of the six-century-old Ottoman Empire. Modern Turkey has inherited much from the people, institutions, and culture of that empire. It has also made such revolutionary changes that it is a new nation. The continuity and the changes are the subject of this book - the rise, grandeur, and decline of the Ottoman Empire, the process of westernization, and the rise and development of the Republic.

The Turkish achievement in the half-century since the death of the Ottoman Empire has been unique. In a pattern quite untypical of developing nations, authoritarian government has yielded to democratic government and competitive multi-party politics. This poses special problems for the Republic. If the Turks can persevere in their efforts to build a strong economy and a stable and enlightened society without returning to authoritarian rule, they will have demonstrated again, as they did in other ways in building the Ottoman Empire, an extraordinary talent. They have centuries of experience to draw on and a new ideal to inspire them, but the road ahead is still rough. They know it and frequently quote the exhortation of Atatürk, founder of the Republic: "Turk! Be proud! Work! Be confident!"

R.H.D.

Washington, D.C., February 1968

v

Preface

to the Second Edition

Since February 1968, when the foregoing Preface was written for the first edition of this history, there have been many new developments in Turkey. The most important of these form the subject of the newly added Chapter 10, which has been almost completely written by Professor C. H. Dodd, formerly of the University of Hull and now Chairman of the Modern Turkish Studies Programme in the School of Oriental and African Studies of the University of London. In first draft this chapter was kindly read by Dr. W. Hale.

I regret the lack of opportunity to make changes in the text of the first nine chapters. Readers will realize, therefore, that references in these chapters to "modern Turkey" and to "today", as well as statements in the present tense, refer to the late 1960s. Many of these statements are still valid in the late 1980s. Others require modification or supplement such as will be found in Chapter 10.

The original bibliography has been amplified in two ways. A selection of important works on Turkish history that have appeared in the last twenty years has been added. Further, the most useful titles on recent and contemporary Turkey are also included.

In Chapter 10 all Turkish words, including names, are spelled as in Turkey today.

R.H.D.

Washington, D.C., July 1988

Note on Turkish
Spelling and Names

Turkish words, including names, are usually spelled here as they are spelled in modern Turkey, with a few changes to indicate pronunciation for the English reader.

The Turkish alphabet is phonetic. Most Turkish consonants are pronounced as in English and most of the vowels as in Italian, but there are a few variations. The Turkish *ö* and *ü* are like the German, or like the vowels in the French *peu* and *tu*. Dotted *i* in Turkish is like *i* in "sit". This dot is omitted here in the case of capital letters, as Istanbul or Inönü. Turkish has an undotted *i* which the type in this book does not indicate. Among the consonants, Turkish *ç* and *ş* are here converted to *ch* and *sh*, as they are pronounced—thus the treaty of Küchük Kaynarja, instead of Küçük Kaynarja (often "Kutchuk Kaynardji" in English). Thus also pasha instead of *paşa*. The Turkish *c* is pronounced like the *j* in "jet"—thus Turkish Cemal is here spelled Jemal, and Kaynarca becomes Kaynarja as above.

In 1934 all Turks were obliged to take family names. When those who lived beyond 1934 are mentioned before that date, the family name is added in brackets—thus Rauf [Orbay]. Mustafa Kemal [Atatürk] and Ismet [Inönü] are so well known that their family names are not added.

Corrigenda

Contents

ix

x

1

Contemporary Turkey

At 9:05 A.M. each November 10 activity in Turkey comes to a halt. Traffic stops. Automobile occupants get out and stand quietly at attention. For five minutes the country remembers in silence the moment of death of Mustafa Kemal Atatürk, creator and first president of the Turkish Republic.

Atatürk died in 1938. Modern Turkey is peopled by a generation and more who know him only through education and tradition. Yet Turkey still lives in the long shadow he cast. His picture is everywhere. Although Turkey has come a long way since his death, the guiding policies which he laid down have fundamentally been followed: the creation and preservation of a territorially limited national state for the Turks; the inculcation of a Turkish national consciousness; the breaking of the hold of Islam over state, law, and education; the westernization not only of material life but of institutions, minds, and customs; the rapid development of the economy; an avoidance of class divisions and growth of a sense of solidarity; a devotion to the republican form of government; and finally, the pursuit of peaceful foreign relations. Atatürk, of course, was not alone in encouraging these policies nor in working them out. Nor could he have achieved what he did without the basis provided by a century of reform effort before him. He was, nevertheless, the chief driving force in the creation of modern Turkey, and some of the above-mentioned aims—especially the nation-state, the secularization, and the republic—were peculiarly his. Together the policies Atatürk laid down provide a convenient frame within which to view modern Turkey.

The Turkish national state. The nation-state of today is compact and limited to territory which is essentially Turkish-peopled. Turkey includes a southeastern corner of Europe, called Thrace, but its bulk is in Asia Minor—Anatolia—on the other side of the vital straits of the Bosporus, the Sea of Marmara, and the Dardanelles. Turkey's total area is just under 300,000 square miles, somewhat larger than Texas, or about the size of France and Great Britain together. This is a far cry from the sprawling, heterogeneous Ottoman Empire out of which, after World War I had shattered its remnant, modern Turkey grew. Republican Turkey no longer bears the old imperial burden. Its territory is more easily governed and defended. Its Anatolian bulk, extending from the lush shores and good harbors of the Aegean Sea across the rugged central plateau to eastern highlands (where Büyük Ağri Daği, known in the West as Mt. Ararat, is the highest point), is essentially the Turkish homeland. This is where the Seljuk Turks, forerunners of the Ottomans, settled. From Anatolia the Ottoman Empire expanded; to it the republican center has returned. The imperial capital was Istanbul, situated on the European shore of the Bosporus. It is still Turkey's largest metropolis with its nearly two million people. The symbol of the republic, however, is its capital on the Anatolian plateau, Ankara, rapidly grown over the past half-century from a small town to a city of nearly one million.

Turkey is for the Turks. The 1965 census reported approximately 31,391,000 inhabitants. A linguistic breakdown of this total is not yet available, but more than 90 per cent must speak Turkish as their mother-tongue, since this was already the percentage reported by the 1960 census. Over six per cent of the remainder in 1960 were Kurdish-speakers. Arabic, Greek, Armenian, Laz, "Jewish," Georgian, Circassian, Bulgarian, and Croatian are spoken by smaller groups. Some of these groups represent peoples conquered by the Ottoman Turks; others are in Turkey today because they fled from persecution by western Christian states, or Tsarist Russia, or Soviet regimes, at various times from the sixteenth century to the twentieth. The overwhelming characteristic of republican Turkey, as opposed to its Ottoman predecessor, is the linguistic homogeneity of its people, despite some differences in dialect and accent. This population is a young and growing one. Well over half are below the age of 15. In the first two decades of the republic there was much concern with underpopulation. Recently the concern has shifted dramatically. The annual growth rate of 2.5 to 3 per cent a year has led the government to embark on a broad program of birth-control.

Turkish national consciousness. The Turks have a sense of national consciousness—of their Turkishness. This does not mean that they are pure Turk in blood descent from their ancestors of Central Asia, despite the fact that some families have taken the surname Öztürk ("Pureturk"). Over the course of centuries there has been much amalgamation through marriage and conversion to Islam with peoples who lived in Anatolia and in the Balkan peninsula. The modern republic has stimulated interest not only in early Turkish history, but in the history of the pre-Turkish peoples of Anatolia, as far back as the Trojans and the Hittites, from whose civilizations and descendants later arrivals, including the Turks, inevitably absorbed various traits. The Turkishness of modern Turks is an awareness of a cultural—particularly of a linguistic—unity, and of a common history; in short, of a common Turkish nationality. The achievement of this sense of unity has come only under the republic. It is not yet complete, nor is it equally felt by all Turks.

During the period of the Ottoman Empire a Turk might consider himself a Muslim, or a subject of the Ottoman sultan, or a native of this or that locality. He would not be likely to think of himself as a Turk, a term which then was used by the educated Ottoman elite to refer disparagingly to an uneducated tribesman or peasant. The common Turkish language had been overlaid by so much borrowing from Arabic and Persian that the literary amalgam used by writers and government officials was incomprehensible to the villager. In later Ottoman days language simplification was begun; the process was speeded up under the republic, with a movement for "purification" that in the 1930s reached its peak by substituting unfamiliar Turkish words even for Arabic expressions in common use. Although the process has slowed down, in the 1960s Turkish words are still being put into use in place of Arabic. Every so often an official notice is circulated indicating a new Turkish word created by government fiat. Language is the most obvious index of Turkishness, but modern Turkish nationalism goes much deeper, to a common loyalty to the nation-state. An educated Turk today will usually think of himself first as a Turk, then as a Muslim or native of a locality. An uneducated villager is increasingly likely to do so.

Breaking the Muslim hold. Modern Turkey is a secular state. The hold of Islam over public life has been broken. This official secularism has not changed the religious affiliations of the people—99 per cent of Turkey's inhabitants are Muslims. Although some of the educated, urban Muslims are quite secular in thought and habit, just as are educated, urban Christians in other countries, the influence of Islam remains strong. The evidences of Islam are everywhere: not only the mosques of the past, but new ones; fasting during the day in the month of Ramazan; boatloads and busloads of pilgrims going to Mecca. There are the everyday expressions like "inshallah" ("if God pleases"); the census figures that show more married women than married men despite the prohibition of polygamy by law; the Koran placed atop the mast of a newly acquired destroyer. Open observance of religious rites and customs has been commoner, and has found more government support, in the years since 1950. Religion can still spark reactionary political movements.

Yet the divorce of government from Islam, instituted under Atatürk in the 1920s, has lasted. Once there was the greatest of the Islamic empires; now there is a secular republic. Once there was a sultan who claimed also to be *calif* of all Muslims; now there is neither sultan nor calif, but a president who holds no religious office. Once the law was based on the *sheriat*, the religious law of Islam; now the law is an adaptation of secular codes used in western Europe. Once education was mainly religious, controlled by the learned men of Islam and supported by funds from pious foundations; now education is secular (even though classes in religious instruction have been restored in primary schools) and the teachers, themselves the product of secular training, are paid by the government.

The westernization of Turkey. Modern Turkey is a part of the western world. In a sense the Turks have faced west ever since they migrated west from the outer edges of China, since they turned their backs on shamanism and Buddhism to adopt Islam, one of the great western religions. In a sense the Ottoman Empire itself was always western, since it took as its base not the classic Arab and Persian lands of Islam but the Byzantine kernel of Anatolia and the Balkans. But from the sixteenth century, a great gulf had developed between the Ottoman Turks and western Europe, a gulf reinforced by but not confined to the differences between Islam and Christianity. The gulf was most visible in technology and industry—in material things, from factories and weaponry to gadgets and clothing. It was almost as obvious, and more significant, in attitudes toward change and progress, science, education, commerce. Conscious efforts, increasingly important, to reduce the gap in one way or another were made by Ottoman rulers and statesmen beginning in the late 18th century. By the end of the first World War much westernization had occurred, but in republican Turkey the pace has been even faster.

Today the material aspect of westernization is immediately visible, particularly in the larger cities. Istanbul now has western-style traffic jams—though if one flees the mass of immobilized autos in front of the Egyptian Bazaar, it is only to be caught in a complete eastern-style jam of horse-drawn wagons in the narrower streets behind it. The electric refrigerator, the radio, the tape-recorder, the washing machine, the latest antibiotics, and all manner of plastic gadgets are increasingly common, and many of them are now locally manufactured rather than imported.

The whole process of secularization has also been a part of westernization. Like the legal system, the state school system has drawn on western—in this case principally French—models since its inception. The schools themselves are not only an index but a major agency of westernization, spreading literacy in the new westernized alphabet adopted in 1928. There is a long way to go, but the literacy is now up to nearly 50 per cent. The universities too are fashioned on western lines. Before World War I there was only one, in Istanbul. By the later 1960s there were seven, including two technical universities. Knowledge of western languages is increasingly widespread, primarily French until World War II, and English thereafter. Borrowed Western words are sprinkled throughout Turkish speech. At one point this process went to excess, with French imports like *fuar* (*foire*), *garshefi* (*chef de gare*), *bröve* (*brevet*). "While trying to save ourselves from the deserts of Arabia and the gardens of Shiraz, we fall into the middle of the Quartier Latin," complained a writer during the war.[1] But Western words remain embedded in popular speech—*futbol*, *parti*, and hundreds of others. One hears today much Turkish folk-music, but as much western music. Avant garde theatre, painting, sculpture, poetry, and novels spring from the westernized artists, some of whom have

[1] Mustafa Namik Canki, in *Cumhuriyet* (July 25, 1942).

now come to the ultimate point of westernization by self-consciously reviving "folklorik" themes of dance, design, and melody.

The westernization of modern Turkey can be measured on a triple comparative scale—geographically, west to east; demographically, city to village; and socially, men to women. In general, the regions nearer Europe are more westernized than those near the Iranian frontier. In 1963, for example, Istanbul had 16,170 private autos and 12,370 taxis; Bingöl province had one private auto and two taxis. This, of course, is primarily a commentary on roads and wealth, but it can serve as a crude index of the degree of westernization in education and attitudes as well. The primitive conditions in the neighboring eastern provinces of Mush and Erzurum were forcibly brought to public attention by the disastrous earthquakes there in 1966.

The city-village contrast can be sharply drawn also in material things, but no less so in attitudes toward religion and society. A sensation was created among the urban, educated elite in 1950 by the publication of Mahmut Makal's little book *Bizim Köy* ("That Village of Ours").[2] The author, a young teacher in a village school, drew a realistic picture not only of the poverty of goods in the village, but of the poverty of mind—of the suspicion, ignorance, and superstition of the villagers. To many city Turks, as to many city-dwellers in all countries, even in the United States, the pockets of poverty and ignorance are simply unknown. Today Turkey has scientists, physicians, entrepreneurs, administrators, scholars, engineers, and merchants who are at the top on any western scale, though still not enough for her own needs; but at the same time she suffers from the social imbalance that characterizes all countries, and the developing countries more than others. The top men and women are concentrated in a few cities. Others seek wider opportunities and better salaries abroad, rather than work in Turkish towns and villages. The "brain drain" is a problem. In 1965 it was estimated that between two and three thousand Turkish physicians were working abroad, while countless villages had not a single doctor.

As for the contrast between men and women, it increases as one goes down the social scale. Professions and commercial employment are freely open to women and many are prominent and successful. A woman is not as free as a man to do as she wishes even in highly educated city groups, but a woman in a small provincial town still is

[2] See reference to the translated version A *Village in Anatolia*, in bibliography.

bound by traditional convention, and may still conceal her face in public. The peasant woman of the village is in the latter respect a bit freer.

Westernization, however qualified, is nevertheless an observable and continuing trend. It has been since the mid-nineteenth century and is now irreversible. It is producing not a simple copy of any western country, but a Turkish synthesis that is *sui generis*.

Economic development. Modern Turkey has a developing economy with all the problems that accompany such a change. About three-fourths of her people are engaged in agriculture, which supplies food-stuffs and the principal export items—cotton, tobacco, fruits. Since 1948 agricultural production has grown by about 4 per cent a year, barely keeping ahead of the population increase. In the late 1960s Turkish agriculture still faced the need to produce more. Partly this was a question of mechanization, of replacing the usual iron-tipped wood plow and squeaky ox-cart with the tractor which has become fairly common—about 50,000 in 1963, as compared to 1,750 in 1948. Partly it was a question of intelligent use and maintenance of this and other machines. The tractor has become a status symbol, and peasant owners sometimes are tempted to use it for racing, tugs of war, or riding into town to the cinema. Partly it was a question of irrigation on the comparatively arid central plateau, of land reform to give landless farmers a stake in the soil, of halting fragmentation of farm plots to create economically viable units. It is obvious, by comparison to late Ottoman days, that an agricultural revolution is under way, but much is yet to be accomplished. Debates in the government and in the press show that the problems are widely recognized.

Industrialization is also rapidly increasing, and the more that agricultural exports earn, the more foreign exchange is available for the necessary investment in machinery. The industrial revolution is only now coming to Turkey. Little large scale industry developed during the Ottoman days, despite sporadic efforts. Now Turkey has two large iron and steel works, at Karabük and Ereğli, the latter opened only in 1965. Electric power is constantly growing; with the laying of the foundation stone for the large Keban dam on the Euphrates in 1966, a significant new increase was in prospect. To manufactures of textiles, cement, glass, and other items there was added in 1965 the first domestic production of an automobile, the Anadol (with a fibre-glass body), and over half of its component parts are locally made. Deposits of iron, coal, chrome, copper, and petroleum are being exploited. In 1967 a 300-mile pipeline from the oil refinery at Batman to the port of Iskenderun went into operation. Industrialization too has its share of problems—the finding of the capital, the locating of industry in economically sound rather than politically or strategically determined areas, the training of skilled labor and managerial talent, the cutting through the red tape of bureaucratic control.

The economy that has developed is a mixture of state capitalism and private enterprise, pragmatic rather than doctrinaire, although *étatism*—state-directed, controlled, and financed development—was in the 1930s the accepted formula, and still continues in part today. Since 1963 two five-year development plans have aimed at an annual growth rate of 7 per cent. The visitor to Turkey today finds both scepticism and a mood of cautious optimism. The problems of economic development are many, but the opportunities also are many. Some businessmen see the country as just on the point of bursting forth—resources are there, skills are developing, the rising material desires of the people await satisfaction. Compared to other Middle Eastern countries, excepting those with the largest petroleum deposits, Turkey has good prospects.

Development of Social Solidarity. Modern Turkey is a society without class prejudices but with deep social divisions. This apparent paradox is explained by the fact that despite the very real differences between various social groups, the Turks do not think of themselves in terms of class—political parties are not organized on such lines, the ideology of the republic has avoided such distinctions, and there is considerable and increasing social mobility. From the early days of the Ottoman Empire it has been possible for an occasional individual to rise by merit, education, favor, or chance from the humblest of circumstances to exalted official posts. Today the touchstone is education. Those who have managed to get a lycée education find new opportunities in government service, industry, and commerce. A lycée graduate was, until recently, automatically an officer when he did his military service. Lycée graduates constitute a small proportion of the population, but the number grows yearly. It is also increasingly common that children of the uneducated are getting an education.

There is, then, an educated elite in Turkey. There always has been an elite in one form or another. It has been the ruling element and the moving element throughout Turkish history. Originally it was composed of military officers and civil servants. In later Ottoman days it began to include more journalists, lawyers, physicians. The Turkish Republic inherited this ruling elite from the Ottoman Empire—over 90 per cent of the general Staff officers and over 80 per cent of the trained bureaucrats of the empire remained in Turkey after 1918, rather than in the other successor states of the empire. Four of the republic's five presidents have been ex-generals. These were men used to leadership, to administration, to dealing with public problems. The republic did not have to start from scratch. Naturally not all officers and civil servants are able, clearsighted, and devoted solely to the public weal. The Turk, like all other humans, complains about the bureaucrat, his procrastination and ability to say no, his fussiness over regulations and bits of official paper. The small official—the *küchük memur*—is the butt of jokes, often regarded as arrogant and self-serving. "The desk makes the man," one will hear. Yet the top leadership has proven remarkably able on the whole. Without the ruling group, Turkish history is inexplicable. In the past two or three decades this elite has included an increasing number of professional men, especially lawyers, and of businessmen.

Most of the elite are found in the cities. It will be obvious from the preceding discussion of Islam, of westernization, and of the economy that one of the principal divisions in Turkish society is between the city and the provincial town and village. Rapid urbanization has recently struck Turkey. The 1955 census reported six cities with populations over 100,000; the 1960 census reported nine; the 1965 census reported fourteen. Cities of lesser size have grown with similar speed. Most of the increase is attributable to emigration from the villages. Each of Turkey's large cities is rimmed by squatters' settlements (*gejekondular*) made up of recent arrivals from the countryside. The squatters seem to represent less the despair of rural poverty than an enterprising search for greater opportunity in jobs and in education. Many of them prefer the big city to the provincial town nearer home not only because of opportunity, but because the town is socially more conservative and traditional than suits their taste. They swell the ranks of the urban underprivileged—the cap-wearers, or *kasketliler*, as opposed to the more sophisticated and wealthier hat-wearers—but they are not an industrial proletariat in the ordinary sense. Quite a few have recently moved on to unskilled or semi-skilled jobs in western European countries, particularly in West Germany, returning after a few years with considerable savings. Labor unions have developed, small strikes have occurred, but any sense of solidarity among urban workers, or massive organization to represent it, still lies in the future. Obviously the city is not a social unit, but today as in the past a collection of quarters or communities. Still, its tone is set by its elite, and the contrast to the village is striking.

Speaking in parliament in 1966, Prime Minister Demirel pointed out that the majority of Turkey's 35,000 villages, where 20,000,000 people lived, lacked roads, water systems, schools, and health services, and that a large number still had no electricity. Many of the villagers live in grinding poverty, walled in by ignorance and superstition. Many suffer from landlessness or landlordism. A contemporary Turkish literature of social concern, much of it in the novel or short story form, portrays sympathetically the peasant lot, castigates the landlord, and sometimes praises the local "Robin Hood" type who sets out to attack injustice. Yet each year more villages are brought into contact with the outside world through road construction, bus service, and radio. There is no mistaking the gradual awakening of villagers to new desires and new demands. It is reflected in Turkish politics since World War II.

Turkish republicanism. Modern Turkey has a republican form of government and a democratic, multi-party political system. These have resulted from a century of evolution, several revolutions, and the wrench from the past provided by the defeat and near extinction of Turkey at the end of World War I. In 1876 the Ottoman Empire was the first Muslim state to adopt a written constitution and a real parliament. The present constitution dates from 1961, after the revolution of 1960. Many variations were tried and much was learned over that time-span. The 1876 experiment created a constitutional monarchy under a sovereign sultan. After the Young Turk revolution of 1908 the sultan's powers were eroded, but only with Atatürk's leadership were the people declared sovereign. Since the founding of the republic in 1923 popular sovereignty has been unquestioned. For more than two decades it was exercised by one party. At the end of World War II multi-party politics replaced the one-party system. It has survived several dangers. Faced by challenges from groups on the extreme right and extreme left, Turkey now confronts the problem of integrating not just a ruling elite but the whole mass of townsmen, peasantry, and urban workers into orderly party politics.

Since the historic elections of 1950, when the Democratic Party achieved a peaceful electoral overturn of the hitherto ruling Republican People's Party, the peasant has discovered his political power. Atatürk once said that "the peasant is our master." Some of the urban elite took this as a humorous exaggeration; they now wryly admit that it is close to the truth. The peasant has retained much of his traditional suspicion of government, which to him has meant simply the tax collector and the recruiting sergeant. But he also wants the material advantages that government can bring—agricultural aid, roads, schools, and health services. For more than a century the government of the Ottoman Empire, then of the republic, had been expanding its sphere of activity beyond the traditional functions of collecting taxes, dispensing justice, maintaining order, guarding frontiers. Now other benefits are trickling down to village level. Politicians make promises to woo the peasant vote. The radio helps. As in other developing countries, a mass society is in process of creation, helped along by the receiving set in the village coffee-house which enables an illiterate generation to jump into national life before it has learned to read the press. Of the 1,816,000 radios registered in Turkey in 1963, nearly a quarter were in the villages.

Political life in Turkey can be stormy—not only debates in the Grand National Assembly, but the sniping at each other by opposing parties and personalities in the press. The conflicts of views can halt action and lead to stagnation. The tradition of one-party rule, further, may not yet be dead. It looks, however, as if the Turks were determined to make multi-party democracy work. Meanwhile the army has taken itself out of politics, but remains on the sidelines as the guardian of the republic. It has intervened in Turkish politics on a number of crucial occasions. The last time was in 1960, when it ousted a Democratic regime that repressed the opposition. Whether the army will intervene again depends on the quality of political leadership and the tone of political life in the republic, and also on the effectiveness of government in coping with economic and social questions.

Turkish foreign policy. Modern Turkey's foreign relations are peaceful, and her international position is good. The Ottoman Empire was perpetually at war with its neighbors. Once the Turks' struggle to assure their independence was won in 1922, the republic has been at peace. Its major aim, successfully achieved, has been to maintain the absolute independence and integrity of the country. Of Turkey's six neighbors (USSR, Greece, Bulgaria, Iran, Iraq, Syria) the Soviet Union has been the greatest threat. At the end of World War II, during which Turkey maintained neutrality, the Soviets exerted great pressure on her for

territorial cessions and for special privileges in defending the Straits.
A history of more than two centuries of such pressures, and of many
Russo-Turkish wars, made the Turks extraordinarily wary. They have
therefore since 1947 accepted considerable American aid for their size-
able army, together with other economic assistance, and are members
of the North Atlantic Treaty Organization (NATO).

Until 1964 Turkish-American relations were close. Thereafter, the
Turkish government, although still friendly to America, entered upon a
detente with Russia, which had abandoned its menacing attitude and
made instead offers of economic assistance. "We are wearing suits of a
different color," said the Turkish foreign minister in 1966, but went on
to say that good neighborly relations with the USSR were possible.
Greece, another of Turkey's neighbors, is also a NATO member. Turkish-
Greek relations were usually good until the tensions caused by the
renewed outbreaks of acute conflict over Cyprus at the end of 1963,
and again in 1967. The Cyprus question also caused anti-American
demonstrations by Turkish students, when America failed to give
support to the Turks on this issue. But the strains in Turkish-American
relations go deeper. The American presence, both economic and military, had become too obvious in Turkey; too great a dependence on any
one power was resented. Again a heritage of the past helps to explain
the reaction: the old Ottoman Empire had been so afflicted by economic and judicial servitudes imposed by the European powers, and by
political or military intervention, that Turks were highly sensitive to
such matters. There must be no derogations from total sovereignty and
total independence.

Turkey's relations with her four other neighbors vary. With Iran they
are generally good. Both countries are members of CENTO, an alliance
for military and economic cooperation. The centuries-old border strife
between Turkey and Iran no longer exists. With Bulgaria, a member of
the Communist bloc, relations have been strained on several occasions
in the recent past, but they are also susceptible of improvement. Iraq
and Syria pose particular problems for Turkey. Both of these Arab states
have in recent years had support from Soviet Russia. The Turks are
aware of the dangers of a squeeze if Russian pressures should be exerted
on these southern Turkish frontiers as well as from the Soviet Russian
border. At the same time, the Ankara government seeks greater understanding not only with Syria and Iraq, but with all Arab states, including Egypt, with which relations have been quite uncordial in the recent

past. Turkey recognizes Israel, which the Arab states do not. Yet Turks feel a sympathy for the Arab-Muslim cause, and in addition want the support of their Muslim brethren of the Arab states on the Cyprus issue. Goodwill delegations from Turkey went out to a number of these states in the mid-1960s. Other official visits followed. Improvement in Turkish-Arab relations faces the obstacle of Arab resentment of the past —the fact that for four centuries they were under Ottoman Turkish rule. Political stability and economic progress in the Arab states would contribute immeasurably to such improvement.

In this world of tensions Turkey presses ahead. The obvious progress made under the republic, and the better understanding of Turkish history now available to the world through scholarly research, have shattered the old western stereotype of the Turk—the "barbarian," the destroyer rather than a builder, etc. The Allied Powers in 1919 replied to the Ottoman delegation to the Paris peace conference in these words:

> There is no case to be found, either in Europe or Asia or Africa, in which the establishment of Turkish rule in any country has not been followed by a diminution of material prosperity, and a fall in the level of culture. . . . Neither among the Christians of Europe, nor among the Moslems of Syria, Arabia and Africa, has the Turk done other than destroy wherever he conquered; never has he shown himself able to develop in peace what he has won by war. Not in this direction do his talents lie.[3]

Such an attitude was unjustified then. It would be impossible now. The Turk has demonstrated in the past, as in the present, an organizing and constructive ability comparable to that of the ancient Romans or medieval Northmen. Like them too, he has valued and continues to value highly the military qualities of courage, endurance, discipline. His sports idols are likely to be the muscular wrestlers who win international and Olympic championships for Turkey. He tends to be frugal of speech, and appears somewhat dour on first acquaintance. But he is also friendly, generous, and at times brilliantly witty and talkative. He possesses also calm self-reliance, practicality, and a basic rationality that relates cause and effect. Generalizations like these are always

[3] Ernest L. Woodward and Rohan Butler, eds., *Documents on British Foreign Policy, 1919–1939* (London, 1946–), Series I, IV, 646.

dangerous, for there are as many kinds of Turks as there are of any other people in this transitory human world. Yet those who know Turkey will attest the truth in such judgments.

The Turk is also conscious of his heritage from ancient civilizations —from the early Turks, from Islam, from the Ottoman Empire, from the West. He lives surrounded by old and the new, by monumental Hittite sculptures, Roman amphitheatres, Byzantine mosaics, Seljuk caravanserais, Turkish folk music, Ottoman mosques, asphalt roads, and high-tension electric cables. The past presses on the present as the present presses on the future.

The Ulus square in Ankara is on a modern boulevard, close by the old quarter of the city. Nearby are the ancient temple of Rome and Augustus, the medieval Byzantine citadel, the fifteenth-century mosque of Haji Bayram, and the modern railroad station. In this section of the city were erected the first public buildings after the nationalist movement planted its government there. A large equestrian statue of Atatürk dominates the square. On its pedestal is carved a relief showing a tree with a massive branch shattered near the trunk, and a new vigorous growth springing from the top: the Turkish Republic growing from the Ottoman Empire. The new Turkey had inherited people, land, religion, and many problems from the old. The republic had risen out of the failures and collapse of the empire, but also out of the empire's experience and progress. That empire itself had a history of six hundred years. It had been created by the Turks. The heritage of modern Turkey goes back, then, through Ottoman times to the Turks of pre-Ottoman, and pre-Islamic, days.

2

From Steppe to Empire

In recent years the Turks have exhibited a particular interest in their origins as a people. Such has not always been the case. Throughout most of the life of the Ottoman Empire, what history the Turks wrote and read was the history of the Ottoman dynasty and state, or the history of Islam. Toward the end of the nineteenth century, however, some Ottoman intellectuals began to take a keener interest in their Turkish-speaking brethren who lived in a vast land belt stretching across Middle Asia from northwestern Iran and the Caucasus through Russian-menaced (and soon Russian-dominated) Turkestan into China. Spurred by western European scholarship, some also began to probe into the ethnic and linguistic past of the Turkish peoples.

This quest for national origins, a part of the development of modern nationalist consciousness, is, of course, not peculiar to the Turks, but it came later to them than to the Greeks, Slavs, and Armenians whom they ruled. It was also more difficult, since the Ottoman and Islamic overlay had so completely obscured the Turkish past. Even Arabs and Persians, who also were Muslims, had kept a greater consciousness of their Arabness and Persianness than had the Turks of their Turkishness. For the Turks, a part of the difficulty lay in the cultured style of writing and even speaking which had borrowed so heavily from the Arabic and Persian vocabulary and forms. The quest for national origins was

15

accompanied by a quest for the simpler, more truly Turkish, tongue.[1]

When the Turkish Republic replaced the Ottoman Empire, the probe into Turkish origins continued, now purposefully spurred on by Mustafa Kemal Atatürk so as to heighten the sense of national identity and solidarity, of uniqueness and pride. Some odd and untenable theories resulted.[2] But the net effect was not only to solidify the Turks' interest in their ethnic past, but to redress the imbalance of their consciousness of their own history. Today the educated Turk is aware not only of his Ottoman past, and of the pre-Ottoman Islamic past, but also of his pre-Islamic Turkish past.

Much of the early history of the Turks is obscure. Some of the obscurity used to be tidied up by legend, or by fictions that embellished the facts. But even relatively modern scholarly theories may be suspect. For example, it is sometimes said that the Turks are part of the Ural-Altaic language group. Philologists today, however, find that the genetic connection between the Uralic tongues (involving Finnish, Estonian, and Hungarian, among others) and the Altaic (including Turkic, Mongolian, Manchu-Tungu, and possibly Korean) has not been scientifically proven. Nor are the relationships among the Altaic languages clear. But it does seem clear that the Turks were once part of a group of Altaic peoples among whom are numbered the Mongols, the Manchus, the Bulgars, probably the Huns, and others. Their earliest appearance in history was in what today would be Outer Mongolia, south of Lake Baikal and north of the Gobi Desert. Chinese sources of the second millennium B.C. refer to what seems to have been a confederation of such nomadic and pastoral peoples, whom the Chinese called the Hiong-Nu. Among them the Turkish element was probably the greatest. A western group of these Hiong-Nu, pushed west by the Mongols, appeared in Europe in the fifth century of the Christian era and are known as the Huns.

Out of the wars of these tribes and tribal confederations on the fringes of the Chinese Empire, there emerged in the sixth century the first group known to be called Turks—Tu-Kiu to the Chinese. An eastern Turkish kingdom was centered on the Orkhon River, tributary to a stream flowing north into Lake Baikal. Here in Siberia have been found the earliest Turkish inscriptions, dating from the 730s. The kingdom was an off-again, on-again proposition, suffering Chinese conquest

[1] On language reform beginnings, see below, pp. 84–85.
[2] For these theories, see below, pp. 135–36.

or internal collapse. Other Turks had pushed south and west into what is now Russian Turkestan, where an ephemeral state achieved a certain splendor as it sat athwart the silk route from China to the West. Envoys from the Byzantine capital of Constantinople attested to its vigor as they sought, by paying tribute, to gain its assistance against Persia. But this Turkish state, like its eastern counterpart, soon collapsed. The area nevertheless remained ethnically Turkish. In religion, though they were touched by Nestorian, Manichaean, and Buddhist influences, the Turks remained largely shamanistic.

In the seventh century began the first of two encounters which were to shape the destiny of the Turks for centuries to come. This was the encounter with Islam. The Arab conquest of Iran in the seventh century carried the creed preached by the prophet Muhammad to the Turkish fringes of Central Asia. Individual Turks then entered the lands of the Islamic califate and became Muslims. In the ninth century, and later, many Turkish fighting men were recruited as slaves for the armies of the Muslim rulers and converted to Islam. Some rose to important administrative positions. The bulk of the Turks, however, still essentially nomadic in Central Asia east of the Aral Sea, accepted Islam in the tenth century.

Islam served as a new bond among all those Turks who professed it. It was not simply a method of worship or a narrow religious creed, but a way of life, theoretically encompassing all man's relations to man, as well as man's relations to God. Law and state, society and culture, were built on and permeated by Islam. With Islam, the Turks also took over the Arabic script. Yet when the Turks accepted Islam, they did not all do so in the same way. Some, prominent among them a group whose chief was named Seljuk, became linked with the orthodox Sunnite form of Islam, and were on good terms with the theologians. Many others, often referred to as Turkomans, who remained more tribally nomadic, were influenced by less orthodox forms of Islam spread by merchants, mystics, and by the *gazi* groups, or "warriors for the faith," with whom they intermingled on the boundaries of the Islamic realm. These were open to influences from the Shiite heresy so prevalent in Iraq and Iran, and to the urgings of popular preachers and mystics. Nor did they forget all their traditional folk-religion. The two aspects of Islam were both to influence later Turkish history.

The universal califate had begun to disintegrate by the ninth century, and by the eleventh century the confusion of competing states and dynasties into which the Islamic world was plunged had shorn the calif in Baghdad of all real power. Various Seljuk groups entered what is now Iran, by invitation or by force. The Seljuk leader, Tughrul Beg, in 1055 took control of Baghdad and, supporting the calif, restored his dignity, though effective power remained with Tughrul and his heirs, who now were granted the title of sultan. As of this point the Turks had not only adopted Islam, but had rescued Sunnite or orthodox Islam from degradation and had become rulers of a major portion of the old Islamic world in the Tigris-Euphrates valleys and Iran. A learned Turk living in Baghdad, Mahmud al-Kashghari, repeated in an encyclopedic dictionary he wrote in 1074 an apocryphal saying (obviously a later invention) of the prophet Muhammad: "God said, I have a host which I have called Turk and settled in the East. If any people shall arouse my wrath, I shall give them unto the power of this host." And, commented Mahmud, this demonstrated for the Turks "a superiority over all other peoples because God took upon himself the naming of them." [3] Whether or not this saying demonstrated a direct connection between the Turks and the Prophet, and the Prophet's God, as Mahmud hoped, it did show how much Islam had become a part of Turkish life.

The second encounter that was to shape Turkish destiny was with the Byzantine Empire. The tribal Turkomans, on whom the Seljuk leaders had often to depend for fighting forces, adopted gazi ways of fighting on the frontiers of Islam against the non-believers, and were more attracted to the north than to the hot climate of Mesopotamia. As a result, Turkoman warriors began raiding into Byzantine lands in what is now eastern Turkey. They found the Byzantine Empire in a period of weakness and internal strife. This proud heir of Rome had attained perhaps its greatest imperial glory in the tenth century, when it controlled a prosperous two-continent realm stretching from the Adriatic Sea to the Syrian frontier. But the weakening of the imperial government thereafter and the discontent of eastern peoples under its rule lessened resistance to the gazi raids, especially in the region of Armenia, which had been newly annexed to Byzantium. By the mid-eleventh century the Turkish raiders had penetrated half-way or more across present-day Turkey, at least to Konya (Byzantine Iconium). The raids brought about a fortuitous northwestern expansion of Seljuk territory. The sultans of the Seljuk empire had intended to drive into Syria and

[3] Robert Devereux, "Al-Kashghari and Early Turkish Islam," *Muslim World*, XLIX, No. 2 (April 1959), 134–35.

toward Egypt, but in order to control the Turkomans and oppose an advancing Byzantine army, the sultan Alp Arslan, successor to Tughrul, marched north. There in 1071 he defeated the Byzantine forces led by the emperor Romanus IV Diogenes at the battle of Manzikert near Lake Van.

By breaking the Byzantine defensive power in Asia, the battle of Manzikert opened the way to expanded Turkish penetration of Anatolia. Raiding Turkomans, again uncontrolled by the Seljuk Sultans, led the new expansion all the way to the Aegean and Marmara shores. The Turks first occupied the countryside, making communication between Byzantine cities hazardous or impossible, and so destroyed Byzantine administration. They frequently were welcomed by Greeks who were unhappy with Byzantine taxes or church control. As more Turks entered Anatolia, the towns and cities were absorbed into the Turkish sphere. The result of this westward expansion was not a single, organized Turkish state, but a congeries of nomadic and gazi groups, short-lived proto-kingdoms intermingled with the older populations of Anatolia in what had now become a vast area of border marches.

Among the embryonic Turkish states that arose, the strongest for a period in the 1080s was one led by a Seljuk chief, Süleyman, who by agreement with the Byzantine emperor Alexius held Iznik (Nicaea) as his capital, not far from Constantinople itself. The Turkish principalities quarreled with each other, upsetting the peace of the countryside, and occasionally the peace of pilgrim routes through Anatolia to Jerusalem. All the while, Turkoman groups drifted in. Thus began the Turkification of Anatolia, and the fateful juxtaposition of Turkish warriors for the Islamic faith with a weakening Christian Byzantium.

The influx of Turks finally called forth Byzantine countermeasures. To oppose the "Muslim barbarians" of the East, as the emperor Alexius conceived them, he appealed to the "Christian barbarians" of the West.

So came the First Crusade to Asia. In 1097 the crusaders conquered Iznik and returned it to Alexius. The same was true of other cities, so that the Byzantines regained control of perhaps a third of Anatolia as the Turks were pushed back. But the Turks were not ejected, and a later Seljuk leader defeated the second Crusade in 1147. Though the Seljuks failed to regain Iznik or their earlier western lands, they held the center of the Anatolian plateau and created there what was known as the Sultanate of Rum. "Rum" originally meant "Rome" or "Roman," but by this time it had acquired the connotation of Greek or

Byzantine because the eastern empire based on Constantinople had styled itself Roman. Competing with other Turkish emirates, especially that of the Danishmends, the Sultanate of Rum gained a temporary stability. Its capital was at Konya.

Here in the later twelfth and earlier thirteenth centuries the Seljuk Sultanate of Rum flourished, its high point coming about 1230. It dominated the central Anatolian plateau and formed a part of the Anatolian balance of power that developed among the Byzantine states of Nicaea and Trebizond (after the Latins of the Fourth Crusade had ejected the Byzantines from Constantinople in 1204), the Seljuk state, and a revived Armenia in the East. Once looked down upon as destructive and interested only in warfare, the Seljuks are now recognized as having attained a reasonably high cultural level. Central Anatolia is still dotted with bits of their roads, their excellent stone bridges, their network of caravanserais (hans), their mosques, their theological schools, and their fortifications. A flourishing trade with Italian city-states brought increased prosperity. It was in Konya too that the famed mystic poet, Jelal ed-Din Rumi, founded the order of Mevlevi dervishes (known to the West commonly as the whirling or dancing dervishes).

Although Turkomans had continued to come from Central Asia into the Seljuk lands of Anatolia, the first wave of infiltration had slowed to a trickle about 1100. The Sultanate of Rum, once established, could usually keep the nomadic tribes in check, and controlled or exploited their gazi tendencies. Toward the end of the thirteenth century, however, came a new wave of Turkish penetration into Anatolia. A disaster for the Sultanate of Rum provided the opportunity. The Mongols, who in earlier raids had bypassed Anatolia, in 1243 defeated the Seljuks of Rum at the battle of Köse Dagh. The Seljuk state never recovered, though the dynasty lasted until 1303. The Mongols did not try to govern Anatolia directly, but simply collected tribute. Their greater interest lay in Iran, where a Mongol dynasty which had accepted Islam, the Il-Hans, ruled. Anatolia was an Il-Han frontier.

Paradoxical as it may seem, the Mongol blow to the Turkish Seljuk Sultanate of Rum led to the increased Turkification of Anatolia. This came about in two ways. First, new waves of Turkish tribal groups migrated from Central Asia into Anatolia, either driven by the Mongols or following in their wake. Second, the weakening of the Seljuk state at its center dispersed power to the periphery. Little Turkish principalities or emirates began to act independently of Seljuk authority. Those

on the Byzantine frontier began again a vigorous war against the un-
believer. This was now easier, since much of the Byzantine military
effort, after the capital at Constantinople had been regained in 1261,
was diverted against the Latin West. The gazi spirit came again to the
fore. Western Anatolia was reoccupied by the Turks, leaving some
Byzantine cities isolated.

After this period, Anatolia became increasingly Turkish in complexion, not only in the districts won anew from the Byzantines, but
throughout the plateau. The Seljuk sultanate had ruled over a mixed
population. The Turks were the warriors, administrators, and craftsmen
in the towns; the Turks were also pastoral nomads. But trade tended to
fall into Greek, Armenian, or Jewish hands. The peasantry, though part
of it was Turkish, had remained in large part Greek—that is, Christian.
But the Hellenization and the Christianization of many of the Greeks
of the central and eastern Anatolian plateau must always have been
superficial—far more superficial than on the Aegean fringe. As ever new
archaeological discoveries are proving, Anatolia had been the home of
civilized man for millennia. One suspects that descendants of the Hittites, the Phrygians, and others, who have been somewhat intuitively
claimed at times by modern Turks as ancestors, must have been mixed
into the populations that were included in the Roman Empire and its
eastern heir, Byzantium. Folk-beliefs of many sorts survived. The Orthodox hierarchy of the Byzantine Empire had often been unpopular
among the common people, especially to the east. Sometimes the people
discovered either an affinity for Islamic as opposed to Greek Orthodox
doctrine or a release from the exactions of their clergy through conquest
by Muslims. Islamicization and Turkification were but aspects of the
same process.

In the later thirteenth and the fourteenth centuries, when Turkish
property seizures or taxation hastened the disintegration of the Greek
church as a social institution in its once-richest Anatolian area, conversions to Islam seem to have particularly increased. The spreading
Mevlevi dervish order had a missionary appeal. Not only common people, but on occasion even Greek priests, monks, Jewish rabbis, and
Armenians accepted Islam. The intermingling of frontier peoples on the
Christian-Muslim borders must also have produced intermarriage. In the
fourteenth century even Byzantine emperors had Turkish princes for
sons-in-law. The result was the spread of Islam as Christianity contracted, though the latter did not disappear from Anatolia. The Turks

increased in numbers, both by immigration and by absorption of local elements.

One of the emirates that laid claim to the heritage of the Sultanate of Rum was centered on Söğüt, a town just north of the modern city of Eskishehir, located in northwestern Anatolia. It was by no means the biggest or strongest of the emirates, and it must be a matter of surprise that not only the greatest Turkish-ruled state, but also the greatest Islamic empire of history, grew from this tiny state. In the 1290s its ruler was Osman, from whose name comes the name of the dynasty: "Osmanli" to the Turks, "Ottoman" to the West. Tradition gives the Ottomans a tribal origin. Accounts of a band of horsemen coming out of the East into Seljuk lands, helping them in a crucial battle, and being rewarded with the frontier march around Söğüt have often been accepted. Later Ottoman chronicles embellished such accounts by inventing a noble genealogy for the Ottomans, leading back through the Oghuz Turks of Central Asia to Noah, that bottleneck of the human race, and so inevitably back to Adam.

Though Osman's family may have had a tribal origin, the Ottoman state grew strong for religious, military, and political reasons rather than because of tribal élan. Osman's principality lay on the Byzantine frontier, the closest to Constantinople of all of the emirates. It attracted from the Turkish hinterland gazi warriors, hoping to spread the faith and to plunder. It became a gazi state, slowly expanding during Osman's lifetime. An early inscription calls Osman a "Sultan of the Gazis." And an Ottoman chronicler of about 1400, writing an account of the dynasty, says "A Ghazi is the instrument of the religion of Allah, a servant of God who purifies the earth from the filth of polytheism; the Ghazi is the sword of God. . . ." [4] The Ottoman emirate also drew other strength from the Turkish hinterland: orthodox theologians, artisan or tradesman brotherhoods with religious overtones (ahi's), dervishes and heterodox preachers. These helped to strengthen the social fabric of the emirate.

Osman's emirate, as it expanded, created both the territorial basis and the administrative organization for an empire that after a half-century spread to Europe. The initial expansion was slow. Osman's successor, Orhan (reigned 1324?–1362?), took the first significant Byzantine city, Bursa (Brusa) in 1326, making it his capital. A few years later Iznik (Nicaea) and Izmit (Nicomedia) fell to the Ottomans. Soon

[4] Paul Wittek, *The Rise of the Ottoman Empire* (London, 1938), pp. 14–15.

after reaching the Marmara shores they crossed over into Europe. In 1345, and twice more within a decade thereafter, Byzantine emperors or contenders for the throne called in Orhan's forces as allies. The Turks saw Thrace, some of them even Constantinople, and they liked what they saw. In 1354 they crossed the Dardanelles to stay, establishing a fortified base at Gallipoli. It is significant that only at this date did the Ottomans begin any important expansion eastward into Turkish territory, taking control of Ankara. Ottoman growth was pendulum-like, west and east, but west always came first. This was partly because of geography and opportunity, partly because of the gazi origins of the state.

Under Orhan's successor, Murad I (reigned 1362?–1389), conquests in the Balkans continued as organized state action, not independent gazi action. Proceeding in campaigns by stages up the Maritsa and Vardar valleys, the Ottomans annexed Bulgar territory, raided into Albania and up the Adriatic coast, and in 1389 at the famous battle of Kossovo defeated a Serb-led coalition. The old, central Byzantine core of the Balkan peninsula was now Turk-dominated. Constantinople was virtually isolated; the Byzantine emperors were in effect vassals of the Turks. Papal appeals for a crusade and Hungarian armed opposition had availed nothing. In another significant action, Murad transferred his capital in 1365/66 from Asia to Europe—from Bursa to Edirne (Adrianople).

Inevitably, the historian seeks an explanation for the transformation within a hundred years of a tiny emirate of march-warriors into a sizable two-continent state which, though it did not yet have Constantinople, had taken over the kernel of the Byzantine empire. No explanation can be final, but several reasons are apparent. For one thing, the opposition to the Ottomans was disunited. Serbs, Bulgars, and Byzantines found it impossible to collaborate in the face of the new threat; rather they tended separately to call in the Ottomans to gain advantage over a rival. The Latin West, which might have sent aid, was also disunited. It was hard to get up a crusade when the French and English were at odds in the first stages of their Hundred Years' War, when Venice and Genoa were in deadly competition with each other, and when the Roman church was itself weakened by the "Babylonian Captivity." To these external reasons for the Ottoman success must be added the Black Death, which swept out of the Crimea to Constantinople in 1347 and continued in a great arc around Europe for the next five years, terrifying

the Greeks and other Europeans but bypassing the Turks. Nor must it
be forgotten that access to Europe was easy for the Ottomans, and that
the prospect of booty appealed not only to them but to other gazis
who were attracted to their standard. In addition, Ottoman rule may
have appeared an easier yoke to some Balkan peoples than the former
Byzantine regime. Christians were as a rule left unmolested in the practice of their religion, though in the early days of gazi Balkan conquest
there were some forced conversions. Ottoman tolerance usually applied
to all who accepted their rule and paid a special tax.

There were also internal reasons for Ottoman success. The family
produced able leaders who generally enjoyed long reigns. The rival
Turkish emirates of any importance were some distance off to the east,
and some of their lands came into the Ottoman orbit by marriage or
other peaceful means. The Turkish hinterland provided the learned
men of Islam (the *ulema*) as well as the Seljuk administrative experience and the artisan brotherhoods. With these aids, the Ottoman
sultans set up a military and administrative machine that proved highly
workable. The process of development is not yet clear, for new research
is pushing back the dates of Ottoman organization. By the time of
Murad I, however, the Ottoman state had added more permanently
organized forces to its irregular and volunteer horse and its irregular
footsoldiers. A system of fiefs carved from conquered territories insured
that the cavalryman holder (*sipahi*) would provide a stipulated number
of horse when needed; this was perhaps adopted from similar Seljuk
practice. A corps of trained footsoldiers—Janissaries (in Turkish *yeni
cheri*, "new troops")—was created, perhaps in the time of Murad I,
but possibly earlier, from slaves who were captured in war, or bought,
or presented to the sultan. The Seljuks also had maintained such slave
troops. The Janissaries were probably no more than a thousand at first,
though the size of the corps grew with time. The vassal Serbs and
Byzantines were obliged on occasion to furnish troop contingents too.
As yet the Ottomans had no navy worthy of the name.

Administratively, the Ottoman state by the time of Orhan had attained complete independence of its nominal Mongol overlords. Orhan
adopted the symbols of sovereignty: he struck his own coinage, there
was mention of his name in the Friday prayers, he had his own flags
or standards and a military band. The energetic Ottoman sultans—the
Arab traveller Ibn Battuta in the 1330s marvelled at Orhan constantly
going around visiting his nearly one hundred fortresses—were assisted

by an administration headed by a grand vezir. One grand vezir early in Orhan's reign may have been the first to be called "pasha," a designation of high civil or military rank. Anatolian territories were divided into provinces (*sanjaks*); some European territories were too, but many at first were made tributary vassal states rather than being totally incorporated into the empire. The sultans after all, even in Anatolia, ruled over a polyglot empire, religiously and ethnically vastly diversified. Like other rulers before them, their interest was in an efficient method of getting money, by tax or tribute, and in levying soldiers and commanding obedience. Uniformity was less important than results.

One suspects also that the polyglot empire and the captive-producing warfare led the Ottomans to rely on slave administrators, as had the Seljuks before them. Slaves born Christian, converted to Islam in youth, trained, and removed from their native regions, would be likely to serve the sultan loyally. Not only slaves, but peasant or nomadic groups were purposely transferred to other regions to settle, to cultivate, and to ensure security. As military contingents from Rumelia (Europe) were often sent to Anatolia and vice versa, so also were settlement groups sent in these transverse directions. After the conquests of Murad I, Balkan peoples—Greeks, Bulgars, Serbs—began to add to the Turkish racial mixture, particularly in the Ottoman ruling class. Conversion and marriage supplemented the mixture already begun in Anatolia.

Ottoman expansion was favored by the almost simultaneous collapse of Byzantine and Seljuk power, leaving a weakened and divided Balkan peninsula and an Anatolia split among competing emirs. Murad's successor, Bayezid I (reigned 1389–1402), often called "Yilderim" or "Lightning-bolt," tried to take advantage of both situations at once. In Europe, he raided north across the Danube, stabbing at the Hungarians. He also besieged Constantinople now and again throughout the 1390s. In Asia he absorbed Turkoman emirates to the south of his holdings, along the Aegean littoral, and also well to the east, as far as Samsun and Sivas. In so doing, he precipitated two military crises, either of which might have been fatal to the Ottomans. The second crisis in its turn brought a third. The result might have been the end of the Ottoman Empire; that this was not the case was partly a matter of chance.

The first crisis came from the West. Frankish knights of western Europe, in plentiful supply during a lull in the Hundred Years' War, mounted a crusade in 1396 to join the Hungarians in an attack on the Turks. The assembled Christian armies were formidable. The Franks, contemptuous of the Turks, caroused their way down the Danube to the fortified Turkish town of Nicopolis. There, heedless of the sensible Hungarian warning, they launched an attack on Bayezid's Turks and his Serb allies which ended in the utter rout of the crusaders. The failure of this last great crusade of the Middle Ages served to confirm the Ottoman domination of the Balkan peninsula. It caused Bayezid to break off his siege of Constantinople, but only temporarily saved the city.

The second crisis came from the Muslim East, and this, ironically, gave the Byzantines a greater respite than the crusade. Timur (Tamerlane) was the source of the new threat to the Ottomans. Bayezid's eastward conquest and absorption of Muslim emirates, using in the process Christian Greek and Serb contingents along with Janissaries, had angered Timur on imperial and perhaps also on religious grounds. Displaced emirs appealed to the great conqueror, heir of the Mongol realm, who had built an Islamic empire from Central Asia to Syria. Timur finally responded. In 1402, at the battle of Ankara, he defeated Bayezid's forces and captured the sultan, who died the next year. Timur did not want Anatolia for himself, though he overran most of it. He cut down the Ottoman power by restoring emirs in eastern and central Anatolia. The Ottoman dominion in Anatolia was set back to where it had been a half-century before.

Timur's defeat of Bayezid, and the latter's death, brought on the third crisis, which was internal. Four sons of Bayezid fought for a decade to determine who would rule what was left of the Ottoman state. Had the civil war among the brothers preceded either the Nicopolis crusade or Timur's attack, or had Timur defeated the Ottomans before the crusaders came along, there is no telling whether the Ottoman state would have survived. But because of Timur's disinterest in direct control of Anatolia, followed by his early death, and because of the disunited Christian West's failure to take advantage of the Ottoman civil war, though the West was well informed about it, the struggle went on free of intervention. In 1413 the one survivor among the contending sons, Mehmed I, emerged triumphant. The Ottoman state could be put together again, though without the easternmost Turkish areas annexed by Bayezid. For the next fifty years the face of the Ottomans was again turned principally toward Europe. Perhaps Timur had done them a favor in reorienting them toward the area of gazi expansion on the Christian frontier.

The combined reigns of Mehmed I (1413–1421) and of Murad II (1421–1451) represent a period of consolidation of the Ottoman state in which warfare of some kind, either in Anatolia or Rumelia, was almost continuous. The state was by no means as yet solid or unitary. The Serb vassals, for instance, regained independence for a short span, and then lost it again. The Hungarians, led by their hero John Hunyadi, harassed the Turks after the Turks had raided across the Danube. One last crusade, a feeble repetition of Nicopolis, and more Hungarian than western, invaded Bulgaria only to meet decisive defeat at Varna in 1444. This was the end of an era; crusades were now dead, despite later western and Byzantine pleas for them. But certain events in this half-century were harbingers of the future. For one thing, there was the beginning of a maritime struggle with the Venetians, who felt their Adriatic and Aegean routes to eastern Mediterranean and Black Sea trade being threatened by the Turks. The Ottomans, who had a small, feeble navy under Bayezid, saw the need to build up naval strength, though only beginnings were made. Another sign of things to come was a Janissary rebellion. In this case the rebellion was incited by one faction in a contest for influence in the sultan's court, but it forecast a turbulent king-making role for the Janissaries in years to come. Still another portent was a dervish-led revolt in Anatolia against the orthodox Ottoman state organization, symptomatic of the religious-political discontent which could on occasion break out among common people when influenced by mystics or Shiite tendencies.

Constantinople had thus far eluded the grasp of the Turks. It had seemed for a time that Murad II might take it. The city itself, with a small surrounding area, was all that was left to the Byzantine emperors, who usually paid tribute to the Ottoman sultans. But Murad's siege in 1422 was unsuccessful, even though he used cannon for the first time against its walls. The Ottoman navy was unable to cut the city's sea routes of supply. Yet the imperial city, once so magnificent, had fallen on sad days despite its valor. Pero Tafur, a Spanish pilgrim-traveller, has left an illuminating account of his visit there in 1437. He admired the great church of Hagia Sophia, the wonderful anchorage afforded by the Golden Horn, the massive city walls. He saw the emperor in a procession of great splendor depart for the Council of Florence, in what proved later to be a vain attempt to win Latin aid by reuniting the Eastern and Western churches. But Pero Tafur found the palace deteriorating, the city's population sparse and poorly clothed, the defenses in need of soldiers despite the presence of some western mercenaries. In effect, the Turks already dominated the city, he said. But the people deserved even worse, he added in a burst of Latin self-righteousness, for they were "a vicious people and steeped in sin." [5]

Pero Tafur's visit to the Ottoman capital of Edirne, a little to the west, gave him the chance for a direct comparison. He was received by Murad II—"handsome, grave, discreet"—and impressed by the sultan's immense body of horsemen and the fine clothes of his retainers. The Turks were in anything but a sad condition. They treat the Greeks cruelly, said Pero Tafur, but are

> a noble people, much given to truth. They live in their country like nobles, as well in their expenditure as in their actions and food and sports. . . . They are very merry and benevolent, and of good conversation, so much so that in those parts, when one speaks of virtue, it is sufficient to say that anyone is like a Turk.[6]

The Turks, while Pero Tafur was there, marched near the walls of Constantinople, terrifying the inhabitants, but passed on without attack. At Murad II's death in 1451, Byzantine Constantinople remained, decaying though it was, a city surrounded by an aura of a thousand-year imperial tradition, inevitably enticing the Turks to conquest. It was also still a potential menace to the Turks if Byzantine intrigues or western naval power could close the Straits or block the Turks' easy communications from Anatolia to Rumelia.

When Mehmed II succeeded his father as sultan in 1451, he made the conquest of the city his first aim. Mehmed proved to be an able organizer. Within two years all preparations were completed, including the rapid construction of Cut-Throat Castle at Rumeli Hisar, which rose within five months in 1452 on the European shore of the Bosporus at its narrowest point, opposite a smaller fortress that Bayezid I had erected on the Asian side. These castles protected passage from Europe to Asia for the Turks, supplementing the passage across the wider Dardanelles to the south. Rumeli Hisar also served, with its cannon that flung huge stone balls, to check assistance that might reach Constantinople from the Black Sea. The isolated city vainly sought aid from the West, at the price of consummating at a ceremony in

---

[5] Pero Tafur, *Travels and Adventures, 1435–1439*, trans. Malcolm Letts (New York, 1926), p. 146.
[6] *Ibid.*, p. 128.

Hagia Sophia the reunion of the schismatic churches, but only a handful of Italian soldiers and a few ships arrived.

Large Turkish forces were assembled outside the land walls of
Constantinople in the spring of 1453. Some huge cannon, the greatest
of which hurled stone balls of 1200 pounds but could be fired only
seven times a day, were cast under the direction of a Hungarian, Orban,
and put in position to batter the walls. A Turkish fleet of little ships
was swept together, anchored in the Bosporus. On April 5 bombard-
ment began. It continued more than fifty days, interspersed with
assaults on the walls which the defenders managed to drive back. Some
defenders were diverted to the harbor walls when the Turks hauled
a number of small vessels overland and dropped them into the Golden
Horn. Still the city resisted, though fear was great, and "the pictures
sweated in the churches." [7] Mehmed's conservative grand vezir, fearful
of new European aid to the Greeks, counselled breaking off the siege.
But the sultan, supported by other vezirs, determined to attack. In
the early hours of Tuesday, May 29, 1453, the final assault began.
After waves of irregulars and foot came Janissaries who mounted the
walls. The last emperor, Constantine XI Paleologus, perished un-
noticed in the fighting. The city was given over to sack by the Turks,
though this was probably not as devastating as the looting by the
Latin crusaders in 1204. Sultan Mehmed, thereafter known to his people as Fatih Mehmed (Mehmed the Conqueror), then restored order
and began reconstruction.

So dramatic an event as the fall of the Second Rome to Muslims,
after centuries of resistance, appeared to later Europeans as a cata-
clysmic event marking the end of the Middle Ages, the start of the
western Renaissance, and the beginning of a search for new trade routes
to the Far East. It led, they thought, to epoch-making voyages by
Columbus and others. Such unhistorical fantasies have now been ex-
ploded, for the Renaissance and the new exploration had long since
begun. Some Europeans at the time of Constantinople's fall did, to
be sure, lament the blow to Christianity and to humanist learning—
"a second death for Homer, a second oblivion for Plato." [8] Another
western reaction was one of fear: would Italy, Bosnia, or Hungary be

[7] Kritovoulos, *History of Mehmed the Conqueror*, trans. Charles T. Riggs
(Princeton, N.J., 1954), p. 35.
[8] Aeneas Sylvius to Pope Nicholas V, quoted in Louise Ropes Loomis, "The
Fall of Constantinople Symbolically Considered," in *Essays in Intellectual History*
(New York, 1929), p. 245.

next? Crusade talk was revived, but it remained talk only. In 1453 and for some years thereafter, however, the principal western reaction seems to have sprung from the common view that the Greeks were sinful and corrupt schismatics who deserved no better fate because they had left the true Roman church. Some westerners saw in the Turkish victory over the Greeks the revenge of the ancient Trojans, with whom the Turks were on occasion identified. So, although Pope Calixtus III could three years later add to the Angelus litany the plea, "From the Turk and the comet, Good Lord, deliver us"—Halley's comet appeared in 1456—the West as a whole was not aroused.

To the Turks, however, the conquest of Constantinople, which they popularly called Istanbul,[9] was more than the capture of an isolated city. It was, first of all, a gazi deed *par excellence,* the taking of a millennial infidel center. Hagia Sophia, its ikons removed and its mosaics covered over, became a mosque, still called Aya Sofya by the Turks. Fatih Mehmed, when he entered the city, prayed there after the Muslim creed was recited by an imam. The conquest brought to the Turks prestige in the old Muslim world from which they had come, and to which they still belonged. Further, Istanbul united, both physically and symbolically, the old Anatolia and the new Rumelia. Its conquest did not mean that the Turks suddenly now became a European power, for they were already that, but it did confirm the fact. From then on not only was the chance for a crusade to save Constantinople for the Greeks lost, but the Ottoman rulers of the city began to be sought out by this or that European ruler or faction, even by the popes of Rome, as allies in the shifting European balance of power.

Yet more important, the city they held afforded the Turks a magnificent naval and commercial harbor and a position at the crossroads of trade. The prosperous Genoese suburb of Galata, just across the Golden Horn from the city, also came under their domination. Sultan Mehmed's actions confirmed this maritime and commercial aspect of the city's importance. He began at once to rebuild the imperial center whose population in the last Byzantine days had fallen to some 80,000. From all corners of his realm he imported artisans, merchants, farmers —Turks, Armenians, Greeks—to repopulate the city and its suburbs. He ordered roads, *hans,* baths, and a fine bazaar to be built, as well as

* "Istanbul" is usually explained as a probable corruption of what Turks heard the Greeks say: *eis ten polin,* "to the city." Byzantines often called their capital simply "the city."

a great mosque called by his name. Throughout the rest of his reign (1451–1481) groups of people from newly subdued regions in the Balkans, the Black Sea shores, or the Aegean islands were sent to live and work in Istanbul.

The reconstruction of Istanbul had more than an economic aspect; it had also an imperial aspect. This was the new capital. With it the Ottomans inherited a tradition of imperial splendor that had clung to the city even in its darkest days, and that could not but affect its new masters. Mehmed now added to his titles the designation "Rum Kayseri" ("Roman" or Byzantine Emperor) and the epithet, "ruler of the two lands and the two seas" (of Rumelia and Anatolia, and the Black and Aegean Seas). Since the Turks had been in contact with the Greeks from early Seljuk times, and in Europe for a century, it would be foolish to think of 1453 as marking a sudden acquisition of Byzantine traditions or practices. How much direct borrowing or inheriting of Byzantine culture there was is still debated; some Byzantine influences had certainly reached the Turks earlier through an Arab filter. The Byzantine imperial tradition was, however, unmistakably associated with the majesty of the capital city. It was majesty of political rule, enhanced by the splendor of a leading cultural center. Mehmed II was himself a highly cultured as well as a warlike man. He is reported to have known Persian and Arabic literature, and to have spoken Serbian and perhaps Italian; whether he knew Greek, as is often stated, is doubtful. He began to collect learned men at his court, among whom a Greek philosopher was a favorite. Istanbul was to be revived as an economic, a political and a cultural center. For the Turks, its conquest symbolized the completion of a transition from frontier march to empire.

3

The Golden Age of the
Ottoman Empire, 1453-1566

Perhaps a century before the Ottoman Turks took Istanbul, the myth of the red apple had spread among them.[1] The red apple was a far-off object of longing, a symbol of something in the infidel world the capture of which would lead toward world dominion. Its immediate focus had been a gleaming, gilded metal ball in the hand of Justinian's equestrian statue that stood before the great church of Hagia Sophia in Constantinople. After 1453 the focus of the myth moved west. The red apple was always in the as yet unconquered Christian lands. Often it was connected with Rome, perhaps with the shiny dome of St. Peter's. It could also be connected with the Christian cities of Buda and Vienna, beckoning not too far beyond the Ottoman frontier.

In the century after Istanbul fell to the Turks, the westward expansion of their empire continued, checked momentarily here and there, but then again regaining its momentum. To it was joined an eastward expansion. The success of Turkish arms stretched the frontiers of their empire from Buda to Basra, from Algiers to Armenia, from Azov to Aden. This success was undergirded by a military and a political

---

[1] The Turkish expression is *kizil elma*, literally "red apple." *Kizil* also means golden, or red-gold, and "golden apple" is the translation favored by Richard Kreutel, *Im Reiche des Goldenen Apfels* (Graz, 1957), pp. 9–11.

32

organization which, developing with the empire, functioned reasonably well until the later sixteenth century. Although one can speak with less assurance about it, a fairly stable and prosperous social and economic order seems to have developed along with the military and political success. And there is no doubt of the unique Ottoman cultural achievement in the same period. Military success, political organization, social order, economic prosperity, cultural heights, all served to stamp the sixteenth century as the golden age of the Ottoman Empire. In times of later weakness would-be reformers were to look back at it with nostalgia. Because the past could not be recaptured, the nostalgic look backwards was to be a hindrance to needed reform. Some of the once-successful military and political forms, of the social and economic and cultural attitudes would in time become burdens—which of course at that time could not be foreseen. This was also true of the vast territorial acquisitions.

As soon as Fatih Mehmed had taken Istanbul and started its reconstruction, he turned his attention to further conquest. Most of it was in Christian lands, though he did annex the Turkish emirate of Karamania in south-central Anatolia. Part of Mehmed's expansion was in the Black Sea area—Wallachia was made vassal, the Greek state of Trebizond was conquered, the Crimean Tartar khanate also was made vassal and with it the Genoese trading center of Kaffa, long a renowned slave mart. The Black Sea was well on the way to becoming a Turkish rather than a Christian lake, although Italian shippers were still for a time allowed to trade there. Mehmed's major expansion came in the Balkans. In part this was a reconquest, and annexation to his direct rule, of areas that had so far been tributary. In part it was conquest of new territory.

Inevitably Mehmed's success thrust him into European politics, particularly as he ran up against the imposing maritime empire of Venice, which was itself involved in European power struggles. Rivals of Venice on the Italian peninsula encouraged the Ottomans. Venice in its turn sought support from the natural opponents of the expanding Ottomans: Uzun Hasan, the Turkoman who ruled in western Iran; the Karamanian emirs; the Albanian hero Skanderbeg. Naval warfare with Venice, intermittent during most of Mehmed's reign, resulted in Turkish capture of some Venetian islands in the Aegean and raids along the Adriatic coast nearly to the gates of Venice. It resulted also in a building up of the Ottoman fleet. Mehmed, says his contemporary biographer, Kritovoulos, had concluded from his studies of history that seapower was the key to success, and ordered many triremes built. The lesson, learned centuries before Captain Mahan, was not lost on Mehmed's successors. Two crucial points eluded Mehmed's grasp: the fortified town of Belgrade on the Danube, and the island-fastness of Rhodes from which the Knights of St. John launched their attacks on Muslim coasts and Muslim shipping. Otranto, a base on the Italian peninsula, was held by the Turks for only a year before they gave it up; plans for an Italian campaign evidently were cancelled,

Such territorial expansion as was achieved during the reign of Bayezid II (1481–1512), Mehmed's successor, was again at the expense of Venice. Most of her ports around the southern edge of the Morea fell into Ottoman hands. Venice, now a declining seapower partly because the Portuguese circumnavigation of Africa opened an all-sea route to the Far East that cut into middleman trade, was now being eclipsed by the Ottomans in the Black Sea, the Aegean, and the eastern Mediterranean. The Ottoman navy was built up by incorporating pirates, both Christian and Muslim, who raided as far west as the Balearic islands in 1501—one of the results of which was the capture from a Spanish sailor of an early map of Columbus. By the end of Bayezid's reign the Ottomans had in effect replaced territorially both the Byzantine Empire, in its essential Balkan and Anatolian nucleus, and the Venetian maritime empire, except for Crete and Cyprus, that Venice had won during the Byzantine decline.

During the war with Venice a new threat to the Ottoman empire, appearing in the East, led to territorial expansion away from Europe. A revived Iranian power under Shah Ismail endangered not only the Ottomans' eastern frontier, but generated disturbances within their borders. Ismail had made Shiism the official creed of Iran, and had made himself the religious rival of the Sunnite Ottoman sultan. Thus he could play upon the Shiite tendencies of various heterodox groups within Anatolia. A large-scale revolt there, led by Shah Kuli, a dervish and sufi, was soon crushed by Bayezid. But the danger of revolt was still possible among the heretics known to the Turks as *kizilbash*—"redheads"—from the red caps that Ismail's followers wore. Bayezid's successor Selim (reigned 1512–1520), called by his people The Inexorable (*Yavuz*), prepared a campaign against Ismail. Reportedly he first had 40,000 *kizilbash* in Anatolia slain. In 1514 he advanced with his Janissaries into Iran, taking Tabriz after defeating Ismail's army at

Chaldiran. Selim might have penetrated farther to the East on this victorious Sunnite military promenade, but his Janissaries, largely of European origin and feeling *dépaysé*, evidently objected.

Instead, then, of conquering Iran, Selim turned south against the Mamluk dynasty of Egypt, which also ruled Syria and which, besides having border disputes with the Ottomans, was about to aid Ismail. The Mamluk sultan and his cavalry were defeated in Syria in 1516, his successor and the Mamluk remnants at Cairo in 1517. The Ottoman success was made possible in large part by their new weapons; they had cannon and muskets, with gunpowder made by Jewish refugees from Spain and artillery expertise furnished by Italian mercenaries. Syria and Egypt thus passed under Ottoman rule which was to endure for four hundred years.

This was part of the old Islamic world, the world south of the Taurus mountains which for centuries had marked the dividing line between Byzantine and Arab, Christian and Muslim. Its acquisition was a break, really an aberration, in the Ottoman tradition of conquest —conquest hitherto confined to the lands that Byzantium had retained in the face of the seventh-century Arab assault. Selim's southward expansion brought new contact with Arab culture, adding to earlier Persian and Arab influences on the Turks. Further, the expansion brought into subordination to Istanbul two of the historic Muslim capitals, Damascus and Cairo, and the three sacred cities of Islam: Mecca, Medina, and Jerusalem. The story is often repeated that the shadow-caliph who had existed in Mamluk Cairo, and who now fell into Ottoman hands, formally transferred his title to Selim. The story is baseless. It was true, nevertheless, that the Ottoman connection with the world of traditional Islam was strengthened. The sultans in Istanbul became the chief power of the old Islamic world, guardians of the holy cities; they now used the title "Commander of the Faithful" (perhaps first adopted by Mehmed II), with greater reason and wider Muslim approval. So, more than a century after reaching the Danube, the Ottoman Turks had reached the Nile and were stretching toward the Euphrates, joining the old world of early Islam to the new world of gazi conquest.

The long reign of Süleyman (1520–1566) was no less filled with wars of conquest. His first care was to remove two blocks to expansion. Belgrade, which had for so long proudly resisted the Turks with Hungarian aid, was taken in 1521. Rhodes, whose obstreperous knights harassed the sea route from Turkey to Egypt, fell to a siege the next year. Secure then in his rear, and with the route to the upper Danube open, Süleyman embarked on a series of campaigns into the Hungarian plain and on into the Austrian lands of the Habsburgs. His advance was motivated not only by a need to satisfy the Janissaries' desire for action and loot in quest of the red apple, and by friction with the Hungarians, but also by European politics. His Most Christian Majesty Francis I of France, defeated at Pavia by His Apostolic Majesty Charles V, the Habsburg Holy Roman emperor, urged the Muslim sultan to war against the Habsburgs. In 1526 Süleyman's army destroyed the flower of Hungarian knighthood at Mohacs and temporarily occupied Buda. Three years thereafter Süleyman again led his forces into Hungary, this time answering an appeal from a candidate for the Hungarian throne for aid against the Habsburg contender. After retaking Buda, he laid siege to Vienna. But without heavy artillery, and hampered by long supply lines and autumn rains, he was unable to overcome the stout resistance of the inner city, and so retired from this farthest point of the Turkish westward advance. Hungary and Transylvania, however, remained under Ottoman suzerainty. The Habsburgs paid tribute to the sultan for the northwestern section of Hungary they retained. Most of the Hungarian plain was placed under an autonomous ruler, tributary vassal to the sultan, and then, after renewed campaigns, was directly incorporated into the Ottoman Empire.

The Ottoman-Habsburg wars were not confined to the Danube valley, but spilled over into naval action that ran the length of the Mediterranean. Throughout Süleyman's reign the fortunes of war fluctuated, but in general the Turkish admirals such as Hayreddin Barbarossa—possibly of Greek origin—succeeded in checking the Holy League which the Habsburgs had formed and which included Venice. As a result, the Ottoman Turks' control was extended along the north African coast to Tunis and Algiers. Their most signal failure was Malta, which held out successfully. The Turkish drive to the west, in addition to giving incidental help to the Protestant Reformation, had aroused the "Turkish fear" in central Europe. This was, however, no deterrent to Francis I of France, who was an ally of the Turks whenever it suited his purposes, and who in 1536 concluded with them a treaty of friendship and commerce that had effects lasting into the twentieth century.

The Habsburg wars also played a part in renewing the Ottoman-

Iranian hostility, for the Habsburgs urged the Persians to war against Süleyman as a counterbalance to the French-Turkish cooperation. In two wars with Iran Süleyman won new success in the region of Kurdistan, though he failed like his father, Selim, to retain Tabriz. He did, however, take Iraq from Persian control and added it to his empire. In so doing, he had incorporated within his empire another of the great capitals of the old Islamic world, Baghdad, though it was now but a shadow of its former self. He also reached the Persian Gulf. This success prompted him to try to break the Portuguese stranglehold on the Persian Gulf and the Indian Ocean trade so that his empire could regain a dominant position as middleman in oriental commerce. The Mamluks of Egypt had earlier tried, but in vain, to oust the western invaders. An Ottoman fleet now reached India from the Persian Gulf, but was driven back into the Gulf by the Portuguese. Other naval efforts against the Portuguese also failed, although Aden and the Yemen, at the southern end of the Red Sea, were occupied. The Red Sea, like the Black, was becoming an Ottoman lake.

When Süleyman, again on campaign up the Danube, died in 1566, the Ottoman Turks could look back on a century of phenomenal territorial expansion since the Second Rome had fallen to them. They had added the Arab world to the Greek world. Even this was not the outer limit of the empire's growth; other lands were to be acquired, well into the seventeenth century. But the Turks had run up against two obstacles. They could not take Vienna. It was a matter of chance, perhaps, in 1529 when the first assault failed; but it was not a matter of chance that Süleyman in his next thirty-five years could mount no second assault. Western arms, western economies and polities, were growing relatively stronger. Nor could the Turks wipe the Portuguese from the Indian Ocean. They operated successfully for a time in the closed Mediterranean with their oar-powered vessels, but could not compete with the Atlantic navigators of western Europe who had outflanked them by circumnavigating Africa. Nor could they share in the commerce that developed on the great ocean routes, even though Mediterranean commerce did not at once collapse. Because the empire of the Ottomans was still one of the greatest powers of Europe, possibly even the greatest in the mid-sixteenth century, it was natural that these portents were not understood. But Europe was making relatively faster economic and technological advances than its Turkish rival, and the fantastic extent of the Ottoman empire, with possessions on three continents and an extraordinarily long coastline, created un-usual problems of external defense and internal cohesion.

For the moment, however, all seemed to be well. The Ottomans had, in the period of the first ten sultans down through Süleyman, elaborated a system of government that allowed them to absorb the conquered territories, achieve a reasonable degree of cohesion, keep order, collect revenue, and maintain effective military forces. At first the usual method of absorbing newly won lands was to leave the local rulers, whether Muslim or Christian, in power, but in a vassal-tributary relationship which obliged them to pay a specified amount annually to the sultan and to provide a stipulated number of soldiers. A few of the outlying areas that came to be known as "privileged," like the Danubian Princi-palities of Moldavia and Wallachia, retained such status. But the usual next step was the direct incorporation of conquered lands under Ottoman rule through the system of military fiefs.

Ultimate title to all land, in theory, was vested in the sultan. He could keep large estates for himself, administered by his own officials to produce revenue for him. He could alienate property to private ownership or pious foundations. But in the period of Ottoman ex-pansion, most arable land was assigned to *sipahis*, cavalrymen, who became fief-holders. The revenues of the fief (*timar or zeamet*), col-lected by the holder, were in effect his salary. The tithe on produce of farmers was his most important source, but there were other dues too. His obligation was to provide, according to the extent and value of his fief, certain numbers of armed fighting men. This method had both Seljuk and Byzantine precedents. Its application by the Ottomans, further, was not always revolutionary. Although local ruling dynasties were ousted when fiefs were established, local gentry and military leaders, even some tribal chiefs in Anatolia and Syria, were given such fiefs and so incorporated into the Ottoman ruling class. Many of them, in the early years, were Christian, though by the sixteenth century this was rare, and most of the Christian fief-holders seem to have be-come Muslim. The right of appointment remained with the sultan; he could and did appoint sons of holders to fiefs, but no hereditary feudal aristocracy of right was allowed.

To calculate tax revenue and assign fiefs, the sultans undertook a meticulous survey of each province. Their agents recorded village populations, land, crops, livestock. Such *defters* (registers) were first made in the fourteenth century, though the earliest that now survives dates from 1431. Conservatives opposed the *defter* when Bayezid I used it, unconsciously echoing the comment of the Anglo-Saxon chronicler on the Domesday Book—"it is shameful to tell" how every ox and cow was recorded. Once an efficient instrument of government control, the *defters* are now a major historical source.

The fiefs were included in provinces (*sanjaks*) which were the basic military and administrative units of the empire. A *sanjak-bey*, the sultan's chief official in each province, commanded the *sipahis* in war, and was responsible for public order and for carrying out administrative and legal decisions. In the early days of the empire there were two governors-general (*beylerbeys*)—one for the provinces of Anatolia, one for Rumelia. As the Ottoman territory expanded, more were appointed.

By the later fifteenth century the character of warfare was beginning to change, because of the new firearms. Cavalry became less important. To organize and train infantry and artillery, the sultans could not depend on the fief system; the job had to be done centrally, and it required cash rather than feudal service. Thus the system of government in the sixteenth century began to reflect this change. Some land that at an earlier time was in *timars* was (at different times in different places) converted to tax-farms—units which would produce cash revenues, under the system know as *iltizam*. Hungary and Syria, when first incorporated, were under the *timar* system, though Syria was changed in 1607. Egypt after the Ottoman conquest was on the tax-farm basis, sending funds annually to Istanbul to support the standing troops.

Of course, from early Ottoman days there had been footsoldiers—irregulars, some regulars, vassal contingents, and the elite Janissaries. As the empire grew and warfare changed, more regular infantry units were organized, and new functions created for them. The Janissary corps grew in size. At the time of Mehmed II it was only about 12,000 strong; estimates for Süleyman's time range up to 40,000. The Janissaries were slave warriors, Christians converted to Islam, and dependent directly on the sultan. At first their ranks were filled with war captives or purchased slaves. Later a system of levying a tribute of boys from Christian subjects was organized. This may have started under Murad I, though the origins are not clear; under Murad II the conscripting system known as the *devshirme* (collecting) seems to have become institutionalized. About every five years boys in their teens or younger were taken from Christian families, screened, tested, trained in various schools, and then enrolled in the Janissary corps. Some, the cream of the levy, were taken into higher palace and administrative training, but the majority entered the Janissary corps or other standing military units. Though it is often stated that the levy applied only to Balkan Christians—and certainly the bulk were Balkan Greeks, Slavs, or Albanians—it is now clear that the levy was also applied to Anatolia at least from the mid-fifteenth century. Janissaries were required to remain unmarried, though in Süleyman's time this rule was being broken. They constituted a very effective fighting force and were feared by opponents of the Ottomans; in battles they were often held in reserve until the crucial moment. They also became, however, a domestic political force. So early as the mid-fifteenth century a Janissary revolt had to be quelled, and with Mehmed II it became customary for a new sultan on his accession to distribute the "Janissary coin" to assure the loyalty of the corps.

From the *devshirme* the Ottoman sultans also drew youths who were trained in various palace schools. The top echelon became pages in the imperial palace, continuing their education in the so-called "inner service." The Seljuks and other eastern dynasties had used slave administrators, and the Ottoman sultans began the practice early. The slaves, after training, occupied high palace jobs, were sometimes assigned *timars*, made *sanjak-beys* or given other major administrative posts. Until the conquest of Istanbul, however, the highest positions, including that of grand vezir, were usually held by born Muslims, often of leading families. Thereafter the new elite of the *devshirme* began to eclipse the older elite, and for two centuries or more grand vezirs almost without exception, as well as provincial governors and top military commanders, came from the *devshirme* ranks. They were products of the palace school that Mehmed II had instituted in his new capital of Istanbul. Here, following a curriculum broader than that of the traditional Muslim school, they learned Turkish, Arabic, and Persian; studied the Koran; absorbed some history, mathematics, and music; became proficient in horsemanship and weaponry; underwent rigorous physical training; learned a craft or trade; and learned etiquette as well. The graduate—in theory a scholar-athlete-gentleman after some fourteen years of training, as well as a sound Muslim and devoted servant of the sultan—was then equipped to take his place as an official of the sultan's household or as an administrator of the empire.

This is the system which occasionally aroused such favorable comment from Europeans in whose kingdoms noble birth was the key to high office. In Süleyman's time the ambassador of Emperor Charles V to Istanbul wrote:

> No distinction is attached to birth among the Turks; the deference to be paid to a man is measured by the position he holds in the public service. . . . In making his appointments the Sultan pays no regard to any pretensions on the score of wealth or rank . . . ; he considers each case on its own merits. . . . It is by merit that men rise in the service, a system which ensures that posts should only be assigned to the competent. Each man in Turkey carries in his own hand his ancestry and his position in life, which he may make or mar as he will.[2]

The slaves from the *devshirme* system were not slaves in the usual sense: they could own property, they had individual rights, but as slaves their lives and property were at the disposition of the sultan alone. Inevitably some Christian youths recruited in the *devshirme* tried to escape, and their families on occasion objected even to the point of revolt. But for those who were palace trained great career opportunities were opened up, and the Ottoman elite through them was continuously infused with new blood.

The growth of the empire made central government considerably more complex. Much of the daily work was carried on by secretaries, or bureaucrats—*kâtibs*—who collectively formed a group that may be called "men of the pen." These included scribes and record-keepers of all sorts, of whom some of the most important were the financial secretaries, *defterdars*, headed by a chief *defterdar* who in the early days of the empire was one of the most prestigious officials. The Ottoman empire was a revenue-collecting organization. This activity took precedence over all functions except the military, and was, of course, necessary to finance the military. The head-tax paid by non-Muslims, customs duties, income from imperial estates, income from mines, tribute from vassal states, and other types of revenue had to be recorded and kept current. Now and again new taxes were invented and imposed. The tendency was to add a new bureau or bureaucrat to keep account of each source of revenue. Thus the bureaucracy grew. Most of its members seem to have been born Muslims, and many were members of the class of *ulema*—those with training in Muslim theology

[2] *The Life and letters of Ogier Ghiselin de Busbecq*, eds. C. T. Forster and F. H. B. Daniell (London, 1881), I, 154.

and law, the "learned." The other major branch of the bureaucracy, concerned with general administration, and in particular with correspondence and imperial ordinances, likewise grew larger.

In the Ottoman view of government, military force was necessary for power, revenue was necessary for military force, public order and well-being were necessary for revenue, and justice was necessary for public order. In addition, then, to the soldiers and administrators who dealt with security and revenue, judges formed an integral part of the governmental system. Each sanjak and each of its subdivisions had its *kadi* (judge), appointed by the sultan and independent of the *sanjak-bey*. He applied the *sheriat*—the traditional Islamic law—as well as other legislative ordinances of the sultan. The kadis were members of ulema, a vital element in Islamic polities. In the Ottoman Empire they were organized by the state into a hierarchy and given official standing greater than they had enjoyed in earlier Muslim states. The law of Islam pervaded the empire. The class of ulema included, in addition, teachers in the schools (which were usually attached to mosques), prayer leaders (*imams*), and interpreters of the law (*müftis*). At the highest level of government in the golden age stood the *kadi-asker*, the chief judge. Originally there was one chief judge, but after the extensive conquests there were two, one for Rumelia and one for Anatolia.

At the apex of the military and administrative hierarchies was the sultan, an individual of the utmost importance in the Ottoman system. He was from the time of Mehmed II as much an autocrat as the conditions and communications of the time would allow. Though the individual characters and qualities of leadership of the first ten rulers, from Osman to Süleyman, varied greatly, all were able men and some obviously had outstanding ability. As a rule each had had administrative and sometimes military experience in a provincial post while still a prince. Son always succeeded father on the throne, but not necessarily the eldest son. There were occasional bloody contests for the succession among brothers, the most dramatic of which was the ten-year struggle among the sons of Bayezid I after Timur's victory. If, after one son became sultan, a brother survived, a real danger was posed to imperial cohesion by the possible contender. The brother of Bayezid II, Jem, had been such a threat, and doubly so because he escaped abroad and his claim might have been used as an excuse for a "crusade" by a coalition of European enemies of the Ottomans. To avoid challenges to the reigning sultan, the cruel custom of fratricide was established. On accession, the sultan had his surviving brothers strangled with the silken bow string; the justification was that public disorder was worse than a few individual deaths. The relatively long and stable reigns of the first ten sultans, averaging about twenty-seven years, may prove the point. The successful brother was frequently the most able, though often he owed his accession to the cooperation of palace officials and the Janissaries. Down to the time of Süleyman, the sultan usually led his armies in person.

The sultan also, to the time of Mehmed II, presided in person at sessions of the imperial council, or *divan*. Thereafter to Süleyman's time, the sultan listened to divan deliberations from behind a screen. In the sixteenth century the divan met four days a week to deal with all government business, in the morning hearing petitions and complaints in public session and after lunch going into executive session. The composition of this small group changed slowly with time. The grand vezir, the sultan's alter ego and chief executive officer, presided. Several "vezirs of the dome" (so named because the council met in a domed chamber of the Topkapi palace), the two *kadi-askers*, the two chief *defterdars* and the *nishanji* (a kind of chancellor or secretary of state) made up the nucleus of the divan, though other officials attended and sometimes participated. The divan had its own secretariat, and headed up other bureaus which together formed the central administration of the empire.

Not only these highest officials of the central administration, but also the military men, the *devshirme* officials, the bureaucrats, and the ulema mentioned above, wherever stationed, belonged to what in Ottoman times was considered the ruling group. This the Ottomans called the *askeri* class, meaning literally the "military" class, although the civilian elite were included as well. The class was not a closed group. Through education, exceptional service, or the *devshirme* one could rise to it, but the tendency for sons of the elite to secure governmental positions grew strong. Those with the rank of vezir or title of pasha, terms which were originally associated with the highest ranks of military command and provincial governorship, stood at the top. There were pashas of various grades, indicated by the number of horsetails on their standards. The sultan alone had six tails, the grand vezir and other vezirs three, beylerbeys two, sanjak-beys one. The title of *efendi* was applied to bureaucrats and members of the ulema. The members of this ruling group served faith and state, in the common phrase, and knew the Ottoman way—which involved knowledge of the complex literary language and of the customs and etiquette of the top level. The *askerî* class was not taxed.

Other peoples in the empire, no matter whether Muslim, Christian, or Jew, paid taxes. There were the *reaya*—the ruled, as distinct from the rulers. Being ruled did not mean being oppressed. It is generally thought that up to the sixteenth century peoples as a whole were better off where Ottoman rule was established than they theretofore had been —better security, more equal justice, taxation not too onerous. Conditions of life, including taxes and other obligations, varied with locality, for the Ottomans absorbed many local customs and practices of the societies that preceded them. The empire was in fact a great mixture of rights, duties, customs, and above all of peoples—perhaps fifty million in the sixteenth century. Each person was presumed to have his rightful status in a group, where he should stay put. There were economic, social, linguistic, and cultural differences among the various groups, but the most important without question were the religious differences under which many of the others were subsumed.

Within the empire the major religious groups, in addition to Muslims, were the Greek Orthodox, Gregorian Armenian, and Jewish. Though a preponderance of the Orthodox were Balkan peasants, and of the Armenians were east Anatolian peasants, and though most Jews were city dwellers, the various confessions were not geographically separated by region, but were intermixed throughout the empire. This confused confessional pattern was partly inherited by the Ottomans; partly it resulted from conquest, conversion, and immigration; and partly it was promoted consciously by the government's practice of *sürgün*—of transporting and resettling various groups for reasons of border defense, local order, sedentarization of nomadic tribes, or economic development. The various elements of the population rubbed shoulders with each other. The mixture impressed foreigners. "In all cyttyes in Turkey," wrote the servant of a travelling English gentleman, "they have iii Sabothes in a weke, the Turks upon Fryday, the Jewes upon Satterday, and the Crystyans uppon Sounday." In a Balkan caravanserai, he says, "You shall have Turkes, Jues, Crystyans, and trewmen and theves all at onc." [3] The Spanish writer Cervantes, who spent some time as a captive in Algiers, found that city similarly mixed: Arabs, Berbers, Jews,

[3] A. C. Wood, ed., *Mr. Harrie Cavendish, His Journey to and from Constantinople, 1589, by Fox, His Servant* (London, 1940), pp. 24-25.

Christians, Turks—and the born Turks made the best officials, he said. Yet despite the close physical proximity, compartmentalization of life by sect was the rule. This segregation resulted not only from the tendency for adherents of any one sect to cluster together in separate villages or city quarters, but from the political institutionalization of the sects by the Ottoman sultans, in what was known as the *millet* system.

The minority religious groups were officially made political by Mehmed the Conqueror. After taking Istanbul, he appointed a leading Orthodox cleric to be patriarch and civil head of all the Orthodox in the empire. The same was done by recognizing the Armenian patriarch and the Jewish grand rabbi of Istanbul as heads of their respective *millets*, or religious communities. The authority granted to the *millet* heads, and through them to their clergy, extended beyond the normal matters of church administration, worship, education, and charity to supervision of the civil status of their co-religionists. Judicial and tax-collecting authority was included, though criminal matters were always reserved for the sultan's judges. The *millet* system was thus an instrument of government.

The recognition of *millet* autonomy by the sultans also reflected the traditional tolerance of Islam for "peoples of the book" who accepted Muslim rule. Tolerance did not, however, mean equality. The most obvious inequality related to conversion. Christians or Jews might freely become Muslims, but for a Muslim to apostatize meant death. Nor could non-Muslims rise to high governmental position unless they became converts. They suffered certain disabilities—no bells were permitted on Christian churches, for instance. But the lot of non-Muslims in the sixteenth century Ottoman empire was usually better than that of religious minorities in western Europe, where Christian persecuted Jew, Catholic oppressed Protestant, and Protestant replied in kind where he could. One evidence is the great influx of Sephardic Jews from Spain and Portugal into the Ottoman empire, bringing with them financial, commercial and political knowledge that was often useful to the sultans' administration and military, as well as to the empire's economy. There seems also to have been considerable immigration of peasants from Germany, Austria, and Hungary, perhaps more from economic than political motives. Non-Muslims were excluded from call-up for military service, but instead paid a special head-tax (*cizye*). Despite the legal inequity involved, the non-Muslims seem to have been happier with this arrangement.

Viewed in economic and social terms, sixteenth-century Ottoman society included the three traditional groups: nomads, peasants, townsmen. The tribal nomads, whether of mountain or desert, were numerous in eastern Anatolia and in the Arab areas. As always, they raided the settled populations, creating problems for tax collection and maintenance of public order. Ottoman documents of the period reveal a sometimes exasperated government trying to keep the tribes in check by reprisal attack, by taking hostages, by making tribal chiefs into officials, or by planting new villages along travel routes. The peasants, the backbone of the empire's economy, worked land which they usually did not own, which formed part of a fief or a tax-farm. The villager was generally poor, his house rude, his agricultural methods primitive and falling behind those of western Europe. His oxen were about half the size of the better-fed western beasts. Yet the empire was agriculturally self-sufficient, and produced grain which could be exported. In the towns and cities were concentrated Turkish officials and garrisons, so that (especially in the Balkan peninsula) town and country presented a Muslim-Christian contrast. In the towns also, however, were the artisans and tradesmen, many of whom were non-Muslims, and the merchants who were even more usually non-Muslims. Artisans and tradesmen were organized into guilds (*esnaf*) which exercised supervision over members and products and were in some places so influential as effectively to control local government. Guilds had also a religious and ceremonial as well as economic and fraternal cast, each with its patron saint. Some guilds were Muslim, some Christian, and some were mixed.

Foreign trade was fostered by the sultans. After the capture of Istanbul, Mehmed II renewed the trading privileges which Venice had held in Byzantine days, and encouraged other Italian city-states. The Black Sea was closed to western Christian merchants at the end of the fifteenth century, but Greeks who were Ottoman subjects carried on commerce there. Turks—traditionally soldiers, administrators, or farmers—were not usually engaged in commerce, but left this to Arabs, to the non-Muslim minorities or to westerners. Though the Portuguese were cutting into the Muslim role as middlemen in the Far East trade, some of this ancient trade survived and revived in the later sixteenth century through Syrian centers such as Aleppo, and through the Red Sea. The transit trade, together with trade with the empire itself, gave western Europeans an opportunity which the French grasped when their political and military cooperation with the Ottomans made possible the treaty of 1536. This commercial treaty—"capitulation" as such treaties came to be known—recorded the privileges of the French in Ottoman dominions: to trade freely in Ottoman ports, to come under the jurisdiction of French law and consuls rather than of Muslim judges, to have freedom of religion, and to be exempt from Ottoman taxes. Similar privileges, freely accorded by a powerful Ottoman empire in order to encourage commerce, and only in part reciprocal, were later secured by other western states. As in the case of the *millets*, law followed the individual rather than the territory. This theory was being discarded in the West, but was still acceptable in the East, and so Europeans obtained extraterritorial privileges that were later to cause the Turks much grief.

Along with trade and capitulations came European ambassadors sent to reside in Istanbul. The first French ambassador arrived in 1535; the first English ambassador in 1583, though at the expense of the Levant Company rather than the crown. The Ottoman dynasty's estimate of its position in the world was made clear in the diplomatic relationship: foreign resident ambassadors were received, but the Turks sent none of their own abroad on a permanent basis—only on special missions. The Ottoman view was, in effect, that the foreigners came in the role of petitioners. European (and sometimes other) diplomats they tended to regard as potential hostages, and sometimes treated them badly. Peace treaties were granted by the sultans as if to suppliants, and not negotiated as with equals. The French monarch was as near an equal as the sultan would recognize. Süleyman wrote to Francis I in the following manner:

> I who am the sultan of sultans, the sovereign of sovereigns, the distributor of crowns to the monarchs of the surface of the globe, the shadow of God on earth, the sultan and padishah of the White Sea [Mediterranean], of the Black Sea, of Rumelia, of Anatolia, of Karamania, of the land of Rum . . . of Damascus, of Aleppo, of Cairo, of Mecca, of Medina, of Jerusalem, of all Arabia, of the Yemen and of many other countries which my noble forefathers and my illustrious ancestors (may God brighten their tombs) conquered by the force of their arms and which my august majesty has likewise conquered with my flaming sword and my victorious blade, Sultan Süleyman Han, son of Sultan Selim Han, son of Sultan Bayezid Han; You who are Francis, king of the land of France, you have sent a letter. . . .[4]

[4] Ernest Charrière, *Négociations de la France dans le Levant* (Paris, 1848), I, 116–19.

The sultans signed treaties in their own capital—others could come to them.

The scorn for Europe did not, however, keep the sultans from using European diplomatic or commercial expertise on occasion. Luigi Gritti, illegitimate son of a Venetian doge, was an influential adviser to Süleyman. Toward the end of Süleyman's reign, and during that of his son, some of the leading Sephardic Jews helped to shape Ottoman policy—especially the "Great Jew" (as Europeans called him), Joseph Nasi. But the Muslim monarch admitted no infidel equal—or Muslim equal, for that matter.

Islam was at the center of Turkish educational life as well as of law and government. Muslim schools produced the educated members of Ottoman society: bureaucrats, *devshirme* officials, physicians, and others. The exceptions to this rule were European refugees or renegades, or the clerical and lay elite of the non-Muslim minorities. Most of the educated were members of the ulema, which included the kadis, the interpreters of law (*müftis*), the prayer-leaders, and the teachers. Heading up the body of ulema was the chief müfti of Istanbul, the Sheikh ul Islam, who began to rise in status during the sixteenth century until he eclipsed the *kadi-askers* and ranked just below the grand vezir. Though often called a "clergy," the ulema were not a priesthood, ordained to sacerdotal office to stand as intermediaries between man and God; the hallmark of the ulema was rather learning. It was learning in the orthodox Sunnite tradition, in the official Islam of the empire. This they studied and in turn imparted in the theological schools (*medreses*) of the empire, where not only the inseparable theology and law but some elements of humanities and science were taught.

Members of the ulema were frequently administrators of pious foundations (*vakifs*), a vast number of which were established to support schools, hospitals, mosques, public fountains, hospices, soup-kitchens, even to build and maintain roads and bridges. Many of the functions that the modern state assumes in providing for public welfare were thus cared for by foundations which were set up by the wealthy of all kinds, including sultans and vezirs. There were also *vakifs* which were set up primarily to insure continuity of income from a property to the founder's family and heirs, and to avoid confiscation, or division as a result of the inheritance laws. The considerable amount of property set aside in this fashion from normal state taxation and control, and from the area of normal real estate transactions, was to cause immense problems in the future.

There was also, in addition to the official Islam represented by the ulema, another and more popular Islam which had flourished among the Turks since the days of the border march. Incorporating Shiite, mystic (*sufi*), and folk-religion elements, even in some cases Christian elements, this unofficial Islam was best represented by the dervish orders. The more important had thousands of members. Some full-time members lived in the *tekkes* (convents); many more were part-time, lay brothers from among the people, who participated in the rites that gave them a greater sense of union or communion with the divine than did the austere formalism and ritual of orthodox Islam. Some of the orders kept closer to orthodoxy; some were much more heterodox. The Mevlevis were an example of the former, the Bektashis of the latter. Organized perhaps in the early fifteenth century, the Bektashis had spread widely, especially in Rumelia, and had become even more influential because of a close connection with the Janissaries. The Bektashis also helped to preserve the popular Turkish language in the face of strong Persian literary influences.

Among the common people Turkish folk-poetry and popular tales had, of course, continued to exist, but the culture of the sixteenth century that impressed the Ottomans then and in later times was more complex and eclectic, the creation and possession of an urban elite. Among the centers of urban culture, Istanbul was supreme. To it gravitated the poets who wrought beautiful verse on Persian models, the historians who celebrated the achievements of the dynasty, the artists who illuminated manuscripts, the ulema who taught in the great *medreses*. Istanbul's houses were of wood, as if to imply that to build anything more permanent was to lay blasphemous claim to immortality, but its major public buildings were of stone—the bazaars, hans, baths, schools, and, above all, the mosques. Aya Sofya's dome was a model and inspiration for Ottoman architects, but the best of them surpassed it in creating vast unobstructed dome-capped space for the long rows of worshippers. The master architect Sinan, a product of the *devshirme* from Kayseri, built in his long lifetime well over three hundred structures of all sorts, scattered from Buda to Baghdad. Two neighboring mosques in Istanbul epitomize his genius. The Shehzade mosque, done early in his career, forms with its modest proportions part of a delightful ensemble that includes some delicately appealing small mausoleums in its garden. The mosque of Süleyman, built two decades later, is among Sinan's greatest, with its airy lightness and spacious grace, again surrounded by *medreses* and tombs.

In some spheres Ottoman cultural achievement was even higher in the seventeenth and eighteenth centuries, but the sixteenth could also be proud of its cartography, its calligraphy, its brocaded textiles, its stone and wood carving, its leather work, its ceramic tile with colorful geometric, floral, and vegetable designs. In Süleyman's time the Istanbul tile works produced nearly three hundred different varieties of tulip patterns alone. Even representational art, though frowned upon by orthodox Islam as close to blasphemy, flourished in a small way with some delightful miniatures. Some of the best among them are colorful pictures of the towns and villages along the route of march of one of Süleyman's campaigns against the Persians.

The sixteenth century was a lively time made livelier by the introduction of coffee, first in the Arab provinces, and about mid-century in Istanbul. An English traveller who encountered it late in the century describes it as "a certain liquor which they do call coffee, which is made of a seed much like mustard seed, which will intoxicate the brain." [5] Though the ulema opposed coffee, and found the coffee-houses to be "meeting places of rascals and ungodly people," [6] its popularity could not be checked. The ulema themselves succumbed to the habit. Tobacco also soon invaded the empire, courtesy of Englishmen, from the New World.

It had been said of the Byzantine Empire in the great days of Justinian that Hagia Sophia was God's, the palace was the emperor's, and the Hippodrome—scene of sport, entertainment, and occasional riot—the people's. Just a thousand years later in the same capital the Ottomans attained a golden age under Süleyman, who is known to the West as the Magnificent but to his own subjects as the Law-giver (Kanunî), for like Justinian he was renowned for his legislation. Süleyman had his palace of Topkapi on the promontory of Istanbul commanding a truly imperial view of Europe and Asia, of the Bosporus, the Golden Horn, and the Sea of Marmara. Here, surrounded by hundreds of artists, and

[5] William Parry, "A New and Large Discourse on the Travels of Sir Anthony Sherley," in *Sir Anthony Sherley and His Persian Adventure*, ed. E. Denison Ross (London, 1933), p. 107.

[6] Uriel Heyd, *Ottoman Documents on Palestine, 1552–1615* (Oxford, 1960), p. 161.

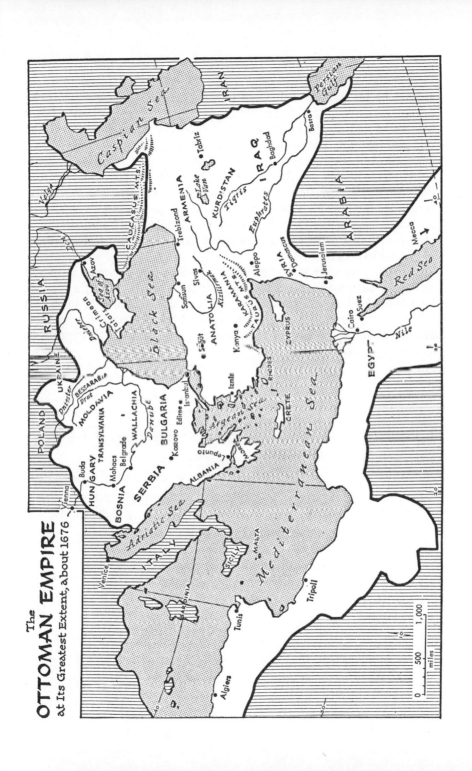

The
OTTOMAN EMPIRE
at Its Greatest Extent, about 1676

POLAND

RUSSIA

UKRAINE

Dnieper

Dniester

Prut

BESSARABIA

MOLDAVIA

Vienna

Buda

HUNGARY

TRANSYLVANIA

Mohacs

Belgrade

WALLACHIA

Danube

Volga

Don

Sea of Azov

CRIMEA

Crimean Tatars

Caspian Sea

CAUCASUS MTS.

Black Sea

Trebizond

ARMENIA

Lake Van

Tabriz

IRAN

Persian Gulf

Basra

Baghdad

IRAQ

Tigris

Euphrates

KURDISTAN

Samsun

Sivas

ANATOLIA

Kızılırmak

KARAMANIA

KARAMANIA

TAURUS MTS.

Aleppo

SYRIA

Damascus

Jerusalem

ARABIA

Mecca

Red Sea

Söğüt

Konya

Izmir

İstanbul

Edirne

Kosovo

BULGARIA

SERBIA

BOSNIA

ALBANIA

Lepanto

MOREA

RHODES

CYPRUS

CRETE

Aegean Sea

Cairo

Suez

Nile

EGYPT

Mediterranean Sea

Adriatic Sea

Venice

ITALY

SARDINIA

MALTA

SICILY

Tunis

Tripoli

Algiers

0   500   1,000
miles

20°

40°

assisted by his slave household of military men and administrators, he ruled. The mosques and the medreses were God's. Here orthodox Islam was served and taught by learned men who also formed a part of the ruling group. The people had dervish orders, guilds, and coffeehouses. They also had the Karagöz (literally "Black-Eye"), the shadow theatre, across whose screen paraded the varied types of the polyglot empire— the artisan, the "gentleman," the provincial characters, the Arab, the Armenian, the Jew. These were the ruled, each representing his appointed station in life. In the Karagöz theatre the people also found overtones of the mysticism with which they felt at home, and satirical comment on the social order.

Though there were important stresses within the Ottoman state and society in Süleyman's time, these were not so apparent as they would later become. The social order had not yet broken down. If there was ever a golden age, this was it; in retrospect it became even more golden. During darker days many of the Ottomans would long to recapture its vanished glories.

4

The Decline of Faith and State,
1566-1792

Sultan Selim II (1566–1574), son and successor of Süley-man, became known to his people as "Drunk Sultan Selim," and to the West as Selim the Sot, for his intemperate and quite un-Muslim addiction to wine. He led no armies in the field. He presents so strong a contrast to Süleyman the Lawgiver, who at 71 years of age forced himself to go on that one last campaign during which he died, that the year 1566 is often taken to mark the beginning of the Ottoman Empire's decline. The date is convenient, but history is not so simple. In so far as significant territorial loss may be taken as a measure, the treaty of Carlowitz of 1699 provides a more rational starting point for decline. If internal decay rather than territorial loss be taken as the index, the starting date may be pushed back into Süleyman's own reign. This can admittedly be done only with the benefit of hindsight, but it is not only the hindsight of the modern historian: Ottoman officials who wrote commentaries on their times, beginning around the year 1600, found elements of disorder in Süleyman's time. Kochi Bey, for example, writing around 1630, was specific about the military and administrative defects in Süleyman's day. To such commentators, dislocation of the traditional order meant decline. They hoped it would shortly be arrested by restoration of the order that had produced the golden age.

At times the decline was checked, but the checks proved to be temporary. The empire continued on a general downward course for more than three centuries. The symptoms became obvious. But how does one explain the complex causes of a decline that was very long, gradual, interrupted, and relative? Compared to other Islamic states—Iran, Mogul India, Morocco—the Ottoman Empire was strong, long-lived, and glorious. It was only in relation to its own golden age, and to the progress of its Christian European neighbors, that the empire declined. The process is not yet well understood; cause and effect, particularly in the interaction of the economic and political spheres, are not easy to distinguish. The decline can more readily be described than explained. The simplest description is to indicate first what happened within the empire, and then the military failures and territorial losses that made the decline externally obvious. The two aspects are interrelated at many points, and the only justification for this artificiality (aside from convenience) lies in the fact that the start of internal decay preceded territorial shrinkage. But first, some European developments need to be mentioned.

In one way, what happened in Europe outside the empire from the sixteenth to the eighteenth centuries constitutes the true history of Ottoman decline. Several momentous developments in which the Ottomans did not share gave the West its relative superiority. They underlie many of the problems of the modern Turkish Republic as it hurries to catch up. One such development has been noted: the commercial expansion that enriched the Atlantic states, to the detriment of the Ottomans. Further, the West developed improved agricultural methods. Its technology too advanced rapidly, as did its industry, both aided by scientific experiment and by the rationalist attitudes culminating in the Enlightenment. None of these things happened in the East before 1800; at best they awoke only feeble echoes there. A further western development made the greatest immediate impact on Ottoman fortunes: fairly strong, centralized national monarchies or bureaucratic empires appeared not only on the Atlantic but on the Turkish frontiers. Such states could concentrate technological and economic forces and eventually could win fairly consistently in war against the Ottomans. In the Ottoman state, on the other hand, a centrifugal tendency soon became evident, and no prosperous and enterprising Turkish bourgeoisie on the western model arose to aid the ruler. Such wealthy bourgeois as existed were either non-Muslims, merchants and bankers, and therefore unacceptable as allies, or already bureaucrats within the ruling group.

Not only in comparison to the West, but also in comparison to their own past, the Ottomans seem doubly to have lost their absorptive and expansionist power—both territorial and intellectual. Simply to state the fact is to raise the question, why? The answer is complex and not entirely certain.

In part, the explanation lies in the breakdown of the governmental machinery of the empire, including the military. It began at the top. The seventeen sultans after Süleyman, from 1566 to 1789, were with few exceptions men of little ability, and in some cases incompetent and mentally defective. Their average reign of thirteen years was less than half that of the first ten sultans. Much of the reason for the decline in the calibre of rulers must be sought in a change in the principle of succession, fortuitously occasioned after Mehmed III in 1595 had his nineteen brothers slain. At his death in 1603 his two minor sons, both inexperienced, were the only direct male survivors of the house. To kill one would endanger the line. Mustafa, the younger, was therefore spared by his brother Ahmed I and kept secluded in special apartments in the harem portion of the palace. Fratricide was thereafter abandoned in favor of seclusion. Mustafa in 1617 followed his brother Ahmed to the throne, and succession thereafter went not necessarily from father to son, but to the oldest surviving male. New sultans who emerged from this seclusion—the *kafes* (lattice or cage) as it was called —had no governmental experience on accession, and had led an idle life in a confinement often physically and mentally debilitating. In the *kafes* they were allowed concubines, but these were either sterilized or their children were allowed to die at birth, so that no sultan could have sons until after his accession; the likelihood was that any sons born thereafter would still be immature when their fathers died. The sultans also gave up the exercise of close control over state affairs. Rarely did they lead armies. Following Süleyman's example, they ceased on all but a few ceremonial occasions to attend meetings of the divan, thus putting more responsibility on the shoulders of the grand vezir. The divan more and more met at the vezir's house. In the mid-seventeenth century the grand vezir was given an official residence, to serve also as office, which became the effective center of government. It was known as the "Pasha's Gate" or later as the Bab-i Âli, the "lofty gate," and in European parlance as the Sublime Porte. "Porte" in time became a term to denominate the whole government.

Although the sultans abdicated day-to-day control, they still appointed the vezirs, and the palace still had enormous influence. The way was then opened for palace cliques and intrigue to advance favorites in public office. The harem began to play a larger role, probably made easier by the fact that in Süleyman's reign his favorite and wife, Hurrem Sultan (Roxelana), had persuaded him to move the harem quarters from the old palace to the Topkapi palace, center of government. She herself made and unmade vezirs. Among the harem women, the mothers of sultans or of heirs presumptive exercised greatest influence, and for three decades or so in the seventeenth century the empire was in fact ruled by women.

The atmosphere of weak sultans and palace intrigue was conducive to bribery and purchase of office as well as simple favoritism. "The heade beinge soe longe sicke hathe weakened all the members," wrote an Englishmen who was in Istanbul forty years after Süleyman's death.[1] He had perhaps heard the Turkish expression, "The fish stinks from the head," which within a few years found its way into the powerful didactic verse of Uveysi, a Turkish poet, who inveighed against corruption among the ruling group. Promotion by merit, which had distinguished the Ottoman administration, became less common. Provincial appointments, of course, were also affected by corruption. An office purchased meant that somehow the officeholder had to recoup his expense and lay up something for the future, so the cycle of bribery and of squeezing out extra money in tax collections was intensified. Frequent shifts in officeholders worsened the situation. The ulema were also affected; some who were ill-trained and ignorant bought office and hired substitutes; kadis became venal as justice was bought and sold. Obviously there were still men of ability and integrity in the government, whether they held office by virtue of merit or purchase. In some periods of crisis capable grand vezirs, among whom members of the Köprülü family in the late seventeenth century were preeminent, made efforts to root out corruption. The downward tendency was nevertheless apparent. In other societies—say, Elizabethan England—there was also large-scale corruption among some high officeholders, but the effects in the Ottoman system were more disastrous.

[1] Sir Thomas Sherley, *Discours of the Turkes*, ed. E. Denison Ross (London, 1936), pp. 4–5.

The products of the *devshirme*—the levy of Christian boys—and palace school were evidently affected by a competing force as well as by the decline of the *cursus honorum* in the face of cash and favors. The competition came from the swollen ranks of the bureaucrats, who seem by the late seventeenth century to have been successful in breaking the monopoly of high office held by the slave administrators. In the next century even more efendis became pashas and governed provinces where once the slave-military group had been supreme. The palace school continued to function, but the *devshirme* itself was abandoned, though at what date is not certain. There is evidence that in some areas the levy was continued into the eighteenth century, contradicting the usual assumption that the *devshirme* was ended in the seventeenth.

Abandonment of the boy levy was directly connected to growing rot in the Janissary corps, which provides one of the most obvious and startling indices of Ottoman decline. The rule of Janissary celibacy was first tacitly, then openly abandoned. Under Selim II Janissary sons were allowed to enroll in the corps. The sons were not slaves, but free Muslims, and it inevitably followed that other free Muslims managed also to enroll, even though the Janissaries tried to preserve a monopoly for their own sons. The size of the corps may have reached 200,000 by mid-seventeenth century, after which there was a drastic reduction followed by another increase. As the numbers grew, the military efficiency declined. Some Janissaries were not on active duty, did not go on campaign, deserted if they had to march, and simply drew pay on the basis of the pay certificate each Janissary held. These certificates became regular objects of commerce, bought up by outsiders who presented them quarterly like bond coupons. Many of the corps members were in reality artisans holding pay certificates. This double identity was breaking down the social order as well as the corps—soldiers and artisans were supposed to be distinct categories. The loosening of the social order, in turn, furthered the weakening of the Janissaries during this period.

The corruption of the Janissary corps helped not only to weaken military might and the social order, but also to injure the Ottoman economy and system of government. In some corners of the empire the Janissary garrisons became the effective local rulers. They tended also to live off the land and people, plundering the empire internally when the booty of conquest was no longer available. "I was allmost in tears every day to see their insolencies in the poor villages through which we pass'd,"

wrote Lady Mary Wortley Montagu in 1717.[2] The concentration of
Janissaries in Istanbul, with its large payroll and frequent demands for
money, was an embarrassment to the treasury. This soldiery also came
to play the role of kingmaker, and for some years in the early seventeenth
century actually dominated the central government. Osman II (1618–
1622), one of the few vigorous sultans, though still in his teens, was
deposed and then executed by the Janissaries, who suspected, rightly,
that he intended to curb their excesses. By 1630 Kochi Bey was complain-
ing of their political power. The corps was now less a threat to foreign
armies than to the empire's own government and people.

With the progressive improvements in firearms, more standing infantry were obviously needed for Ottoman military strength, but corrupt and unwarlike Janissaries were hardly the answer. With the improvement also in shipbuilding and navigational techniques, a stronger
navy was needed to control the lengthy coastline, but the navy too fell
into disrepair. Long periods of maritime truce abetted the decline, and
the Ottomans were late in converting from oar-powered galleys to sail-
ing vessels, the uses of which they never fully mastered. To round out the
picture of military decline, the fate of the feudal sipahi must also be considered. The cavalryman was no longer so vital a part of the armed forces.
After the sixteenth century an accelerating effort was made to turn
fiefs, as they became vacant, into state land that would produce cash
to support standing troops. The effort was frequently unsuccessful. Some
former fiefs were leased in tax-farm, and often produced less revenue
than desired. Some were put under lifetime tax-farm. Former fiefholders
under such arrangements got almost an hereditary right to the properties.
Some "sword-fiefs" were bestowed as "shoe-money" on harem favorites
or others, draining away financial support needed for the armed forces.
Some fiefs, by illegal means, became almost the equivalent of private
property. From fiefs that continued to exist as such, the horsemen often
failed to report for duty when called. Early reform-minded critics sometimes felt that the purity of the old system should be restored, but this
was obviously not the needed answer.

The disorder in the fief system was in fact part of an economic and
social transformation in which the empire was involved from the late
sixteenth century on. A class of local notables (*ayan*) and lords of the
valley (*derebeys*), having by one means or another secured control of

---

[2] *The Complete Letters of Lady Mary Wortley Montagu*, ed. Robert Halsband
(New York, 1966), I, 310.

former fiefs, grew up in parts of the Balkans and Anatolia. They exerted great local political and economic influence, sometimes keeping private armies. Some founded "dynasties," and by pressure got vezir or pasha rank from the Porte. Local government was in their hands. They amassed wealth at times, but were likely to squeeze the people less than a short-term governor or tax-farmer might because their permanent interests were bound up with local prosperity. The weakened central government could not control these changes. The fief system was effectively ruined, though it continued in name until the nineteenth century. Local government eluded central control—even more so in outlying Arab areas where bedouin tribal leaders, ambitious Ottoman governors, Lebanese mountain princes, descendants of the Egyptian Mamluks, or Barbary beys could easily defy the sultan's authority. The imperial treasury suffered, as did the empire's economy as a whole.

These changes were accompanied by other economic shifts, some of which are still little understood. It is not difficult to see how an empire geared to war and raid yielding booty from beyond its frontiers would begin to suffer when long wars at increased cost brought more frequent defeat and little or no spoils. The need for cash to pay more standing troops and an expanding bureaucracy is no mystery, nor is the aggravation of fiscal difficulties by bribery, peculation, or the spendthrift habits of sultans—some of them supporting harems with wildly expensive tastes. But the inflation that seems to have begun in the middle of the sixteenth century, and to have continued thereafter, presents more difficult historical problems. Prices of certain staples, such as grain, evidently increased tremendously through the eighteenth century. This may reflect the competitive demands of growing urban markets. It also reflects the influx of new silver from the mines of the Americas which in the later sixteenth century began to inflate prices throughout the Mediterranean. The effects went beyond commodity price indexes. Ottoman coinage was based on silver. The new silver bought gold at a comparative advantage, and the empire began to be drained of it. The administration, not knowing how to deal with inflation, on several occasions resorted to debasement of its own coinage, which in the end intensified the inflationary spiral. Military men and bureaucrats on fixed pay suffered from the higher cost of living; here is one more reason for Janissary fractiousness and an occupational sideline, and for bribery among officials.

The economy of the empire suffered in other ways as well. Although profits from the middleman role in European trade for eastern silks and spices had continued through the sixteenth century, they declined thereafter. A long series of Turkish-Persian wars hindered caravan safety. The British, French, and Dutch then looked rather to the sea route around Africa. By the seventeenth century the East India Company could bring goods from India via the Cape to London and reexport them to Istanbul or Izmir for sale there at prices cheaper than the Levant Company could manage by direct trade with India. As for the exchange of Ottoman and European goods, this too turned to European advantage. An unfavorable Ottoman balance of trade developed as European manufactures became better and cheaper, and as their importation was facilitated by new and extended capitulations which the European powers began not only to insist upon but to abuse. Many non-Muslim Ottoman subjects got certificates of protection from European diplomats, benefitting thereby from some immunities, and creating a situation destined to become bitter in the mouths of the Turks. Meanwhile, industrial production in the empire stagnated both because of the outside competition and because of the restrictive practices of the guilds.

Agricultural production in the empire suffered also, for many reasons: the breakdown of the sipahi-peasant relationship, the lack of peasant incentive to produce what tax-farmers would only take away, the failure to develop better cultivation practices or to found new farm villages in the border areas (as the Habsburgs and the Russians were then successfully doing). In fact, as far as village settlement is concerned, the opposite was the case: contemporary accounts are unanimous in pointing to a growing rural depopulation, deserted villages, peasants driven off the land by increased taxation or extortion. Depopulation perhaps also resulted from the bubonic plague and other diseases which spread in the empire beginning in the sixteenth century, though these probably affected the cities more than the countryside. There are also indications of a falling birthrate, and emigration. Revenue for the government declined, or at least failed to grow, as productivity declined. Peasant movements or risings, usually called Jelali revolts, occurred in parts of Anatolia at various times, expressing discontent with the economic order. So did peasant movements in or migrations from the Balkans. In the latter case there were overtones of Christian discontent with Muslim landlords. In Anatolia, there were heterodox Islamic overtones mixed with resentment of rule by the Ottoman upper crust. The Persians sometimes gave the heterodox protection in the Ottoman border regions. An English observer of such risings predicted in 1605 an Ottoman decline: "And nowe that the Turkes finde that by rebellinge they can dischardge them selves of that serville yoke with whyche the Ottomans have so longe, tiranised over them, there will cum (& that speedily) a greate dissipation in that Empire. . . ." [3]

To political and economic problems were added others which are yet harder to judge rightly. One must remain still in the form of a question: was there a moral decline? Various foreign observers, now more scornful of the Ottomans than frightened by them, emphasized their vices rather than their virtues, and thought they perceived a decline in character. Drunkenness, pederasty, prostitution, and coffee-house society provided them with examples. Ottoman self-criticism agreed with some of these views, but pointed more urgently to corruption, bribery, and love of luxury in high places. Leaving unanswered the question whether throughout the empire there was a decline in morals, it is probably true that such a decline did occur in Istanbul (perhaps even as a carry-over from the decadent Byzantine days), in some other major cities, and particularly among the ruling group. Presumably this was a reflection of the breakdown of traditional systems and values, and of an increase in the "worldliness" a modern historian fastens on the eighteenth century.[4]

In some of its aspects the Ottoman decline from the later sixteenth century to the end of the eighteenth may seem to echo similar trends in the later Roman and Byzantine empires. The similarity extends also to intellectual life. Here also the Ottoman Empire experienced a decline, but not immediately. The golden age of culture extended beyond Süleyman's time, and was succeeded by a "silver" age. Sinan's greatest masterpiece, for example, the mosque of Selim II in Edirne, was completed only in 1575. The great "blue mosque" of Ahmed I in Istanbul was a seventeenth-century product, and other mosques in the eighteenth century "baroque" period continued to have charm. Poetry of the classical Persian-influenced school is considered to have reached its peak a century after Süleyman. Miniature painting, too, exhibited originality and talent down to the early eighteenth century; some of the best of this period represents with fidelity and vivid color tradesmen, artisans, and entertainers—the common people—as well as the rulers.

The body of ulema, however, did exhibit an intellectual decline that

---

[3] Sherley, Discours, p. 8.
[4] Niyazi Berkes, The Development of Secularism in Turkey (Montreal, 1964), pp. 26–30.

had unfortunate consequences. Many in the higher ranks were more interested in material gain than in learning. The medrese curricula became narrower, the receptiveness of ulema to new ideas less common. Compared to their own earlier standards, with individual exceptions, they fell short. Palace-school graduates tended to be better educated than the ulema. Most of those Muslims in the empire who could read and write were medrese products, and the resultant drag on progress of mediocre education was great. The chief function of the ulema was, of course, to maintain order—which to them meant the traditional order and was synonymous with justice—by upholding the sacred law of Islam. An ignorant or narrowly educated ulema would do this unimaginatively. Innovation, always looked askance at in Islam, became their enemy. Yet innovation was badly needed.

The theory has been advanced that in the long run it was unfortunate that Selim I and Süleyman had been able to repress Shiite heresy and rebellion within the empire, for this meant that orthodox Islam could harden without having to meet the intellectual challenge of vituperation and dialogue that prevailed in the West, where neither Catholicism nor Protestantism could suppress the other. Therefore Sunni orthodoxy could become intellectually lazy, resistant to new ideas, and, in its ossification, disinterested in or contemptuous of infidel western intellectual advance.[5] How much merit this theory has in explaining the cause of intellectual stagnation remains to be proven. Certainly the heterodox dervish orders remained influential within the empire.

It would be unfair to blame the ulema alone for the unhealthy intellectual attitude prevalent among the Ottomans, though the ulema did much to encourage it. It was an attitude which proclaimed the superiority of the world of the true believer over the world of the Frank infidel. It found its justification in the Ottoman successes of the past, which became an intellectual millstone around the neck of would-be reformers. Why should not the same methods, once corruption had been rooted out, again prevail? Why borrow from the Frank, except possibly a few techniques and inventions? Thus in a period when the West was making rapid progress, the Ottoman mind was relatively stagnant. This comparative rather than absolute backwardness was the most disastrous phase of the intellectual attitude. The Ottoman empire was in and

---

[5] See William H. McNeill, *Europe's Steppe Frontier, 1500–1800* (Chicago, 1964), pp. 36–37.

of Europe, and had to reckon with it. There were always highly cultured men in the empire, including members of the ulema, who were receptive to new ideas. But they were exceptions and could not easily prevail in the face of the general attitude which was nourished by those administrative, provincial, Janissary, or ulema groups whose selfish interests seemed best served by the situation as it was.

The foregoing catalogue of Ottoman weaknesses yields a picture of almost unrelieved gloom. One must constantly be reminded that the decline was slow—a matter of two and a half centuries, sometimes checked, and relieved by occasional reform and progress. This is illustrated partly in the Ottoman experience of warfare and territorial shifts between 1566 and 1792. The period began with both failure and success. Under Selim II and his vigorous grand vezir, Sokollu Mehmed Pasha, a raid into Muscovite territory failed to achieve the victory necessary for digging a Don-Volga canal. A plan to dig a Suez canal had to be abandoned because of a Yemeni revolt. Then, when in 1571 the Ottomans were besieging Venetian-held Cyprus, their fleet was badly beaten by combined Christian fleets at Lepanto in the last great ram-and-board action of galleys. But while the West celebrated its victory and failed to press its advantage, the Ottomans took Cyprus and kept it (for three centuries), even forcing an indemnity from Venice. Sokollu Mehmed is said to have told the Venetians that they had lost an arm which would not grow back, whereas only the Ottoman beard had been shaved and it would grow back stiffer than ever. The fleet was in fact rebuilt within a year.

Thereafter a new pattern of warfare developed. By the end of the seventeenth century the Ottomans confronted an extended arc of opponents on their periphery—Venice, Austria, Poland, Russia, Iran—some of whom acted together on occasion. When one considers also that European maritime strength had driven the Ottomans from the Indian Ocean and had gained in the western Mediterranean, it becomes apparent that they were boxed in on all sides. The periphery was far from Istanbul, however, and the Ottomans at first did not do badly. The seventeenth century began with the treaty of Zsitva Torok in 1606, concluding a war against Austria. Territorially it was favorable to the Turks. But it was a symbol: the first treaty concluded outside of Istanbul; a negotiated compromise rather than a grant of peace by the sultan to Christian suppliants; the result of diplomatic negotiation to which the Ottomans for the first time sent envoys with full powers and wherein the Habsburg monarch was for the first time treated as the sultan's equal.

In the renewed wars with Iran, fighting ranged back and forth across the border areas, a sort of eastern Lotharingia. Iran was never a constant threat. The major significance of Turco-Persian wars beyond the religious element was the mutual waste of strength, recalling how Byzantines and Persians had similarly weakened each other just before the Arab onslaught a thousand years before.

The real threat in the seventeenth century came from the West and North. While the threat was still intermittent and young, the Ottomans achieved their greatest territorial expansion: Crete was taken from Venice in 1664 after years of fighting; Podolia and part of the Ukraine were seized from Poland in 1676. Then came the turning point. It was, significantly, marked by a Russian victory in 1681 that took away most of the newly-won Ukraine. A long war in which Austria was the constant opponent, joined at times by Poland, Venice, and Russia, began in 1682. The next year the Ottoman armies advanced to the gates of Vienna, as in 1529, but this time they were defeated by the Christians rather than by the weather. A slow retreat began across the plains of Hungary, punctuated by more defeats, while Peter the Great of Russia in separate action took Azov. By the treaties of Carlowitz in 1699, the Ottomans lost Podolia to Poland, Hungary and Transylvania to Austria, the Morea to Venice. Only the last of these losses proved temporary. The others were permanent and marked the beginning of a continuing Ottoman territorial shrinkage, more than a century after the domestic decline was well advanced.

The defeat of 1699 revealed clearly that the Ottomans now had to contend with two major opponents on their frontiers. Both the Austrian and the Russian states were becoming internally more solid just at the time when the Ottoman empire was becoming less so. The Austrians were the greater immediate danger, for they were on the Danube. The Russians were still north of the Black Sea, separated from Ottoman lands proper by the vassal Khanate of the Crimean Tartars. Both conflicts were to shape Turkish destinies, but the Russian became increasingly the more important. During the eighteenth century the result of two Austrian wars was to stabilize the common frontier at the Danube and the Sava, with Belgrade remaining in Ottoman hands.

Austria gained nothing more from the Ottomans until Bosnia was occupied in 1878. Her involvement in other European wars, and later her own internal minority problems, blunted Austria's advance. But the scope of the Russo-Turkish conflict in the eighteenth century went far beyond the earlier border clashes in the Tartar or Cossack areas north of the Black Sea. Three Russian wars in that century culminated in the victory of Catherine the Great, sealed by the treaty of Küchük Kaynarja in 1774. Though the partition of Poland, forced by Prussia, diverted Catherine and saved the Turks from a worse defeat, the war and the treaty set the tone for Russo-Turkish relations in the future.

During the war, Catherine's policy had included championing the Christian Orthodox in the Ottoman dominions and trying to rouse the Greeks to revolt. A Russian fleet from the Baltic failed to take the Morea, but destroyed an Ottoman fleet in the Aegean Sea. In the treaty of Küchük Kaynarja, Russia now obtained the right to build "a public church of the Greek ritual" in Istanbul, and to make representations to the Porte on its behalf, the Porte promising for its part "to protect constantly the Christian religion and its churches" So was laid the base for later exaggerated Russian claims to act as legitimate protector of the large Greek Orthodox millet in the Ottoman empire. Territorially, the Russians evacuated most of what they had overrun, but retained some strategic points on the north shore of the Black Sea. The Crimean Tartars were declared independent, and the Porte was obliged to accord special treatment to Moldavia and Wallachia. Commercially, the Russians were granted the right to trade on the Black Sea, through the Straits, and throughout the sultan's empire, as well as to establish consulates. Diplomatically, Russia was now to have a permanent minister at Istanbul.

Küchük Kaynarja was thus more than the camel's nose under the Ottoman tent; it was head, forefeet, and hump. The Russian desire was whetted for control of Istanbul—which they called Tsargrad, the Emperor's City, as did all Slavs—and the Straits connecting the Mediterranean and Black Seas. Catherine, within a decade, worked out a plan to partition European Turkey with Austria and Venice, reserving for herself what is now Roumania and for her grandson, named Constantine in memory of the last Paleologus of 1453, a small restored Byzantine empire centered on Tsargrad. Though she failed to realize the grandiose scheme, she annexed the Crimean Khanate outright in 1783.

The fourth Russo-Turkish war of the century obliged the Porte in 1792 to recognize the annexation and the further extension of Russian rule westward to the Dniester River.

Several consequences flowed from the Russian victories. The Black Sea, heretofore closed to Christian-flag shipping, was no longer a Turkish lake. Russia created naval bases and fortresses there, and her merchantmen could trade freely in Muslim ports. (At exactly the same time, the Red Sea, heretofore closed to Christian shipping above Jidda, also ceased to be a Turkish lake; British shippers were docking at Suez.) Ottoman Greeks were given the right to trade under the Russian flag; with this prerogative some Greek shippers began to gain wealth, to broaden their contacts, and ultimately to serve as a stimulus to a Greek national revival that within a half-century would rise to confront the Ottomans. For the Ottomans the defeats conveyed a particular lesson: they were no longer one of the greatest European powers. Europe had feared them less and less since the second retreat from Vienna in 1683. In place of the "Turkish fear" of the sixteenth century there had arisen in Europe the "Turquerie" style of the eighteenth, with its imitations of Turkish kiosks and decorative forms. Europe could enjoy Turkishness; the Viennese could laugh in 1782 at the premiere of Mozart's opera, "Abduction from the Seraglio." But until 1739 at least the Ottoman empire was, though weakening, a great power, as well as an element in the European balance so carefully cultivated by the French monarch. Küchük Kaynarja showed conclusively that the Ottomans had lost their great-power status. The peace of Jassy in 1792 confirmed it.

The obvious further lesson for the Ottomans was that they needed reform, at least military reform, to regain their position. Since the West, now including Russia, was superior in arms, the Ottomans would have to borrow from the West in order to oppose it. The process of westernization had begun in a small way early in the eighteenth century. Toward the end of the century it became even more necessary.

5

The Beginnings of Westernization,
1789-1878

The process of westernization is still going on in Turkey today. It has given rise to a debate that is also not yet ended. Turks have been asking themselves whether basic westernization has been achieved, or whether it has until now been superficial only. If the latter, where has the historical process gone wrong? Or is the whole concept a false one? Is it really possible to graft elements of an alien culture onto a Muslim society? Can a viable synthesis be achieved? Can institutions and techniques be borrowed without a total transformation of attitudes and customs? Many of these questions were raised in the nineteenth century also, and they were implicit in the westernization process from its beginnings.

The reign of Sultan Selim III (1789–1807) is often taken to mark the start of westernization. But beginnings of the westernizing tendency have been pushed back by some Turkish historians to the early eighteenth century. Here again, as with the dating of the Ottoman decline, one selects a dividing point only at peril to the truth of historical continuity. The Ottomans had never been totally cut off from the West, even in matters beyond the formal contacts provided by war, diplomacy, and commerce. They had copied some western military and naval advances and had borrowed somewhat in the fields of geographical and medical science. But their absorptive capacity declined after the fifteenth century, and intellectual or cultural transfer was minimal. Paradoxically the Ottomans were by the eighteenth century farther than ever from the West, and at the same time closer to it than ever. There was on the one hand a technological, intellectual, and psychological gulf, measured by the distance between western scientific and economic progress and rational attitudes and the relative stagnation of the East. On the other hand, there was a military, diplomatic, and commercial intimacy, measured by the force that western nations could concentrate on the Ottoman frontiers, and by the growing economic and political influence which the Europeans, helped along not only by shipping and wealth but by the capitulations, could exercise within the empire itself.

The two aspects of the paradox were brought into focus by the obvious need for reform after the second retreat from Vienna and the treaties of Carlowitz. Before that time Ottoman reformers had considered principally the internal weaknesses of the empire, as the institutions of the golden age decayed, and their proposals therefore looked back toward restoration of the pristine state of those institutions. Also largely backward-looking had been the actions of earlier reformers— Sultan Murad IV (1623-1640), for instance, or grand vezir Mehmed Köprülü (1656-1661), whose aims had been to root out corruption and whose weapons had been the executioner's sword and confiscation of ill-gotten property. But, after the treaties of Carlowitz (1699) and Passarowitz (1718) confirmed western military superiority, the moment had come when reform proposals might be western-looking. In the latter year Nevshehirli Ibrahim Pasha, who favored such a tendency, entered on a fairly long grand vezirate (1718-1730). In that year also a memorandum pointing out the need to catch up with western military progress was given to Sultan Ahmed III. It may therefore be reasonable to take 1718 as marking the beginnings of westernization.

Three characteristics of the eighteenth century reform efforts soon became apparent. One was that most of the inspiration for westernization came from French sources and models; France was both the epitome of western civilization and the traditional ally of the Ottomans. The second characteristic was that, naturally, most of the reform effort went into improvement of military training, techniques, organization, and weapons. Finally, it became apparent that reform could produce reaction from vested interests, even to the point of violence—reaction which could more easily be justified in the public eye if the reforms were of infidel origin.

These characteristics can all be seen in the first part of the eighteenth century, in what is commonly called the "Tulip Era," a time of comparative peace, and of a passion for tulip-growing. The Ottoman elite began to take an interest in various superficialities of French life, and occasionally in more fundamental aspects. Yirmisekiz Chelebi, sent on a diplomatic mission to Paris in 1720, was instructed to investigate French technology in order to see what might be useful in the Ottoman empire. He reported on scientific institutions, machinery, and even the theatre with a certain curiosity and wonder which approached approbation. His son, who went along, was instrumental in getting permission for a Hungarian convert, Ibrahim Müteferrika, to set up the first printing press in the empire to produce books in Turkish. Heretofore printing in Turkish or Arabic had been banned, though presses of the non-Muslim minorities existed. Ibrahim Müteferrika, by decision of the Sheikh ul Islam, was allowed to publish books of a non-religious character only. He produced seventeen, mostly on scientific and military subjects. Among them was a treatise of his own which emphasized the need of the Ottoman empire to understand Europe and to acquire better military methods, and which pointed to the example of Peter the Great in building up his fleet with the help of western experts. A revolt in Istanbul in 1730 cost Sultan Ahmed III his throne and the grand vezir Ibrahim Pasha his life; in part this was a protest against the "Frank" ways that had become fashionable in higher circles. But the printing press survived for a time. Further, a French adventurer, the Count Bonneval, who turned Turk as "Ahmed Pasha," was taken on as military adviser to reform the corps of bombardiers. A school of military engineering was established in 1734, though it did not last long in the face of Janissary pressure.

This period of mild "Enlightenment," if such it may be called, tapered off in mid-century despite the willingness of another grand vezir, Ragib Pasha (1757–1763), to consider innovations—he had been willing even to allow a foreign physician to do autopsies, which Muslim law forbade. The printing press was abandoned in the 1740s. Military reform also lost momentum, partly as a result of the long period of peace between 1739 and 1768 which was as fatal to military development as the earlier long maritime truces had been to naval development.

Then in 1774 came the humiliating defeat by Russia, which proved conclusively the superiority of western arms. The pattern of reform begun in the early eighteenth century was resumed toward its end. A new French adviser, the Hungarian-born Baron de Tott, who, significantly enough, did not become a Muslim like Bonneval, was employed toward the end of the war to train artillery and engineer units. New military schools were established, the printing press was revived, more translations of French military or technical books were undertaken, a more rapid trickle of westerners, especially Frenchmen, came to Istanbul for unofficial or official reasons. The grand vezir Halil Hamid (1782–1785) was friendly to them and to the westernizing reforms. But conservatives, alarmed by the influx of men and ideas from infidel lands, as well as by signs that France hoped herself to dominate the eastern Mediterranean, drove him from office and killed him. A sign affixed to his corpse identified him as "enemy of sheriat and state."

The conservatives had, however, no better plan to strengthen the empire, and the new war against Russia and Austria that began in 1787 brought new defeat. Selim III was therefore confronted on his accession in 1789 with the same problems: western superiority, domestic conservatism. Selim's instincts were those of a reformer, and he was not averse to some western models. While still heir he had already corresponded with Louis XVI, hoping for French assistance against Russia. Very soon he inaugurated the first permanent embassies in western capitals, which served the triple purpose of diplomatic negotiation, of reporting on western progress, and of training young Turkish bureaucrats in French. The French influence continued to be strong in Istanbul, though it fluctuated as the Napoleonic wars brought Paris and Istanbul into alliance or opposition.

Two years after his accession, Selim asked for memoranda on needed reforms from a group of advisers. Some of the memoranda touched on questions of tax-collection, coinage, and fiefs, but the major concern was with direct improvement of the armed forces. Among the advisers were several who could see no better way than to reshape the Janissaries in their original form. Others thought that radically new military organization was necessary. Though western models would be acceptable, none of the advisers advocated anything more than the westernization of externals or techniques; there was no consideration of such fundamentals as education, industry, or agriculture. The major westernization of Selim's reign was accordingly in the military field, and was rather a continuation of than a break from the mild beginnings made earlier in the century. The various army corps were reorganized, and some were given new training and better weapons. Greater attention was devoted to technical military schools and to translations, and the very small number of Turks who knew French increased somewhat. In 1793, and again two years later, lists of desired military and technical advisers were sent to Paris.

Selim's principal effort in military rejuvenation was the creation of a new corps, the *nizam-i jedid* (literally, "new order"). The Janissaries had done poorly in the Russian wars, and it had proved impossible to make them adopt new weapons and tactics—hence the decision to train a new corps which might in time replace them. The start of the *nizam-i jedid* had actually been made by the grand vezir Koja Yusuf Pasha while he was still at the front in 1791. After peace with Russia the next year, Selim proceeded cautiously, getting the approval of some leading ulema, including the Sheikh ul Islam, for the new venture. An infantry regiment was trained well outside the city, to avoid friction with Janissary and popular conservative sentiment. With imported rifles, European-style drill, French or other westernized instructors, and clad in blue berets and red breeches, the corps made progress under Selim's eye. Some artillery was added, some cavalry in a second regiment, then provincial units and a provincial recruiting system, so that by 1807 there were almost 25,000 of the newly trained soldiers. The corps was financed in large part by seizing and diverting the revenues of fief lands.

Despite occasional troubles, the corps seemed a success; some small units performed well in minor engagements. But the new corps was never amalgamated with the rest of the armed forces, nor was it ever put to a real test. This may have been due entirely to Selim's own lack of vigor. When some Balkan *ayan* revolted in 1805 against the extension of recruiting for the corps to their region, Selim yielded to their attack on Edirne. Instead of ordering resistance, he removed the corps and appointed the Janissary chief as grand vezir. In 1807, a conservative revolt against Frankish innovation in Istanbul led Selim to dissolve the *nizam-i jedid* rather than use it. Even so, he was deposed. A year later he was dead, having been killed by his successor, Mustafa IV, when provincial troops from the Bulgarian Danube marched on the capital to restore him. Mustafa IV was in his turn slain, and the troops enthroned Mahmud II (1808–1839). Their political leaders reinstituted some of the reforms. But a new Janissary rising killed several of the reformers and turned the control of government back to the conservatives. Mahmud II was himself spared because he was now the only surviving prince of the house of Osman.

It should be pointed out that Selim III had other cares in addition to his new army corps. Napoleon invaded Egypt in 1798, proving once again western superiority and showing that the Ottoman empire was just as vulnerable in the south as in the north. Besides calling in question the disinterestedness of French advisers in Istanbul, the invasion gave Russia a chance to become the ally of the Ottomans. As an ally, Russia won the right to maintain a naval squadron and a base in the Mediterranean, together with the right of passage for her warships through the Straits—a very favorable situation which in later years she hoped to restore. Once the French were out of Egypt and friendly French-Ottoman relations re-established, Napoleon urged the Turks in 1806 to war against Russia, but then deserted them in 1807 by concluding peace with the Tsar. Selim was probably not fully aware how much his own position depended on the French emperor and Tsar Alexander, who could not agree within whose sphere of influence Istanbul and the Straits should fall. Alexander called Istanbul "the key to my house." But it was indicative of how much of Turkish history would be determined from the outside rather than by internal events.

When Selim died, and a year and a half later when Mahmud II was forced to accept conservative domination, the situation seemed equally bad: a war with Russia, French friendship gone, the new army a failure, and reforming zeal cut down along with many of the reformers. The residue of westernizing reform was minimal. A few of the Ottoman elite had learned French, which opened up avenues to more than merely military knowledge. Some had accepted the secularism and externals of Frank civilization, though few were touched by the flaming ideals of the French revolution, which actually influenced Greeks in the empire more than Turks. There was also a lesson to be learned by those who would—that reform, particularly of western inspiration, could succeed only if the conservative opposition were shorn of its Janissary support.

Mahmud II was a ready learner, but he could not risk early action. He had the war with Russia on his hands until 1812, when he was fortunate to conclude a peace that cost him only the province of Bessarabia. Conservatives and Janissaries dominated his capital. Nor could Mahmud at the start exercise much authority outside Istanbul; his empire was, as Lamartine is said to have remarked, a "confederation of anarchies." His first efforts, therefore, were aimed at reasserting central control over the provinces. By force and guile the power of most derebeys was broken, and more obedient provincial governors appointed.

In six areas, however, Mahmud's strength was unequal to the task: Arabia, Egypt, Serbia, Greece, Moldavia-Wallachia, and Algeria. Four different sorts of challenges to Mahmud and the integrity of his empire were involved, only one of which was successfully overcome for a time. This latter challenge was Wahhabism, the puritanical Islamic reform movement that had spread in Arabia along with Saudi political power in the eighteenth century, and had by 1806 won control of Mecca and Medina. The Wahhabis were beaten back, ironically, only by the troops of the governor of Egypt, who himself represented a second and rather more serious type of challenge, Islamic but westernizing. Mehmed Ali was the self-made strong man of Egypt. Profiting by the post-Napoleonic chaos that allowed him to eliminate traditionalist rival groups, he built a centralized regime in which he was ruler, reformer, and chief merchant. His western-style army, after some false starts, was rapidly enlarged, and other westernizing reforms pursued with relative, though sometimes temporary, success. Mehmed Ali's repeated assertion that he was a loyal governor concealed neither his ambition nor the growing power with which he could directly threaten Sultan Mahmud.

The other two challenges, which ultimately were to destroy the empire of the Ottomans, came from the West rather than the East: nationalism, and the attacks of the great powers. The nationalist virus spread first to the Greeks, then to the Serbs and Rumanians. When British, French, and Russian naval squadrons brought aid to the Greek rebels at Navarino in 1827, and when a Russian invasion in 1828–29 drove nearly to Istanbul, Greece attained an autonomy that was soon converted by the powers to independence. The treaty of Adrianople (Edirne) in 1829, in addition to giving Russia strategic territory in eastern Turkey and at the mouths of the Danube, affirmed Serbian autonomy under her own prince and gave Russia influence in Moldavia and Wallachia that helped spur these Rumanian principalities toward national consciousness and independence. Algeria was simply invaded and taken over by France in 1830.

When Mahmud's empire was thus battered, Mehmed Ali in 1831 seized the chance for a direct attack, which drove through Syria and across Anatolia to Kütahya, threatening Bursa and Istanbul. Casting about wildly for help, Mahmud finally accepted the Russian offer. As allies this time, Russian troops disembarked on the Asian shore of the Bosporus just to the north of "Tsargrad," and stayed as protectors until Mehmed Ali accepted a compromise peace that left him in control of all Syria and Adana as well. The Russians stayed on even longer, until Mahmud had agreed to a formal defensive alliance, the treaty of Unkiar Skelessi of 1833, pledging the sultan to consult Russia on all matters affecting "tranquillity and safety." This was a new phase of Russian policy, but just as menacing as the old one of attack and partition. The Ottoman empire was now to be preserved as a Russian sphere of influence, and if the "sick man," as Tsar Nicholas called him in that year, should die, Russia would be chief heir. The policy laid down in Unkiar Skelessi remained desirable in Russian eyes even into the Soviet period. At the time, however, it called forth the British counterweight which, through the rest of the century, often helped to save the Turks from the Russian embrace. Unkiar Skelessi, said the foreign minister Palmerston, would make the Russian ambassador in Istanbul "the chief cabinet minister of the Sultan." He set about not only to counter Russian diplomacy, but to encourage the Ottoman empire to strengthen itself through reform.

Mahmud II needed encouragement less than he did opportunity and resources. The nationalist revolts, the great-power attacks, and the rivalry of Mehmed Ali emphasized the need for reform, but provided little opportunity and chronically drained resources. And there was always the conservative opposition to be reckoned with, backed by the Janissaries. Mahmud had already made a start, however, in 1826, when momentarily the war against the Greek rebellion seemed to be going well: he had determined to replace the Janissaries with a new army corps. The Janissaries had rebelled rather than fight the Russians, even burning houses in the capital, and had required bonus pay simply to march against the Greeks. Proposing not to extirpate the corps, but to retrain the Janissary units piecemeal and incorporate them into a modern army, Mahmud had carefully secured pledges of cooperation from leading officials, including the ulema. When the drilling of a few officers in new, tight-fitting western uniforms began, however, the Janissaries in Istanbul rebelled. Counterattack by loyal troops and volunteers resulted in the massacre of several thousand Janissaries on June 15, 1826. Then Mahmud declared the corps abolished, and announced the formation of a new one, the "triumphant soldiers of Muhammad." Provincial Janissaries too were disbanded. Their Bektashi dervish allies were suppressed. Janissaries continued to exist, even to meet in groups in some cities, but the corps, in the sense of an organized force to oppose westernization, was eliminated by this "auspicious event," as the massacre is known to the Turks. Mahmud also took the occasion to eliminate the last feudal sipahi units, and shortly abolished all remaining fiefs. Such cavalry as was needed was now salaried.

Mahmud's new army was built up under a new commander, the *serasker*, who combined the functions of commander-in-chief and minister of war. European manuals and instructors helped. In the 1830s a group of Prussian officers, headed by Helmuth von Moltke, was hired to improve the Ottoman defenses and to assist with troop training, thus beginning an oft-renewed connection with German military advisers. The navy was similarly refurbished, principally by expert American shipbuilders who turned out in Istanbul some of the finest frigates afloat, and by British naval advisers. Other western influences, at first scientific and linguistic, came with the new technical schools which Mahmud founded. In the medical school, which was principally designed to turn out army doctors, French was the language of much of the instruction. In the military academy also, French was taught. Some of the graduates of each were sent to Europe for further study. The military forces thus began to include a growing number of officers who would themselves in later decades be agents of further westernization.

In addition to the new armed forces, Mahmud was engaged in the 1830s in creating a new bureaucracy. Here too destruction of the old preceded or accompanied introduction of the new. Old palace positions, many of them now sinecures, were abolished. The bureaucrats, often with new job titles, now depended more on the sultan than on tradition for their authority. Mahmud began to convert old offices into westernstyle ministries; in addition to the serasker there were soon ministers of foreign affairs, of the interior, and of the treasury. The council of ministers was intended to resemble a European cabinet, and the grand vezir to be rather a first minister than the old-style absolute deputy of the sultan. For a brief period even the title of grand vezir was abolished in favor of prime minister (*bash vekil*). Though the change in title was temporary, the change in the nature of the post persisted. Mahmud made strenuous efforts, often unsuccessful, to eliminate bribery and to pay adequate fixed salaries to all officials who, as might be expected, were glad to have the salaries, but loath to give up other douceurs. He gave the officials greater security by abolishing the practice of confiscating property. He regulated their dress, putting them into European trousers, black boots, frock coat, and a new hat, the fez, instead of the turban. He founded an official gazette, first with a French and then a Turkish edition, in which appointments and regulations were announced, and to which officials had to subscribe. The *Takvim-i vekayi* (Calendar of Events) represents the start of Turkish journalism.

Education of the new bureaucrats also occupied Mahmud's attention. In the field of education generally change was difficult, since this was the traditional province of the ulema. The usual primary school taught the Arabic Koran by rote, along with smatterings of reading and writing. The higher school, the medrese, was almost entirely religious in curriculum. Neither school could produce a modern-style civil servant. But to change either would arouse unending controversy. Most broadly educated men were self-educated, through private study. Most bureaucrats learned while working as clerks in government offices, beginning in their teens. This continued to be so for many years. But Mahmud did create at the end of his reign another "higher" school to educate officials, in which French and other secular subjects were taught. He also finally closed the palace school, which had outlived the devshirme.

Two other channels for acquiring French and some knowledge of western learning developed also in Mahmud's reign, in addition to the specialized military, medical, and civil service schools. One of these was the diplomatic service. The permanent embassies of Selim III in Europe had been discontinued after his death; Mahmud II re-established them, and the number of young Turks who had the chance to learn while serving abroad was increased. The other channel was the new translation bureau created at the Porte, to take care of increased diplomatic correspondence in French and to train Turks in that language. The dragomans (interpreters) of the Ottoman government had for more than a century been Greeks. After the Greek revolt they were unwanted. The chief dragomans appointed after the Greek rebellion were at first non-Turkish converts to Islam, since few Turks knew western languages. With the establishment of the translation bureau, more and more Turks came to know French. Just as European military pressures had spurred creation of western-style military schools, so European diplomatic pressures spurred establishment of the translation bureau.

The translation bureau and the diplomatic service became nurseries which produced many of the leading Ottoman statesmen of the nineteenth century. These men constituted a new elite developing within the bureaucracy—the elite of the French-knowers, whose importance to Turkey down into the present century can hardly be exaggerated. They tended to be the movers, the reformers. This new split in the bureaucracy came to be paralleled by a division within the officer corps in the army, setting those who had a western-style education, and who usually knew something of a European language, apart from those who had risen from the ranks. Society as a whole was thereby also rendered less cohesive than before. The traditional dichotomy between the ruling group and the ruled persisted, but the illiterate villager was now separated from an elite that looked to the West for its models by an even greater gulf than that which had separated him from the bureaucrats of the old style.

Despite the fact that many of Mahmud's reforms were only partly successful, and despite the superficial character of westernization that did not concentrate on fundamentals of general public education and economic productivity, the changes he wrought were momentous in their consequences. The various starts toward westernization were continued thereafter. Further, he had destroyed old powers and created a new one. The Janissary power was gone. The local dynasts' power was greatly crippled. The Bektashi influence was at least checked. Mahmud had, as well, weakened the power of the ulema by withdrawing some official duties from their supervision and by creating a government inspectorate to control the vast revenues of the pious foundations, heretofore largely under ulema control. These were powers that had in the past limited the sultan's authority, and, of course, sometimes had overwhelmed it. After Mahmud, the power of the central government was much greater. It resided in the palace and the Porte. By the end of his reign Mahmud had considerable personal power, dominating the new bureaucracy he created as his early forefathers had dominated the slave administrators they had created. None of the new bureaucracy were slaves, however, and some felt that the sultan had become an autocrat, a threat to their own security and to the welfare of the state. When Mahmud died in 1839 the Porte, center of the bureaucracy, began to prevail over the palace.

Bureaucratic supremacy was easier to establish because Mahmud's successor, Sultan Abdülmejid (1839–1861) was only sixteen at his accession, and grew to be a mild, well-intentioned, fair-minded man. The dominant figure in government for the next decade and a half came to be Mustafa Reshid Pasha, who in 1839 was foreign minister. Reshid had already served as ambassador in Paris and London, knew French well, and was quite familiar with European politics. He leaned not only toward curbing the sultan's power, but also to westernizing reform, of which he became the leader. His views, and his haste, aroused much opposition among more conservative officials, and they succeeded at times in ousting him from his tenure of the foreign ministry or the grand vezirate. But in 1839 he was able, because of a crisis, to rally official backing for a remarkable reform proclamation. Renewed hostilities with Mehmed Ali of Egypt had again threatened the empire's integrity, and European support was needed. A reform proclamation would help to attract such support by demonstrating that the empire could make progress and was worth saving. In these circumstances the Imperial Edict (*Hatt-i sherif*) of Gülhane was issued on November 3, 1839.

The edict combined old and new. It blamed the decline of the empire on non-observance of Koranic precepts and imperial law, but pointed to the remedy as "new laws" and "complete alteration" of former usages. Specifically, it promised security of life, honor, and property through equal justice; more orderly tax collection in place of tax-farming; and a fair and regular system of military conscription. These reforms, it continued, would apply equally to all subjects, of whatever religion. A Supreme Council which Mahmud II had appointed to draft legislation was charged with working out details of the reform measures and provided with western-style rules of parliamentary procedure for its deliberations. Though the promises of the Gülhane edict had been adumbrated in the time of Mahmud II, this pronouncement in the most solemn form marks the start of a period of forty years known in Turkish history as the *Tanzimat*—the reordering or reorganization.

More than any other period of Turkish history, except perhaps the recent Menderes decade, the Tanzimat has been the subject of argument. Its leaders were severely criticized in its own day by young Turkish intellectuals. Its reforms have been castigated by modern Turkish historians as shallow and over-hasty westernization, or else as insufficiently drastic. The Tanzimat has also been praised as the seedtime in which new ideas and institutions got their start, and without which later reformers under the empire and the republic could not have succeeded. There is truth in all these views. But the fundamental truths are that the empire really had no choice but westernizing reform if it was to continue to exist in the modern world, that drastic westernization was impossible because it would have shattered society, and that therefore the process had to be cautious and piecemeal. Even so, old habits of thought and action were badly jolted. Undoubtedly some things could have been better done. But modern Turkey is inconceivable without the Tanzimat's acceleration of the westernizing process long since haltingly begun, directly inherited from Mahmud II, and given new impetus by Reshid and his disciples.

The bureaucrats, in particular the "French-knowers," dominated the Tanzimat period. Until 1871 their influence was greater than the sultan's. They were called autocrats by their enemies. The charge was untrue, but they did form an oligarchy which became as enamored of power and the emoluments of high office as any ruling group before them. The best of them, among whom Reshid's disciples Âli Pasha and Fuad Pasha were outstanding, were statesmen of real ability. Their primary aim was to save the Ottoman empire. To do this, they had to know Europe and to be able to deal with the powers, for the empire now existed on European sufferance. When Mehmed Ali threatened the Porte in 1839-40, and was backed by France, the other four powers united to drive him back into Egypt and agreed to end Russia's special position laid down in the treaty of Unkiar Skelessi. When the Porte, caught in the middle of a religio-political battle for prestige between Russia, self-proclaimed protector of the Orthodox, and France, self-proclaimed protector of Catholics, stumbled into the Crimean War against Russia in 1853-56, it emerged victorious because of the aid of British, French, and Piedmontese arms—the first Ottoman victory, if such it may be called, over Russia since 1739. At the peace of Paris in 1856 the Ottoman Empire was technically restored to great power status, and admitted to the Concert of Europe by the powers, who further engaged to observe the empire's independence and integrity.

The European powers in the Tanzimat period were also more meddlesome than ever in Ottoman domestic matters, though in the Paris treaty they blithely promised not to interfere. They pressed for reforms of all sorts, particularly for the rights of Christian minorities; they insisted on their capitulatory privileges; and they supported one Ottoman statesman against another. European ambassadors in Istanbul, and some of the consuls in provincial cities, exercised great influence at times. The Ottoman statesmen had to try to keep the favor of at least a majority of the powers, use their backing when necessary, and still blunt their influence inside the empire whenever possible. Since the Russian views on Ottoman reform generally favored Christian autonomies which portended ultimate decomposition of the empire, the statesmen leaned more heavily on the other powers, and especially on the counsel of France. Though some were attracted by English political and economic institutions, their instincts and cultural background generally led them to French models.

Certain broad characteristics of reform, visible under Mahmud II and intensified in the Tanzimat period, reflect the western inspiration. Probably the most significant was the expanded area of state activity. No longer was the state simply an administrative machine to dispense justice, collect revenue, and raise armies; it was now involved in such matters as education, public works, and economic development which in large part formerly fell outside its purview. In addition, while military reform continued to receive attention, after Mahmud II it was no longer the one overriding concern; westernization in law, administration, diplomacy, and education seemed as important. Third, the secular character of reforms became increasingly apparent, as new forms from the secular West were superimposed on the Islamic community and the non-Muslim millets. Islamic and western institutions, especially in education and law, then existed side by side in what is sometimes regarded as a fatal dualism, but may be also regarded as inevitably part of a difficult process of gradual historical growth and change.

A fourth characteristic of the westernizing reform was the tendency for government to treat the subject as an individual, rather than as a member of a group which found sanction for its status in tradition. This aspect of westernization was part of the drive toward secular equality given formal expression in the Gülhane edict—equality under law of all Ottoman subjects regardless of sect. The statesmen hoped to create an "Ottomanism" (Osmanlilik) which would counteract separatist nationalistic tendencies among the minorities and help to preserve the empire intact by winning stronger allegiance of all subjects to a beneficent imperial government. The official policy of Ottomanism encountered a major obstacle in Muslim objections to what they regarded as unnatural equality between true believers and subject unbelievers. An even greater obstacle was the continued existence as separate legal entities of the Christian millets whose rights the great powers frequently supported, and whose members ultimately were more attracted to separatist nationalisms.

All these characteristics were encapsuled in another solemn reform edict, the *Hatt-i Hümayun* of 1856, in the preparation of which three European ambassadors as well as Âli Pasha and Fuad Pasha played a leading role. There was now no reference to the Koran, as in the 1839 decree, but much said about equality of individuals—yet the rights of the scparate millets were also specifically confirmed. There was also a secular emphasis on progress and prosperity. The establishment of banks, and the improvement of public works and communications, of commerce and agriculture, were promised; the empire would draw on "the knowledge, the skills, and the capital of Europe."

The Crimean War itself had already, indeed, vastly increased European influence in the empire. Soldiers, concessionaires, and rabble had streamed in from the West. European customs—clothing, forks, chairs—spread in the seaboard cities. More important, the telegraph reached Istanbul in 1855, in time for the first message to tell Paris and London that the Russian stronghold of Sebastopol had fallen. The telegraph network soon spread farther into the empire, facilitating not only contact with the West, but also quick checks by the central government on actions of provincial officials, and equally quick reference of local problems to the capital. The railway age started at the same time with construction of some short lines by foreign concessionaires; owing to difficult terrain and construction costs, rails expanded more slowly than the telegraph. The Crimean War also initiated the Ottoman government into another of the mysteries of westernization—foreign loans secured by bond issues. Within two decades the external debt had run so high that bankruptcy ensued.

Understandably, the Tanzimat achievement between 1839 and 1871 was quite uneven. Economic progress was abysmally slow. Agricultural production improved little if at all. (Egypt's exceptional profits from cotton sales during the American civil war were quite atypical.) Efforts to attract skilled European farmers as colonists failed. The tax burden on the peasantry remained heavy; tax farming was twice declared abolished, but in fact was not, as direct collection produced neither more revenues nor fewer abuses. An effort to regularize land tenure by a new code in 1858 often had the unintentional effect of throwing legal title into the hands of a large owner rather than the actual peasant cultivator. The extent of roadbuilding and bridgebuilding varied greatly from province to province. No large-scale industry was established, and only a few smaller manufactures. European imports meanwhile, facilitated by treaties that limited the Ottoman protective tariff to eight per cent of value, increased—to the detriment of domestic crafts.

In education the accomplishment was much greater, though fitful. Twice during these years, in 1846 and 1869, commissions of westernized Ottoman officials drew up comprehensive plans for an educational system reaching from primary school to the university. Progress in actually establishing new schools, however, was slow. One of the characteristic aberrations was the attempt to start a University of Istanbul before sufficient secondary preparation was available. A few good secondary schools were nevertheless begun, and, under French influence, the outstanding lycée of Galatasaray gave boys of all sects a western instruction in French. Some special schools for women, for the poor, and for teacher training were founded as well, and in 1859 a new civil service school was established, where incipient bureaucrats studied public and international affairs. The Faculty of Political Science in Ankara today is its lineal descendant. The educational residue of the Tanzimat was a more westernized group of officials, a somewhat better-educated elite, the start of a state school system, and increasing secularism in education. For although the Koran schools and medreses continued, the government schools were officially divorced from ulema control and placed under a secular ministry of education. The educational gulf between the medrese product and the higher government school product was, if anything, widened, as the medreses tended to be filled with the uprooted from backward villages and the new schools with more westernized urban youth.

The development of law during the Tanzimat was similar in several respects to that of education. The religious law continued to be applied in the traditional kadi's courts, and, where needed, in various newly created state courts. But other law, beginning with the commercial and then the penal, was remade in codes which drew heavily on western, particularly French, examples. The religious law of obligations and contracts was maintained, but codified on western principles by a commission under Jevdet Pasha, a liberally educated member of the ulema. Religious law bearing on the civil status of individuals—matters of marriage, divorce, inheritance, and the like—remained untouched, for it was the most sensitive area. The result was then two kinds of law, with the western slowly growing greater. There were also two kinds of courts—sheriat courts supervised by the Sheikh ul Islam, and state courts organized into a hierarchy by Jevdet, who was appointed head of a secular ministry of justice. The dualism caused a certain amount of confusion, some of which was inevitable. But the westernizing and secularizing trends were clear. The effort to provide equal justice under one law to Ottoman subjects of all creeds was, as it turned out, not only theoretical, but erratically translated into practice. The one step that was not and could not then be taken, in view of the ingrained Muslim sense of what was right, was to adopt a western civil code, although Âli Pasha seems to have toyed with the idea of transplanting the Code Napoléon.

Westernization of administrative practice as well as of the upper bureaucracy continued in the Tanzimat period. One index is the increasing separation of powers, as judicial functions were divorced from executive functions on several levels, and as the legislative function was in part delegated by the sultan to various appointed councils evolving from the Supreme Council of Mahmud II. Another index is the transformed provincial government, which underwent various changes to emerge in the 1860s with a new hierarchical structure of vilayets (provinces) and subdivisions closely modeled on the French structure of departments. Provincial governors (valis) with extensive powers were appointed by the central government, but associated with them were advisory administrative councils and provincial general assemblies meant to give the inhabitants a voice in public affairs. Some governors, notably Midhat Pasha in the region of Bulgaria and then of Baghdad, were successful in making the new system work. Others were not, and it became clear that the character and enlightenment of the official was at least as important as, and probably more important than, the system. As in all countries, but especially in one like Turkey which has attempted rapid westernization, how to supply enough competent and dedicated public servants has been a continuing problem. The vilayet system lasted, however, into the republican period.

Another foundation for governmental development was also laid during the Tanzimat period with the introduction of the representative principle—in provincial councils, in provincial assemblies, in courts —based on an indirect system of election in which both Muslims and non-Muslims shared. Even the Council of State, the French-model form in which the law-drafting agency was recast in 1868, was enlarged to contain representatives of various creeds and of the provinces as well as the capital. The representatives were appointed, not elected. But the years of experimentation with some kind of representation, whether in provincial or central government, later served as valuable precedents when proponents of a constitution sought to create a chamber of deputies.

The Ottoman empire lost no territory during the Tanzimat period, and even gained a little as a result of the Crimean victory, but the reform period failed to pull its segments firmly together. Instead, the empire became even looser at the joints. Egypt gained special status under the hereditary rule of Mehmed Ali's family. The Lebanon was endowed with its own regime after massacres in 1860 that brought French intervention. The Yemen was held with great difficulty, and Tunis professed close allegiance to the sultan only to ward off the threat of French control. Serbia and Rumania, with great power assistance, attained complete internal autonomy. Among groups of Greeks, Bulgars, and finally, even Armenians—the last often called the "loyal millet" by the Turks—distinct trends toward separatism grew rapidly. The concept of Ottomanism, despite the advances made toward equal treatment of all subjects, never won their general acceptance. In an age of growing nationalism the Ottomanist goal was perhaps unrealistic, yet the Ottoman leaders had to try to make it work. Had there been no great powers, they might have succeeded; but the empire did not exist in a vacuum. The crisis that began in 1875 with the revolt of Slav subjects in Herzegovina and Bosnia led to great-power intervention that soon proved the point. The crisis also brought to a head discontent with the government of Sultan Abdülaziz (1861–1876) which, after the death of the dominant Tanzimat statesman, Âli Pasha, in 1871, had become increasingly capricious and unpopular.

Critics of the government had available to them by this time a new channel of expression, the newspaper press. Beginning in the early 1860s, independent journalism developed rapidly. This was part of a vigorous Turkish literary renaissance in the post-Crimean years, a phase of westernization that put down strong roots. Western forms in poetry, drama, the novel, and journalism began to attract members of the Ottoman elite. Translations of western works were speedily followed by original Turkish writing influenced by the new forms. Some of the writers, convinced that clarity was preferable to the harmonious but turgid elegance of the official Ottoman style, strove to write so they could be more easily understood, to use more Turkish words in place of Arabic and Persian, to shorten sentences, to clarify spelling. A daring few proposed giving up Arabic characters, which were basically unsuited to representing Turkish sounds, in favor of Latin letters. Western influences were evident also in subject-matter, especially in articles on what might be called "useful knowledge"—on child care, political economy, and transportation, for instance. Western influences were evident also in modes of thought about the nation, government, and progress. Book production increased, but the burgeoning newspapers and journals provided the major vehicles for expression.

Among those who pioneered in these fields, especially in journalism, were a group of young intellectuals who called themselves for a time the New Ottomans (*Yeni Osmanlilar*). Almost all were under forty and had been in government employ—many in the translation bureau —and knew some French; most came from good families of the Ottoman elite. In addition to literary interests they had in common a dislike of the top bureaucracy, especially of Âli Pasha. They called him a tyrant, and in the years 1865 to 1867 conspired to remove him from office. They advocated "constitutional government." Their journalistic barbs and secret plotting brought an official crackdown, whereupon the leading New Ottomans escaped to Paris. In a number of western havens, including London and Geneva, they again published newspapers which were smuggled back to Istanbul through the foreign post-offices which the great powers maintained there under the capitulations. *Hürriyet* (Freedom), the most important of their papers, attacked Âli's administration because it had not prevented European intervention and increased autonomy in some of the imperial provinces, because it conceded special privileges to the Christians, and because it had pursued secular reforms in disregard of the traditional law and culture of Islam.

The New Ottomans were by no means traditionalists, for they harped constantly on the need for economic development, scientific knowledge, and modern education. But their arguments also harked back to what they considered the democratic tradition of Islam as the basis for a constitution, which to them meant some kind of a representative assembly as a check on administrative authority. The ideas of the individual New Ottomans often differed, especially on political matters, and the group itself soon lost its cohesion. Namik Kemal, the most influential and respectable among them, was, however, consistent in his demand for an elected chamber of deputies representing all Ottoman subjects equally, and for separation of legislative and executive powers. Sovereignty, he said, belonged to the people. All this, further, could be done within an Islamic framework. "Our only real constitution is the sheriat," he wrote after returning from exile. And again, "the Ottoman state is based on religious principles, and if these principles are violated the political existence of the state will be in danger." [1]

The New Ottomans' influence on Turkish thought and literature reaches down to the modern republic, which looks back to them as spiritual ancestors. In no aspect of thought were they more influential than in the development of patriotic sentiment. They were not, and could not be, Turkish nationalists, even though some were interested in the Turkish past and the Turks of Central Asia, for they ardently wished to preserve Ottoman soil intact. What they inculcated was pride in country, devotion to the Islamic Ottoman empire created by their forefathers, and a fierce desire to defend it against attack or rebellion. Into the word *vatan* ("home"), which from mid-century had been used as the equivalent of the French *patrie* ("fatherland"), they poured a deep emotional content. [2] A play by Namik Kemal, entitled *Vatan* and produced in Istanbul in 1873, aroused such enthusiastic street demonstrations that the fearful government closed it down. This Ottoman patriotism contained the seeds of a future Turkish nationalism. It marked also the hint of a transition through which the West had already progressed: allegiance to the symbols of a religious community or a ruling dynasty was being replaced by devotion to the sacred soil of a state and to the sovereignty of its inhabitants. Not until the Turkish Republic was well established was the shift completed, however, and some individual Turks have not gone so far even today.

After Âli's death the New Ottomans discovered that the increasingly personal government of Sultan Abdülaziz, who changed officials constantly, was even worse. Additional resentment built up against the government because of economic distress, the growth of Russian influence within the empire, and the repudiation of interest payments on the Ottoman debt. When government action against the Bosnian revolt of 1875 was so lethargic as to allow its spread, and when pan-

---

[1] From *Ibret* (a newspaper), nos. 46 and 24, November 5 and October 4, 1872, respectively; quoted in *Tanzimat* (Istanbul, 1940), I, 844–45, and R. G. Okandan, *Umumî âmme hukukumuzun ana hatları* (Istanbul, 1948), I, 98, n.23.

[2] While "fatherland" is the usual western term equated to *vatan*, Turks will usually translate it as "motherland."

Slavic pressure from Russia was exerted in favor of the Balkan rebels, the cup was full. A small group of top-level bureaucrats headed by Midhat Pasha, and supported by officers of the new army and navy, acted as had Janissaries in the past and deposed Abdülaziz on May 30, 1876, in a bloodless coup. When his liberal-minded successor, Murad V, suffered a nervous breakdown, he was in turn deposed just three months later in favor of his brother, Abdülhamid II.

During the summer of 1876 a constitution had been under discussion. Abdülhamid having promised to promulgate one, the discussions were accelerated through the fall in an atmosphere of growing patriotic and fanatically Islamic reaction against pan-Slavism and European intervention. A commission of ulema and civil officials under Midhat Pasha's chairmanship produced a constitutional draft at the end of November. Much wrangling ensued in the council of ministers, especially over enumeration of the sultan's prerogatives. Abdülhamid, when the draft in final form was submitted to him, was dilatory, but in the end he approved it after a clause was added giving him power to exile any who endangered state security. Midhat was appointed grand vezir on December 19, 1876. Four days later the first written constitution in Ottoman history was promulgated in a ceremony held in a rain-swept square in front of the Sublime Porte.

The constitution breathed western influence throughout. It provided for a council of ministers, an appointed senate, an elected chamber of deputies, an independent judiciary, and a bill of rights. The constitutionalists pinned their hopes to the elected chamber, although the ministry was not, as Midhat had first proposed, responsible to the chamber, but to the sultan. The sultan, in fact, retained the powers of approving legislation, appointing ministers, and convoking or dismissing the chamber—in fact, his ultimate control could hardly be doubted. This form of government might be described as "limited autocracy." Though the liberal Belgian constitution had provided some inspiration, it is quite possible that the more monarchist Prussian constitution furnished just as much. The sultan was also declared to be calif, and his person to be sacred. Though the title of calif had been used by some Ottoman rulers, and had even been formally included in some treaties from the eighteenth century on, no sultan had made much of it until Abdülaziz in his last years. Abdülhamid would soon attempt to give it new luster.

The constitution of 1876 also emphasized again the equality of all

Ottoman subjects—in civil liberties, in all legal rights, in office-holding, and as members of the chamber. Islam was designated the religion of state, but beyond this, and the sultan's title of calif, references to millet distinctions were eliminated. Obviously the constitution was part of a great effort to hold the empire together in a period of crisis. This was apparent also in the first article, which stipulated that the empire —including privileged provinces such as Rumania—was a unit which could never for any reason be divided. Midhat and his supporters hoped indeed to use the constitution as a weapon against the great powers whose delegates were at that very moment convening in Istanbul to propose reforms for the revolt-wracked Balkan provinces. Like Reshid Pasha in 1839, Midhat wanted to show the powers that the empire was capable of reforming itself and dealing with its own problems. Many of the European diplomats naturally considered the document to be insincere, perhaps a ruse. It was not. But the powers acted on their own assumptions and proposed the adoption of a reform plan which the Porte then refused.

The consequence in April, 1877, was a new attack by Russia, claiming to act in the name of Europe, on both the Balkan and Caucasus fronts. Such ideological color as the Russians had introduced into the three earlier Russo-Turkish wars of the nineteenth century had been religious—protection of their Orthodox brethren. The war of 1877 had a racial, pan-Slav color. After the Russian advance, held up for six months by a brilliant Turkish defense of Plevna, drove through Edirne to the outskirts of Istanbul in early 1878, a pan-Slav peace was forced upon the Turks. The treaty of San Stefano obliged the Turks to recognize the complete independence of Rumania, Serbia, and Montenegro. It created a large self-governing Bulgaria. For herself, Russia took Bessarabia and the strategic districts of Kars and Ardahan in eastern Turkey. On both wings, but particularly in the Balkans, the Ottoman Empire was badly hurt.

Turkish losses affected British and Austrian interests as well; both were wary of Russian influence rapidly creeping toward the Mediterranean, and desirous of supporting the Ottomans as a block to Russian expansion. While the defense of Plevna had failed in the end, its valor served to renew British admiration for the Turks as opponents of the Russian bear. A strong British stand, supported by other powers, induced the tsar to agree to an international congress at Berlin to review the peace. The congress met in June, 1878. Much of the treaty of San

Stefano was confirmed, but the large Bulgaria was chopped back to a smaller size; Serbia and Montenegro were also reduced; and Austria was allowed to occupy and administer Bosnia and Herzegovina. By separate agreement forced on the sultan, Britain also gained the right to administer Cyprus and use it as a base in return for a promise to defend Turkey against Russia. Thus, as so often in modern history, Turkey's fate was determined from the outside. She was still a heavy loser, but something had been saved.

The constitution, meanwhile, had not been forgotten. Under a provisional electoral law, which used the councils of the vilayet organization as electoral bodies, a chamber of deputies had been chosen. It held two sessions in Istanbul, from March to June 1877 and from December of that year to February, 1878. Its legislative accomplishments were few, largely because of foot-dragging by Abdülhamid and the ministers in proposing bills or agreeing to those passed. But the chamber acquitted itself well on the whole. Some deputies indulged in sterile debate or bombastic pronouncements. Most, however, not only stuck to the point at issue but displayed independence of mind and a constructive outlook. The differences that arose between Muslim and Christian deputies were overbalanced by the general agreement to seek the welfare of the empire. In the second session, which came at the time of the Russian breakthrough toward Edirne and the capital, the deputies were remarkably outspoken in their criticism of the government for inefficiency, corruption, and the general conduct of the war. This aroused the sultan.

Abdülhamid had never, so far as one can tell, been a strong partisan of the constitution, though he had promised one in order to gain the throne, and perhaps had actually favored the final draft since it gave him such extensive powers. He had, however, weakened the original draft. He had also in February, 1877, before the chamber could convene, exiled the grand vezir, Midhat Pasha, who probably hoped to use the constitutional regime to attain his original desideratum of rule by a ministry responsible to the parliament rather than to the sultan. Then, when the chamber proved to be so independent-minded, Abdülhamid realized how obstructive to his rule a parliament could be, and how much a focal point for popular resentment it might become. He determined to get rid of it. One of the last straws was a bold declaration made by Haji Ahmed Efendi, a master tailor who had been elected to the chamber from Istanbul, at a special council called to meet at the palace to discuss the critical end-of-war situation. "You ask our advice too late," said the tailor to the sultan. "The Chamber declines all responsibility for a situation with which it has had nothing to do. . . . None of its decisions has been carried out. Let me repeat: the Chamber refuses to accept any responsibility for the conditions which have caused the present difficulties." [3] Sultans were not used to being spoken to by tailors in this fashion. The next day Abdülhamid prorogued the chamber. It was not reconvened for thirty years. The best commentary on its potential effectiveness was the simple fact that the sultan so acted. The constitution remained in abeyance, a beacon for future reformers to look back to.

[3] Hakki Tarik Us, *Meclis-i meb'usan 1293/1877 zabit ceridesi* (Istanbul, 1940-1954), II, 401. Translated in Robert Devereux, *The First Ottoman Constitutional Period* (Baltimore, 1963), pp. 243-44.

6

From Autocracy to Revolution: The Era of Sultan Abdülhamid II, 1878-1909

Sultan Abdülhamid II has not fared well at the hands of historians. Both within Turkey and without he has been judged largely on the basis of his opponents' views. The Young Turks and their intellectual heirs in the modern republic have represented him principally as an autocrat who stamped out freedom between the first constitutional period of 1876 to 1878 and the second constitutional period that began with the revolution of 1908. Westerners, under strong impressions of the massacre of Armenians in the 1890s, have seen him not only as a tyrant but as the "bloody sultan," "Abdul the damned." Abdülhamid's undoubted personal idiosyncracies, which grew during his long reign to include a secretiveness and suspiciousness that may have verged on paranoia, serve to reinforce such views. Yet these judgments fail to see the whole man or the whole era. Abdülhamid certainly left his stamp on his age more indelibly than did his three predecessors in office on theirs, and almost as indelibly as Mahmud II did on the early years of the century. It was, however, the stamp of one who was at the same time an autocrat, a represser, a reformer, an Ottoman patriot, and a victim of circumstances.

Events in the first few years of Abdülhamid's reign, both domestic and external, help to explain something of his attitudes and actions. From the circumstances connected with his accession to the throne,

91

Abdülhamid learned to be suspicious of anything that smacked of conspiracy. He had, after all, gained power only as the result of the two depositions of 1876 that Midhat and a small group of bureaucrats and officers had contrived. He naturally wished neither to be beholden to the self-appointed kingmakers nor to suffer the fate of his predecessors. One of these predecessors, Sultan Abdülaziz, had committed suicide after being deposed, but Abdülhamid may have convinced himself that it was a case of murder by the kingmakers; at any event, he developed a fear of assassination. Murad, Abdülhamid's deposed older brother and immediate predecessor, still lived, confined in a palace. By 1878 there had been more than one abortive plot to free him and restore him to the throne. Ali Suavi, an erstwhile New Ottoman, had led one such attempt; a Greek Freemason of Istanbul had led another.

Meanwhile, in the chamber of deputies there had been a move to recall Midhat Pasha from exile. Midhat was ultimately allowed back as governor of Syria and then of Izmir, but reached the capital only in 1881 as a prisoner on a trumped-up charge of having had Abdülaziz murdered. His trial, a farce, did no credit to Sultan Abdülhamid. Upon conviction, Midhat was sentenced to exile in Taif in Arabia, and there in 1884, presumably on Abdülhamid's direct orders, was strangled. Namik Kemal and some of the other 1876 conspirator-constitutionalists were kept in provincial exile until their deaths. Probably Abdülhamid never lost the fears generated in these early years. Midhat had been murdered, but Murad survived until 1904 and from time to time it was rumored that he had completely recovered from his nervous breakdown and could again assume the responsibilities of the sultanate.

The external events of Abdülhamid's first years of rule were equally unfortunate. At Berlin in 1878, Rumania, Serbia, and Montenegro had been declared independent and were lost to the empire for good, and Bulgaria—though somewhat smaller than Russia wanted—was made autonomous. Bosnia-Herzegovina was occupied by Austria, and Cyprus by Britain. Russia, in addition, had taken for herself strategic frontier areas in Europe and Asia. In 1881 the European powers, carrying out a promise made at the Berlin Congress, obliged the Ottomans to give Greece a considerable northern extension of territory, including the breadbasket of Thessaly. In the same year France occupied Tunis, making it a protectorate. In the next year Britain occupied Egypt. While Egypt, long lost to direct Ottoman rule, remained technically within the empire even while it was under British control, no

arrangement for British evacuation was ever completed after Abdülhamid's failure in 1887, because of French and Russian pressure, to
ratify the Drummond Wolff convention which would have provided
for such an evacuation. Egypt remained a sore point throughout
Abdülhamid's reign, and the Turkish newspapers were forbidden to
speak of it. As late as 1906 Britain forced Ottoman recognition of an
administrative boundary line between the Mediterranean and the Gulf
of Aqaba that deprived the Ottoman land forces of any direct contact
across the Sinai peninsula with the Suez canal. It is true that no
other territory was irrevocably lost between 1881 and 1908, but in
1885 autonomous Bulgaria annexed Eastern Rumelia, and Abdülhamid
was unable to find sufficient great-power backing to undo the move. As
a consequence of all these losses, the sultan was warier than ever of
the intervention of the European powers, eager to keep intact what
territory remained, and worried lest revolt among any minority group
give opportunity for new defections which one or more powers might
support.

Under the impact of such events Abdülhamid gathered authority into
his own hands. It was essentially a period of personal rule: power was
shifted back from Porte to Palace. The sultan did not intend to be
dominated either by a bureaucracy or by a parliament, and made skill-
ful use of circumstances to achieve his ends. He had already, within six
months of his accession, used the constitution to oust Midhat from the
grand vezirate and to exile him. The small group of constitutional reformers were too stunned to raise any effective protest. Thereafter, for
six years. Abdülhamid allowed no grand vezir to become entrenched in
office. In that span there were sixteen tenants of the grand vezirate.
Several were not titled grand vezir but prime minister; they were not,
however, allowed the broad powers that western usage of the term
usually implies. Only with Said Pasha's tenure under the old label
of grand vezir, beginning at the end of 1882, did terms of office of a
year or more become usual. Abdülhamid had apparently found men
he trusted somewhat, and both the domestic and foreign scenes grew
calmer.

A year after Midhat's exile, Abdülhamid had used the dangerous situation at the end of the Russo-Turkish war as an excuse to get rid of
the parliament. From 1878 to 1908 he ruled without calling a new
chamber, though the constitution was never officially revoked and
continued to be printed in the imperial yearbook. The thirty years of

autocracy were probably illegal, for the constitution—which Abdül-hamid had himself accepted and promulgated—provided specifically that if the sultan dissolved the chamber a new one had to meet within six months, and stipulated further that no provision of the constitution could be suspended on whatever pretext. But the constitution estab-lished no sanctions to force the sultan to act; on the contrary, it de-clared the sultan to be non-responsible.

Among his Muslim subjects as a whole, these acts were not necessarily unpopular. Parliamentary government meant nothing to the masses, but respect for the duly girded scion of the house of Osman did. The autocrat was generally thought to be well-intentioned, bent on pater-nalistic help to his people. In his earlier years Abdülhamid probably had such good intentions. He was also reputed to be of better character than his two predecessors—frugal rather than spendthrift, abstemious of alcohol, physically and mentally healthy, pious. Some who saw him at the start of his reign carried away the impression of an intelligent, progressive ruler, but a ruler who meant to save the em-pire and improve it by ruling himself.

Abdülhamid seems consciously to have courted popularity. This was particularly true in the emphasis he gave to his position as calif, and to the promotion of Islamic solidarity. The previous ideological emphasis of the government on Ottomanism was now gradually eclipsed by an emphasis on pan-Islam, which grew stronger as Abdülhamid's reign continued. In part pan-Islam was designed specifically to ensure the allegiance of his Arab subjects. Abdülhamid brought a number of Arabs into his immediate entourage, built or rebuilt several important mosques in Arab cities, and encouraged the pilgrimage to Mecca. The most striking physical evidence of the pan-Islamic trend was the con-struction between 1901 and 1908 of the Hijaz railway, from Damascus to Medina—800 miles completed without calling on European capital. No other railway in the empire had been an indigenous product. Some Arab and religious leaders gave only qualified support to Abdülhamid's claim to be calif, and some, like the Senussi order in Tripoli, were quite antagonistic. Abdülhamid himself was wary of Arab leaders who might oppose him; he kept Husayn, the later Sharif of Mecca, in forced residence in Istanbul, far from the holy city. It seems probable that the Islamic emphasis did help somewhat to knit parts of the empire to-gether, though its results are hard to estimate.

The Islamic emphasis had also two other effects, both more readily identifiable. First, an outward show of piety was encouraged without bringing renewed inward vigor to Islam. The important currents of modernizing Islamic thought, or of purifying belief and practice, originated in regions outside Abdülhamid's control, as in India or Egypt, and on the periphery of his domain. Religiosity, obscurantism, and superstition were more characteristic of the capital and the Turkish areas. Medreses were thronged, but not reformed, while dervish convents multiplied. The other effect was an increase in anti-westernism. This was probably intentional on Abdülhamid's part, in an age when the imperial expansion of the European powers—especially Britain, France, and Russia—into Africa and Asia was subjugating more and more Muslims to foreign rule. Like Abdülaziz in the early 1870s, Abdülhamid used the reaction to western incursions to win at least a sentimental allegiance to himself as calif. Pan-Islam of this type was calculated to increase the international prestige of the Ottoman ruler; as a byproduct it undoubtedly increased his stature among the masses of his own subjects. Abdülhamid found a supporter in Kaiser Wilhelm II, who, in order to improve Germany's world position vis-à-vis Britain, France, and Russia, encouraged Abdülhamid's claims to the califate on two visits to the sultan in 1889 and 1898. On the second occasion Wilhelm, speaking at Saladin's tomb in Damascus, proclaimed himself the friend of the world's 300,000,000 Muslims. In this respect Abdülhamid's Islamic emphasis brought at least temporary rewards.

In addition to a palace-centered autocracy and the propagation of pan-Islamic doctrine, Abdülhamid's methods of rule included the use of censors, police, spies, and exile. He seems to have trusted almost no one. Two sets of censors, one in the Porte and the other in the palace, checked on each other as well as on the press. Newspapers were frequently suspended or suppressed. Periodicals and books coming from abroad were particularly suspect, and although the Ottoman government could not control the foreign postoffices in Istanbul and other cities through which much of these materials came, its spies sometimes succeeded in opening their mails. Some local newspapers were subsidized by the government; some local and foreign journalists were able to blackmail the sultan into sizable "gifts" by playing on his fears of adverse publicity. Informers turned *jurnals*, or reports, in to the sultan's officials,—reports which often accused innocent people of subversive activity. Students in schools operated by European or American missionaries and philanthropists within the empire were closely watched, and Turks were at times forbidden to attend such institutions. Students in the higher Ottoman schools were also watched, especially after 1890. Meetings, even private and social, were often suspect. By means of Ottoman embassies, consulates, and informers abroad, the government kept a constant check on Turkish exiles and emigrants from among the minorities. The censorship and espionage gave rise to fantastic stories, many fabricated but many undoubtedly true. It was, for example, dangerous to use certain words—constitution, dynamo, Midhat Pasha, Murad, prince-heir, Macedonia—as well as certain chemical formulas.

Especially after the later 1890s Abdülhamid became the prisoner of his own fears and suspicions. He tended more and more to seclude himself in his palace compound at Yildiz, outside the capital. The effect of this suspicious atmosphere on Turkish intellectuals was to make them lead a kind of double life—a conventional public one and a furtive private one. Newspapers sometimes had a different form of double life, employing special hacks to write paeans of praise for the sultan while trying otherwise to report reliable news, occasionally risking suspension.

Of course, new ideas could not be kept out of the empire. Once the door had been opened to westernization, it could not easily be shut. Knowledge of the West and of modern thought, particularly in science and literature, increased apace. Journals, compelled to avoid political subjects, continued what they had begun in the Tanzimat period— translating French literature, experimenting with fiction and other literary forms, popularizing useful and scientific knowledge. Ahmed Midhat, a prolific writer of books and articles as well as a newspaper editor, was particularly successful at this. Though originally a protégé of Midhat Pasha, he acquiesced in the regime of Abdülhamid and even curried favor with him, thereafter enjoying various official posts. Other writers and editors who fell afoul of censorship sometimes resumed their journals under a new name and sometimes continued their work in exile. The number of readers, meanwhile, increased with the slow rise in literacy as more schools were opened.

In the field of education Abdülhamid was a reformer, though a bit inconstant, in the Tanzimat tradition. Primary schools hardly advanced at all. But the number of higher elementary schools and lower secondary schools was increased during his reign; many of them were in the provincial capitals and larger towns. Military preparatory schools, whose graduates might go on to the higher military schools, were also established in a number of provincial centers. Students in the schools outside Istanbul not infrequently imbibed opposition to the top echelons of the established regime along with their education, as the revolution of 1908 was to prove. Some of the higher special schools, like the civil service academy (*Mülkiye*) and the military academy, were increased in size, while a law school and a new medical school were added to the roster. The law school ultimately became a faculty of the University of Istanbul which, although thrice still-born in the Tanzimat era, finally opened successfully in 1900. In the higher schools, despite the Hamidian watch on them, currents of discontent developed among groups of students who were exposed to a western-style education in sciences, mathematics, French, and even in history on occasion. Secularism rather than religiosity characterized both the students and the curricula.

The military schools, like most of the other higher schools, were intended to produce well-trained men for the Hamidian establishment —at least competent technicians if not broadly educated statesmen. In this respect Abdülhamid was forward-looking. Efficient armed forces were necessary if the empire was to survive. The navy did not make much progress, although its tonnage and firepower were imposing. Throughout most of Abdülhamid's reign, the great ironclads remained at anchor in the Golden Horn. It would seem that the sultan was afraid to let the fleet out of his sight, even for training cruises; possibly he recalled vividly that the navy minister had employed his ships to cover the palace from the Bosporus when Abdülaziz was deposed. But the army was another matter; it was especially necessary for provincial garrison duty to prevent rebellion among minorities. In 1883 the German officer and military historian, von der Goltz, was hired to reorganize the Ottoman army. His twelve years' work produced results that were demonstrated in the victorious war of 1897 against Greece.

In other material ways also the empire under Abdülhamid moved in western directions. European funds financed the tram lines, mine works, and public utilities. Most of the monetary profit, therefore, migrated out of the empire; the empire, however, profited from the increase in material conveniences, as well as from skills and knowledge that percolated in with them. The telegraph network, which had been started at the time of the Crimean War, was vastly expanded under Abdülhamid II, reaching to the uttermost parts of the empire. This had a double political significance. New lines, simplified codes, and trained operators enabled the sultan to keep a closer check on provincial affairs. On the other hand, the educated technicians who manned the telegraph offices would later, in many instances, coöperate with Young Turk and Kemalist opposition to the Istanbul government. The telegraph also provided the means by which political dissenters could in the future bombard the government at long distance with threats and reform demands.

Just as striking, though far shorter in mileage, was railway construction. Here again Abdülhamid continued the westernizing trend inaugurated during the Tanzimat. In that era the lines built by European concessionaires were short, but opened the productive hinterland to nearby port cities. Istanbul and Edirne were linked to the European railway network via Vienna only in 1888. Thereafter Abdülhamid, evidently more interested in the political and strategic than in the economic advantages of railways, contracted with German groups to build lines into Anatolia, first to Ankara and then to Konya. Both were operating by the mid-nineties.

In 1903 the Baghdad Railway Company, which was controlled by the Deutsche Bank, gained a concession to extend the line beyond Konya through the Amanus and Taurus ranges to the Euphrates River and on to Baghdad. Its route was dictated by Turkish strategic interests which required the line to stay away from the Mediterranean coast for protection; similarly, Russian pressures required that no railway be built in northeastern Anatolia without their consent. The Baghdad Railway began to open up new areas to commerce and shortly to show a profit so long as the difficult mountain terrain, where construction costs rose sharply, was left unpierced. It also turned the German interest, originally economic, into a political one. Germans began to speak of their Baghdad railway "sphere," and eventually the line became the subject of great-power controversy. It represented the strongest German link with the Ottoman Empire. German investment and trade in the empire soon came to rank third, behind the British and French. For the sultan, the railway represented a steel link with distant provinces, and a means of military transport.

Railway construction and other economic enterprises were fostered in part by an institution which had its origins in the Ottoman treasury crisis of 1875–76. Since the government's credit was affected, and it had difficulty meeting the payments on its vast external debt, it agreed in 1881 to an arrangement with European holders of Ottoman bonds. The

Ottoman Public Debt Administration accordingly was created, under the control of a council representing the foreign creditors. To the Public Debt Administration were assigned revenues from various taxes and monopolies for service of the debt. The Administration collected and disbursed the revenues and also became an agent for other tax collections. By its efficient operation it enhanced the material welfare of the empire, trained many employees (a great number of whom were, however, Greeks and Armenians), restored the empire's credit, and produced a surplus for the Ottoman treasury. Yet a quasi-public agency managed by foreigners represented an infringement of Turkish sovereignty which was not forgotten by Turkish nationalists in later years.

Despite the educational and economic progress of Abdülhamid's reign, opposition arose from two distinct sources. One was discontent with the sultan's repressive rule among educated Turks. A few of these men had been connected with the New Ottomans two decades before; most knew them only through the writings of authors such as Namik Kemal. Occasional objectors to Abdülhamid's authoritarian regime escaped to Europe in the early 1880s, but it was only toward the end of the decade that discontent among student groups—especially in the military and military-medical schools—provided a focus for opposition. In 1889 a few military-medical students founded the secret organization which came to be the Committee of Union and Progress (CUP), which was often called the Young Turk group. Others, including some civil officials, joined. In touch with western ideas, angered at the absolutism and espionage of the regime, antagonized by its obscurantism, protesting western diplomatic and military intervention in their country, these liberals of their day were also both Ottoman patriots and critics of the privileges extended to sons and relatives of the Hamidian elite. Not a few were of provincial origin.

The other type of opposition originated in the growing particularist or nationalist ideas of non-Turkish groups. Among some of the educated Arabs a cultural revival led to a growing consciousness of Arabism, even momentarily in Syria to thoughts of autonomy. A similar localism began to develop in Albania. The Greeks of Macedonia and Crete looked to union with their fellows in independent Greece, who encouraged the movements. The Bulgars similarly coveted Macedonia; while one group worked from outside Macedonia in autonomous Bulgaria, the Internal Macedonian Revolutionary Organization (IMRO), formed in 1893, agitated within that province for revolt against the sultan. And among the Armenians, now spurred by their own cultural renaissance to a new consciousness of national identity, revolutionary groups sprang up. These groups contemplated the use of force to gain the autonomy that their representatives at the Congress of Berlin had failed to secure. It was the Greeks, Bulgars, and Armenians—more advanced in self-consciousness than the Arabs and Albanians, and closer to the center of the empire—who caused Abdülhamid the greatest concern. He employed in the early 1890s the so-called Hamidiye regiments of irregular Kurdish frontier forces against the Armenians.

As a result of these separatist movements, the Ottoman Empire was confronted in the years 1894 to 1897 with a first-class domestic and international crisis. Risings and protest demonstrations by Armenian revolutionary groups, though disapproved by the Armenian urban elite and the ordinary peasant, were followed by massacres in which many innocent Armenians lost their lives. The great powers of Europe began to discuss reform measures that might be imposed on Abdülhamid's government. Bulgar violence in Macedonia provoked Greek counter-agitation. Meanwhile the Greeks in Crete rose in revolt, demanding union with Greece; the resultant massacres of Christians there so inflamed the public in Greece that Athens sent military help to the rebels, and, in 1897, declared war on the Ottoman Empire. The Ottoman army decisively defeated the Greeks—it was the only victory of Abdülhamid's reign—but was kept from further advance or territorial annexation by the concerted action of the powers, who actually forced the Turks to acknowledge Cretan autonomy under Prince George of Greece. The Ottoman Empire gained only an indemnity payment for its victory.

The empire, however, was the victor by default in larger questions of intervention or even partition by the European powers. Dissension among them prevented more than minimal agreement to try to preserve calm and the status quo. Lord Salisbury, gloomily questioning the sixty-year-old British policy which assumed that the Ottoman Empire could be revitalized and preserved, suggested common action to coerce Sultan Abdülhamid, but found no support among the other powers. Russia, who twenty years before had been anxious to strip away sections from the empire, was now so involved in Far Eastern adventures that she would do nothing for the Armenians, and agreed with Austria to keep the Balkans quiet. In St. Petersburg the proposal of the Russian ambassador in Istanbul, that Tsarist forces be prepared to seize a base on the Bosporus, was quietly shelved. A mild reform scheme which was worked out by some of the powers for the Armenian vilayets in the east lacked teeth and produced no tangible result. Again, the fate of the Ottoman Empire was determined from the outside, even if this time by inaction. The Armenian and Macedonian problems were left unsolved. Abdülhamid's domestic repression increased, and so did his emphasis on the claims of the califate.

During this period of domestic and foreign crisis, covert criticism of Abdülhamid's regime mounted. The secret cells of five into which the Committee of Union and Progress (cup) was organized had spread to include students and graduates of the civil service, veterinary, and other higher schools. Governmental repression bred clandestine opposition; opposition bred repression. In 1895 the government arrested some cup members. In 1896 a cup plot to overturn the government was betrayed. Further arrests, prison sentences, and exiles followed that year and the next. Those who could, escaped to Europe or to Egypt. Living in Paris already were some individual liberals of varying origins, notable among them Ahmed Riza, who had been partly educated in France, and was an intellectual disciple of Auguste Comte. Like the positivists he believed in orderly evolution. He believed also that Islam was flexible enough to facilitate such evolution. With some of the escapees, Ahmed Riza began in 1895 the publication of a newspaper named *Meshveret* (Consultation) in both Turkish and French editions. Its program called for preservation of the Ottoman Empire, opposition to all foreign intervention, reforms, Ottomanism, the re-establishment of the constitution of 1876, the borrowing of western science while maintaining eastern civilization, and forswearing the use of violence. The paper was smuggled into the hands of Ottoman readers through the foreign postoffices.

A journalist and Public Debt employee of Caucasian origin and Russian education, Murad Bey, fled Istanbul in 1895. He had submitted a memorandum on reform to Sultan Abdülhamid which brought no results. In Egypt he began to publish again his paper, *Mizan* (Balance), which was also smuggled back into the empire and found somewhat greater approval than *Meshveret* because of its more Turkish tone. Going on to Europe, he joined the cup group, but he and Ahmed Riza did not get along harmoniously. Murad Bey, the more popular of the two, became leader of the cup in Europe, operating from Geneva while Ahmed Riza stayed in Paris. But in 1897 Mizanji Murad—his nickname was derived from his journal—was lured back to Istanbul by an agent of Sultan Abdülhamid who promised amnesty for CUP members. The sultan did not keep his promise. Other CUP members were also induced to make compromises with the sultan, though Ahmed Riza, a stubborn individualist, stayed on in Paris. The defection of Murad Bey took the heart out of the clandestine movement in Istanbul. Groups remained active in the Balkans, in Cairo, and in Geneva, but their coordination, always tenuous at best, was reduced nearly to zero.

In 1897 and 1898 Abdülhamid's regime seemed to have attained a new plateau of security. The prospects of any immediate foreign intervention in Armenia and Macedonia were past—the attention of the powers was directed to the partitioning of China and to the Anglo-French contest then brewing in the Sudan. The sultan's army had returned victorious from Greece. The German Kaiser visited his friend the sultan-calif, new railway building was being projected, pan-Islamic propaganda seemed increasingly effective. The Young Turks in exile were at odds, and those in Istanbul arrested or quiescent. Abdülhamid's rule became even more repressive of new thought.

Yet the appearance of quiet and security was deceptive. The half-secret intellectual life of educated men in the major cities persisted. The newspapers and magazines that confined themselves to non-political subjects to avoid censorship continued, nevertheless, to provide at least a general knowledge of the material world of the West, and of its scientific progress; this tendency was fundamentally subversive of the regime's anti-western obscurantism. New glimmerings of a nascent Turkish nationalism, which might eventually be subversive both of Ottomanism and of pan-Islamism, appeared in the guises of a revised interest in the Turkish language and Turkish history, of reaction against Arabism in literature, and of resentment against the minority revolts. The Greek-Turkish war of 1897 furnished the occasion for an outburst of patriotic sentiment that carried Turkish nationalist overtones. "I am a Turk, my religion and my race are mighty," wrote the poet Mehmed Emin [Yurdakul], using the word "Turk" as a proud slogan, although it had traditionally been applied by the Ottoman elite to the ignorant or the peasant. Interest in Turkishness was reinforced by renewed interest in the Turks outside Ottoman frontiers, especially in Russia, and by interest in the Asian-Mongol past. The books of Léon Cahun, who glorified this past, were translated; some ran serially even in the Hamidian press. But true Turkish nationalism was still a wave of the future, and did not seriously bother the Hamidian regime. When in 1904 a Russian-born Turk, Yusuf Akchura, published in a Cairo journal an article pointing to Turkism as perhaps a more effective unifying force than the Ottomanism of the Tanzimat and early Hamidian eras, or the Hamidian pan-Islamism of the moment, he attracted little support.

Of more immediate importance was the fact that in Istanbul and the major provincial cities the Young Turk papers, smuggled in from Europe and carrying their criticism of the regime, were still being read. So were the proscribed works of Namik Kemal and others of the older generation of New Ottomans; their works passed from hand to hand, their poems were memorized. New poems by intellectual opponents of the Hamidian regime also appeared. These of course could not be published, but they circulated in manuscript, arousing a secret excitement. The most famous of them was entitled "Mist." Written by Tevfik Fikret, a western-oriented and humanistic moralist, it described the veil of darkness that had settled over Hamidian Istanbul. Tevfik Fikret's poem "Tarih-i Kadim" ("Antiquated History") further attacked the tyranny of the traditional Islamic state and preached an idealistic pursuit of reason and truth. His appeal to the discontented was electric.

While the intellectual ferment continued under cover within the empire, the Young Turks in exile got sudden and unexpected encouragement. Damad Mahmud Pasha, a brother-in-law of Sultan Abdülhamid, escaped to Paris with his two sons at the end of 1899, and, praising Ahmed Riza, wrote a public letter vigorously condemning the sultan. His son, Prince Sabahaddin, in 1902 helped to organize in Paris a small "congress of Ottoman liberals" which attracted Turk, Armenian, Albanian, Arab, Jewish, Kurd, Greek, and Circassian delegates. Though the congress called for restitution of the constitution of 1876, for equality of all Ottoman subjects, and for preservation of Ottoman integrity, it laid bare the diversity of views among its participants. Sabahaddin and Ahmed Riza thereafter split apart. While the latter remained more Turkish, the more ecumenical Sabahaddin became convinced of the need for studying social science, and persuaded of the virtues of Anglo-Saxon political decentralization and personal initiative. Until 1907 the two men followed separate paths.

Meanwhile, within the empire itself new cells of opposition to the Hamidian regime sprang up, particularly in 1906 and after; some were in Istanbul itself, one was in Damascus (with which Mustafa Kemal was associated), and a large number were in the Balkan territories still under Ottoman rule. Macedonia was fertile soil for such protest groups. The city of Salonika became a center of the movement. Abdülhamid's control was weaker there than in the capital, his censorship less effective; in addition contact with European ideas was easy, a Freemasonic lodge existed, and Jewish citizens of Salonika could help with finance and communications.

Above all, Salonika was the base of the Third Army, many of whose officers were enrolled in the secret cells. These men, products of the western-style military schools, were incensed not only that pay was often in arrears, but that in Macedonia the Bulgarian guerrilla activity had increased and had resulted in great-power intervention in the form of a European-officered gendarmerie with the threat of a further weakening of Ottoman control. Patriotic sentiment and resentment against the sultan led to the formation of the secret "Ottoman Freedom Committee" in Salonika in 1906. One of its founders was Talât Bey, son of a poor family of Edirne, who had learned French in an Alliance Israélite school and had risen to be chief clerk of the Salonika post and telegraph office. Though Salonika and Paris were in touch by 1907, and together adopted a new charter under the name of Committee of Union and Progress, coordination was loose at best. The two groups did agree on a restoration of the constitution, and Ahmed Riza came to accept, though reluctantly, Salonika's aim of overthrowing Abdülhamid—but not the dynasty—by force if necessary. A second congress of Ottoman liberals met in Paris at the end of 1907, but had no direct effect on the course of events in the empire. The Paris intellectuals were outdistanced by the practical men of Macedonia. By 1908 the CUP claimed a cell membership of at least 15,000 in Macedonia.

It was the disaffection of the army officers that brought results, though it cannot be denied that the atmosphere created by outside events was favorable. In addition to the Young Turk propaganda smuggled in from Paris, Geneva, and Cairo, the conspirators were encouraged to act by other and diverse events: Japan's defeat of Russia in 1905, which seemed to prove that a westernizing Asian people could achieve success even in the face of European great-power opposition; the victory of the constitutional movement in Iran in 1906; and the meeting of the British and Russian sovereigns at Reval in 1908, which seemed to portend further great-power intervention to quell the renewed unrest in Macedonia.

Ferment within the army seems actually to have triggered the 1908

revolt. In 1906 and 1907 some army units had mutinied to secure over-
due pay. By the latter year, Abdülhamid's spies were aware of the greater
political conspiracy brewing in Salonika, though evidently they underes-
timated its extent. A series of investigations caused a wave of spontaneous and perhaps unrelated revolts among Macedonian army units, starting in late June and early July of 1908. Major Enver and Adjutant-
Major Niyazi, defying authority, took to the hills. General Shemsi
Pasha, sent to put down the mutinies there, was shot in broad daylight
before the eyes of a crowd as he emerged from a telegraph office in
Manastir after reporting progress against the CUP to Istanbul. His assas-
sin was a uniformed army officer. Units of the Third Army began
declaring for the constitution, and finally on July 23 the director of the
military academy at Manastir made a fiery speech for the constitution.
On the same day the CUP leaders in Macedonia demanded of Sultan
Abdülhamid by telegraph that he restore the constitution of 1876. The
sultan was now directly threatened with a political revolt led by army
officers. Such events were not unknown in Ottoman history, but now for
the first time the leadership was a reasonably large group of middle-level
officers who were the products of the western-style military schools.

After some hesitation, Abdülhamid decided to preserve his throne by
restoring constitutional government. On July 24 a three line official
notice of parliamentary elections, carrying no headline, was inserted in
the Istanbul papers. The populace of the capital, generally ignorant of
what had transpired in Macedonia, did not know what to make of this
until the next day, when journalists wrote joyous articles on the restoration of the constitution. Then the dam burst. Revolt had become
revolution. Wild rejoicing brought people into the streets. Members of
the ulema fraternized with Greek and Armenian priests. The CUP motto,
"Liberty, Justice, Equality, Fraternity," appeared everywhere. Justice
was in the oldest tradition of Islamic and Ottoman government. Equality and fraternity reflected the Ottomanism of the Tanzimat period.
Liberty meant a parliamentary check on autocracy, but it might mean
more, and in some of the provincial cities especially it seemed to mean
freedom from interference by the Christian powers, with Islamic and
xenophobic overtones. To the untutored, liberty sometimes meant li-
çense: for small boys to break windows, for their elders to refuse tax payments. The true meaning of the revolution had yet to be revealed. The
sultan, however, had for the moment not only kept his throne but
gained in popularity. He appeared, finally, before a crowd at his Yildiz

palace on July 26 to promise "common accord," and so escaped what might have been a nasty situation had his guards cleared the palace courtyard with gunshot as some wished. Any ideas of deposing him had to be laid aside since the reverence of the masses for the sultan-calif was inbred in the common soldier, whom CUP-oriented officers might not have been able to control.

At first the revolution seemed to mean a glorious new lease on life for the Ottoman Empire. Outward signs pointed to this: the disappearance of beggars and packs of dogs from the streets, and new public works programs, including another bridge over the Golden Horn. A few upper-class women began to abandon the veil, though public reaction soon put a stop to this. The most detested of the palace camarilla fled or were interned. The sultan was obliged to proclaim an amnesty, give up his spy system, and abolish censorship; a flood of newspapers, books, and cartoons resulted as the pent-up subterranean private life saw the light of day after many years. Throughout the autumn of 1908 exiles returned, among them Prince Sabahaddin, bearing the remains of his father for ceremonial reburial, and then Ahmed Riza. The Macedonian officers were less in evidence, although a few individuals like Enver Bey and Niyazi Bey emerged as popular heroes. The CUP as such stayed in the shadowy background of Salonika; its central committee remained secret, though the CUP was consolidating itself, and was trying to influence both the army and the forthcoming elections. What direction it might take was uncertain. Three plays performed soon after the revolution symbolized the cross-currents of the time. One was Namik Kemal's Vatan, with all its Ottomanist patriotism. Another, "The Awakening of Turkey," glorified the exile group, in particular Sabahaddin, and was somewhat broadminded and dépaysé. Still another, by a Third Army officer named Kâzim, praised the Ottoman Golden Age, Islam, the army officers, and in particular Enver.

Hopes for a new lease on life were subjected to two rude shocks. On October 5, 1908, the vassal state of Bulgaria proclaimed its complete independence, including Eastern Rumelia, and thus secured control of a vital stretch of the railway to Europe. On the next day Austria-Hungary annexed outright the provinces of Bosnia and Herzegovina which she had occupied since 1878. The Macedonian officers had been aiming at the preservation of the empire, especially in the Balkans, and had hoped for a more favorable attitude on the part of the powers now that Abdülhamid's autocracy was being replaced by a more liberal, constitutional regime. Both their aim and their hope were deceived. Out of the ensuing diplomatic crisis that engulfed the European powers, no redress was forthcoming for the Ottoman government; the only means of Turkish pressure was a voluntary trade boycott which was fairly effective against Austria, manufacturer of red fezzes for the Turkish market. The boycott helped the Ottomans to make the best bargain they could, giving up both areas permanently in return for financial compensation. In the settlements, Austria and Bulgaria recognized the sultan as calif of Muslims in the lost provinces, and Austria in addition promised to favor an end of the capitulations among the powers. Both the pro-calif and the anti-capitulation gambits were to be used again by the Young Turks.

Despite these shocks, the election system created by the 1877 Chamber of Deputies was set in motion in the fall of 1908. The voters chose electors who in turn elected the deputies, one for each 50,000 males of a sanjak. The elections produced some friction and charges of irregularities, but they also led at times to joyous celebrations of the new freedom. Voting urns were carried in public procession like the ark of the covenant. The resultant Chamber was reasonably representative of all elements in the empire. Most deputies were CUP-supported or otherwise related, though the CUP still hid itself and disclaimed the status of a political party. On December 17 Abdülhamid came to open the session and hear the reading of his speech from the throne. Ahmed Riza, his critic during two decades in exile, was elected president of the Chamber. The revolution now meant, to all appearances, at least some parliamentary limit on autocracy and the resumption of progress toward constitutional government from the point where it had been broken off in 1878.

Any such assumption was cast in doubt by developments in the early months of 1909. Liberal opposition to CUP domination of government grew and attracted a number of deputies. More important at the moment, however, was a reaction among common soldiers and theological students that fed on rumors that the new regime was irreligious, violating the sheriat. The soldiers also resented control by the officer group educated in the westernized military schools; they preferred men who rose from the ranks. On April 13, 1909, this blind discontent burst forth in a revolt of common soldiers; few officers were involved. The soldiers invaded the Chamber, ousted the CUP-installed government, and took control of the capital. But the revolt was innocent of a political program.

Abdülhamid, though he has been accused of fostering the counter-revolution, probably simply gave it support after its start because he overestimated its strength. At once troops loyal to the new regime began to move to put down the rising. As the communications revolution had provided the telegraph, by means of which the original CUP success was achieved in July, 1908, so now it furnished the means to stamp out the violent conservative reaction. General Mahmud Shevket Pasha and his army marched on Istanbul from Salonika—by railway train. On April 24, after sporadic fighting, they secured control of the capital. The religious reaction had reached also into the interior. In the region of Adana and northern Syria, Armenian-Turkish conflicts arose, and in the several days following April 13, some thousands of Armenians were killed, as well as numerous Turks. Once the CUP regime was restored, it hastened to make judicial and financial amends for these unfortunate events.

The greater question was, however, whether Abdülhamid could continue as sultan. It was not clear at the start of the march from Salonika whether his overthrow was intended, since the declared object was simply to save the constitution. But the CUP turned against him. The restored parliament debated his deposition, and also, significantly, whether to declare it simply in the name of the nation or to get a *fetva* from the Sheikh-ul-Islam authorizing the move. In deference to religious opinion, the latter course was followed. The "nation" however sent a parliamentary delegation of four, including one Jew and one Armenian, to inform the sultan of the parliament's decision. Abdülhamid was sent into exile at Salonika. In 1876 he had come to the throne as the result of a coup led by political figures and army officers; in 1909 he lost his throne in the same fashion. Yet the beginning and the end of his reign offer a significant contrast. At the beginning he had convened the chamber of deputies and then had dismissed it. At the end he had again convened the chamber, and it dismissed him.

Mehmed V, younger brother of Abdülhamid, was installed in his place. On accession Mehmed declared that he would follow the sheriat, the constitution, and the "will of the nation" which had selected him. Apparently the revolution had been saved, perhaps even the empire, and popular sovereignty was just around the corner.

7

From Empire to Republic,
1909-1923

The Young Turk revolution of 1908 had twin objectives: to curb Sultan Abdülhamid's autocratic rule, and to preserve the Ottoman Empire's integrity. By 1918, when the Young Turk era ended in the chaos of defeat, CUP rule had proven to be as autocratic as the sultan's, and the empire had been destroyed. In an immediate sense, then, the Young Turk regime failed. In the long run, it not only transmitted to the future the progress made in the preceding hundred years, but also contributed to the institutional, ideological, and social development that underlay the emergence of the modern Turkish nation and Turkish republic. This achievement was the result of much travail. Three problems in particular became increasingly urgent. None was finally resolved, but all had to be confronted. First, what was to be the nature of Ottoman government, now that the Young Turks had deposed Abdülhamid? Second, how was the identity of the empire's citizen-subjects to be defined; what unifying concept could there be? Third, how was territorial integrity to be defended, and how were frontiers to be stabilized? These three problems were inextricably intertwined.

After 1909 Ottoman government was in flux. Mehmed V reigned, but he did not rule. A constitutional amendment in August of that year severely limited the sultan's power to dissolve the chamber of deputies. Now the grand vezir appointed the ministers, and the cabinet was collectively responsible to the parliament for its actions, along conventional western European lines. Political discussion grew apace with the reflowering of journalism. Parties, splinter groups, and coalitions formed in the chamber of deputies—thirteen of them between 1908 and 1913. This did not mean that complete popular sovereignty had yet arrived, even though the deputies were elected representatives. The revolution of 1908 had been essentially a coup d'état within the elite, rather than a mass movement; this had been confirmed by the successful repression of the attempted counter-revolution in 1909. The palace had been eliminated as the fount of political power, but the central government still was in the hands of an elite—which was broadened during the Young Turk era—of army officers, bureaucrats, and some professional men. The ulema, a number of whom held seats in the chamber, were influential, though they were never dominant.

Throughout the Young Turk era the influence of the CUP became ever more pervasive. Though it was not yet in 1909 a political party, five of its members, including the capable interior minister Talât Bey and the brilliant finance minister Javid Bey, were in the cabinet. CUP influence was also exerted from the outside. Secret CUP congresses were held yearly in Salonika until 1912, when the loss of Macedonia to Greece forced their transfer to Istanbul. In the chamber the CUP had attracted as of 1908 a majority of deputies, but a good many drifted away over issues of policy or personalities. The CUP, affected by internal divisions, was itself no monolith; the chamber was even more divided. Nevertheless the CUP managed to assert more authoritarian control over government after a temporary setback when a Liberal Union of deputies had challenged it in 1911. The "big stick" elections of April, 1912, held under much CUP pressure, allowed the return of only a handful of opposition deputies. Another CUP setback came later that year, when a group of dissident army officers forced on the chamber a new "Great Cabinet" that would have limited the role of the army in politics. But the setback was avenged in January, 1913, when Enver, one of the heroes of 1908, staged a new coup in which his opponent, the minister of war, was murdered. Thereafter the CUP controlled the government, transformed itself into a political party, and built up its organization in the provincial towns. The trend was again toward authoritarianism rather than toward democracy. It was also clear that army officers were in politics to stay.

Many of the parliamentary and party arguments in these years revolved around the question of centralized or federalized structure for the empire. The CUP tended to favor the former, Liberals the latter. Such arguments reflected one aspect of the deeper question of defining the essence of the political entity and the identity of its citizen-subjects. Three trends of thought were evident. One proclaimed Ottomanism as the cohesive force, another stressed Islam, and the third emphasized Turkish language and culture. The lines between the three concepts were not always sharp. Each, moreover, was mixed in the minds of its adherents with varying degrees of emphasis on rapid westernization, moderate westernization with preservation of traditional ways, or resistance to westernization. The three poles of orientation were nevertheless clear enough to be identified and argued about.

Ottomanism was the heritage of the Tanzimat era, postulating the equality of all Ottoman subjects—of whatever religion or language—and their loyalty to a common government. This was the creed of the Young Turk revolution of 1908, strengthened momentarily by the joyful fraternization that followed restoration of the constitution. Yet by 1909, the appeal of Ottomanism began to wane. Christians in the Balkans, the Greeks in particular, found it less attractive than nationalism. So, shortly, did Muslim Albanians and Muslim Arabs. Another essential reason for the decline of Ottomanism, aside from the separatist tendencies among non-Turks, was that under the Young Turk regime, Ottomanism began to shade into Turkism. A law of 1909, forbidding all political associations formed on national or ethnic lines, could be interpreted as pure Ottomanism in practice. But when it was followed by efforts at Turkification, even to the point of trying to force Arabic script and Turkish language on Albanians, resistance to a Turkish-oriented Ottomanism grew.

The Islamic emphasis found its political expression in opposition to rapid westernization, and also in the doctrine of pan-Islam, a heritage from the later Tanzimat period and more especially from Abdülhamid II's time. Was not Islam the bond that should cement peoples of the faith together—Turks, Arabs, Albanians, Kurds, and others all under the califate? Islam cannot be split up into nationalities, argued the ardent Islamists. The doctrine may have had some appeal to Muslims outside the empire who looked for support against European powers, but within the empire this doctrine too ran into the hard facts of growing Arab and Albanian self-consciousness. Secret Arab societies aiming at local cultural and political autonomy, or even at independence, sprang up. Albanians indulged themselves in a series of risings against control from Istanbul. And an embryonic Kurdish nationalism also existed.

If neither Ottomanism nor Islam could provide a workable definition of the nature of the state and the identity of its inhabitants, and if the principal obstacle to each doctrine was the increasing separatist or nationalist feeling among both Christians and non-Turkish Muslims, the logical recourse for Turks would seem to be emphasis on Turkish nationalism as the rallying point. Some of the seeds of Turkish patriotism (though not a full-blown nationalism) had been planted in the Tanzimat period, especially by the New Ottoman writers. The seeds had sprouted somewhat during the reign of Abdülhamid II, particularly at the time of the Greek-Turkish war. But a true nationalism was slow to develop among Turks, who were, after all, rulers of a polyglot empire they had created and wanted to keep. Most Turks still thought of themselves as inhabitants of a locality, as Muslims, or as subjects of the Ottoman sultan, rather than primarily as Turks. Yet during the Young Turk period, consciousness of Turkishness developed apace. Often it developed in the form of pan-Turanism.

Pan-Turanism looked to the cultural, and possibly to the political, unity of "Turan"—all Turkic-speaking peoples. Large groups of these peoples lived in the Russian Caucasus and Central Asia, in Kazan on the Volga, and in the Crimea. Well-educated Russian Turkish writers like Ismail Gasprinski (Gaspirali) and Yusuf Akchura encouraged pan-Turkism. Some came to live and work in the Ottoman Empire. They contributed, along with Ottoman Turks, to the *Türk Yurdu* (Turkish Homeland), a periodical established in 1911 in Istanbul to promote "an ideal common to all Turks." In the next year a new organization, the Türk Ojaklari (Turkish Hearths), was founded to foster adult education and to popularize Turkish culture. Pan-Turanism was, however, impractical as a political ideal, despite occasional waves of enthusiasm for it, and despite the fact that Enver Pasha became one of the most prominent enthusiasts. Its cultural emphasis served principally to increase a sense of Turkishness among Ottoman Turks. Turkism rather than pan-Turanism was destined to become the vital force.

The man who became the "philosopher" and major journalistic exponent of Turkism was Ziya Gökalp. Born and educated largely in the eastern border region at Diyarbakir, he had been a CUP member in the 1890s, had been exiled from Istanbul, and in 1909 became a member of the CUP central committee. Originally his views had been quite Ottomanist, but they became much more Turkish with time. Pan-Turanism was less attractive to him than Turkism for the Turks of the Ottoman Empire. The political revolution of 1909, he believed, had to be supplemented by a social and cultural revolution which would make every man conscious of belonging to the Turkish nation. Islam, in his view, was necessary to Turkism, but needed to be modernized. Aspects of European science, of European "civilization" in general, could be and had to be borrowed. But Islam and European additions both had to be merged into Turkish culture—and Turkish culture derived from the essential ethos of the people, who had to break through the accretions of Ottoman culture that obscured the true Turkishness. His slogan came to be Turkification, Islamization, modernization; but the greatest of these was Turkification. The word "Turk" began to be used by a growing number of Turks to describe themselves. Babies were given names taken from early Turkish times, in place of the more usual Muslim names of Arab origin.

The changes in Ziya Gökalp's thinking, and in the more general thinking about national identity, as well as changes in government of the empire, were profoundly affected by the third major problem that the Young Turks had to face—defense of the empire's integrity and frontiers. In addition to Albanian risings and active discontent expressed by almost all minorities excepting Jews, two attacks from the outside confronted the Young Turk regime. In 1911, Italy, fabricating an excuse to enlarge her colonial African empire, invaded the Ottoman province of Tripoli (present-day Libya). Then, as Italy neared victory in the Tripolitan war, a league of Balkan states took the occasion to attack the remaining Ottoman territories in Europe. The Balkan war that began in October, 1912, was disastrous for the Turks, who by the end of the year were driven from all but a few strongholds. Bulgarian troops were not far from Istanbul when an armistice was arranged. The coup d'état of Enver and Talât in January, 1913, resulted from a suspicion that the "Great Cabinet" would make peace. But when the CUP government renewed the war, it suffered further defeat. By the treaty of London of May 30, 1913, the Ottoman government had to cede to Bulgaria, Serbia, Greece, and Montenegro all its European territory excepting a strip to protect the Straits and Istanbul itself. The island of Crete was lost as well. Though Edirne was regained in a second Balkan war when the victors quarreled over their spoil, the Turks were still heavy losers. And they had already lost Tripoli and the Dodecanese Islands, including Rhodes, to Italy.

The Balkan wars had brought the Ottoman Empire under a CUP government that soon became a virtual dictatorship. The assassination of the grand vezir Mahmud Shevket later in 1913, in circumstances still obscure, further gave Enver and his colleagues a pretext to exile a number of opponents. By 1914, the government was effectively run by a triumvirate: Enver as war minister, Talât as interior minister, and Jemal as navy minister. Said Halim, the grand vezir, was less influential. Javid was still essential as minister of finance, but carried less political weight. The Balkan wars had also killed Ottomanism as a practical doctrine. The Balkan peoples had resisted Ottomanism, and the Ottoman defeat meant that now the empire was less polyglot. Conversely, Turkish patriotic sentiment and Islamic sentiment were increased, due to the emotions of war, the sympathy for the Turkish refugees who streamed into Istanbul from the Balkans, and the increased homogeneity of the empire. The defeat induced among Turks a reassessment of their position. "Our defeat means the final victory of modernism in Turkey," proclaimed one of the Istanbul papers.[1]

Westernization had in fact been stepped up under the Young Turk regime, both consciously and as events dictated. This was reflected not only by political parties, parliamentary forms, and the increasingly important role of the press, but by the hiring of European advisers for finance, customs administration, irrigation, law, and of course, military and naval training and organization. Public works were supported, the Baghdad railway made progress, new schools were opened. Secularism increased. Islam could be more openly discussed. A newspaper in 1913 even dared to run a series of articles on the question of whether the prophet Muhammad was an epileptic. One of the indices of change was a modest advance toward the admission of women into public life. More educational opportunities for them were opening up, some began to work unveiled in hospitals as nurses during the Balkan wars, and the press began to discuss women's rights. A few ardent feminists appeared, two of whom edited a *Woman's World* magazine in 1913. One of the editors went aloft in an army plane to bomb the populace with feminist literature.

[1] *Sabah*, date of issue not given, quoted in Ahmed Emin [Yalman], *The Development of Modern Turkey as Measured by Its Press* (New York, 1914), p. 109.

It is impossible to know how the Ottoman Empire might have developed if it had had time to recoup and strengthen itself after the defeats in Tripoli and in the Balkans. But the short period of peace ended when the empire became involved in the great war of 1914–1918. Probably, although not certainly, the Ottoman Empire could have stayed neutral in the conflict that broke out in early August, 1914, between the Central Powers, Germany and Austria, and the Entente powers, France, Britain, and Russia. Many Turks favored Britain and France; but the fact that the historic enemy, Russia, was allied with the two western democracies rendered any belligerent association with the Entente difficult. Neutrality was the preference of most Turks and of a majority of the cabinet in 1914. Yet before the year was over, the Ottoman Empire was at war on the German side. The choice proved to be fatal to the empire, and the consequences crucial for the rise of modern Turkey.

The choice was essentially Enver's. Enver Pasha was a Germanophil, but also undoubtedly thought that Ottoman interests could best be served by siding with the powerful Germans against Russia. He was always somewhat of a dreamer about pan-Turkish expansion into the Russian Caucasus. In July of 1914, he approached Germany for an alliance. The Germans had not expected this, but the Kaiser favored seizing the chance, and so the alliance was secretly signed on August 2, to operate against Russia. Only Said Halim and Talât knew of the treaty before it was signed, and the former, at least, was fundamentally opposed to a war against the whole Entente. An element of miscalculation on the Turkish part may have entered in, for a war against Britain and France was neither desired nor popular. The treaty was kept secret for nearly three months, during which Ottoman forces were mobilized and the Straits closed. But Ottoman preparedness for major war was a long way off, and the cabinet was still split on the issue of actual belligerency. With the stalemate on the western European front, however, Germany intensified her pressure for Ottoman military action. Her leverage was increased by the fact that two German warships, the *Goeben* and *Breslau*, escaped to the Straits and were added, complete with officers and crews, to the Ottoman fleet by an ostensible purchase. Enver Pasha finally ordered the fleet, under command of the German admiral Souchon, to hostilities against Russia in the Black Sea. On October 29, 1914, the ships bombarded Russian ports. Several cabinet members, including Javid Bey, resigned when they learned of the attack, but the die was cast. Formal declarations of war on Turkey by Russia, Britain and France followed early in November.

The war obliged the Turks to fight on a half-dozen fronts. Only a few of the operations were offensive—two ineffectual raids on the Suez Canal and an initial advance on the Caucasus front into Russian territory. In the later years of the war, several Turkish divisions served on loan on the Rumanian and Galician fronts in Europe. But most of the Turkish operations were carried out to protect Ottoman territory. Aside from the small Macedonian front, the major continuing operations took place in Iraq against British invasion, in Arabia and, eventually, Palestine and Syria against Arab revolt and British invasion, and on the Trans-Caucasus and East Anatolian front against Russian invasion. As always, the Turkish soldier proved to be a brave and durable fighter. A few Turkish armies were under German command for varying periods of time, but most were under Turkish command. Germany never, despite assertions to the contrary, dominated Ottoman policy. The Istanbul government was able to get much gold and other financial aid, defense specialists, and ultimately war material, by bargaining with Germany. Enver Pasha retained final control of the whole war effort as the sultan's deputy commander-in-chief. One of the most disastrous actions in the war, of which Enver took charge himself, was the midwinter attack of 1914-15 on the Russians on the eastern Anatolian front. Over four-fifths of this "pan-Turanian" army were casualties. Enver returned to Istanbul and took no further combat commands. The defeat seemed to end all practical value of the pan-Turkish ideal, though it arose again briefly after the Russian revolutions of 1917.

The war also dealt another blow to the pan-Islamic ideal which, coupled with earlier reverses in the Young Turk era, laid it to rest forever as a concept which could revitalize the Ottoman state. Sultan Mehmed V, in his quality of calif had, before the Balkan wars, been sent to religious ceremonies in Salonika and Kossovo in an effort to hold Albanian loyalty. The attempt was fruitless. The peace treaties with Italy in 1912, and with Greece and Bulgaria in 1913, had reasserted the concept, first expressed in the eighteenth century, of the sultan as calif of Muslims outside his own domains; but this was cold comfort when all Ottoman political control in the ceded territories was lost. During the Great War much emphasis was put, by Enver in particular, on the pan-Islamic strategy. It worked to the extent of alarming the

British, French, and Italians about security in their Muslim colonies, and encouraging guerrilla warfare in Tripoli against the new Italian masters. But the "Islamic" strategy of attack on the Suez Canal twice failed. The crowning blow to pan-Islamism was the wartime attitude of Arabs within the Ottoman domains. The sultan-calif, with the endorsement of leading ulema, proclaimed the *jihad*—the holy war—against the Entente powers in 1914. The Arabs failed to respond. Quite the contrary, by 1916 a significant group of Arabs, led by the Sharif Husayn of Mecca, had made a secret agreement with Britain looking to the post-war creation of an independent state out of the Ottoman Arab lands, and began to attack their Turkish rulers. Islamic unity was a mirage, and pan-Islam was worthless as a political doctrine.

The most successful Turkish operation of the war was the defense of the Straits against an attack by British Empire and French forces that began in February, 1915. The initial British naval assault narrowly failed to penetrate the Dardanelles. It was followed by troop landings on the Gallipoli peninsula which led to bloody fighting. A Turkish army under the German general, Liman von Sanders, held the heights against the attacks of nearly a half million Allied troops. It was here that the Turkish army officer, Mustafa Kemal, then a colonel, made his reputation as a capable and tireless division commander. The Allied forces clung to the beaches, but finally accepted defeat and withdrew in January, 1916. The Straits and Istanbul had been saved, at least for the moment.

While the battle for Gallipoli was at its height, and while the Russians were pushing into eastern Anatolia, the cup government began to deport the Armenians. Uprooted from most of Anatolia except the western cities, they were sent to northern Syria or Iraq. One of the great tragedies of the war ensued, as more than a half million lost their lives from massacre, exhaustion, malnutrition, and all the hazards of the long march under primitive conditions. Talât, minister of the interior, explained the deportations as a military necessity, since some Armenians were cooperating with the Russians and the danger of revolt behind the Turkish lines in the East had to be averted. He admitted that excesses had occurred, and that innocent people had perished. German officials protested the deportations, but not vigorously, preferring to keep the wartime alliance in working order. Undoubtedly the Armenians suffered both because the bulk of them lived in Anatolia, intermingled with Turks and Kurds in the Turkish homeland, and because recent Turkish experience with other Christian minorities in the Balkans had aroused an extreme sensitivity to revolt and territorial loss.

By 1917, British and British-Arab attacks, despite such early Turkish successes as the victory at Kut near Baghdad, had forced the Ottoman armies into retreat on the Syrian and Mesopotamian fronts. These withdrawals were momentarily counterbalanced by the Russian collapse, so that in 1918, the Turks regained what they had lost to Russia in 1878 and drove beyond into the Transcaucasus. One unit even penetrated to Baku on the Caspian. But these gains could not produce a victory when the Ottoman allies—Germany, Austria-Hungary, Bulgaria—were weakening and asking for armistice, and when numerically superior British forces pushed the Turkish armies back to the north of Syria and Iraq. On October 30, 1918, the Ottoman government signed the armistice of Mudros. The armistice terms opened the Straits and its forts to the Allied powers, stipulated demobilization of Turkish armies except for frontier defense and internal security forces, and allowed the Allies to occupy any strategic point in the empire if their security were endangered. On November 13, 1918, Allied warships anchored in the harbor of Istanbul.

The effects of the war went far deeper than simple military defeat. For one thing, the cup government was destroyed. Talât Pasha, who had become grand vezir in 1917, resigned some two weeks before the armistice, and, along with Enver and Jemal Pashas, was slipped out of Istanbul on a German ship. Considerable cup organization and local leadership remained, however, and could help in the later building of a national resistance movement. The war period had, further, served to develop more Turkish nationalist sentiment. If pan-Islam and pan-Turanism were ineffective, Turkism remained. A language law of 1916 obliged business firms to keep books and correspondence in Turkish. This "economic Turkism" was accompanied by efforts to train more Turks for commercial and technical jobs. At the start of the war the Ottoman government had unilaterally abolished the hated capitulations, and had wrung from Germany consent to this assertion of national sovereignty. The victorious Allied powers refused to recognize the abolition, but the Turks' desire to reassert complete economic and legal sovereignty remained strong. In many other ways during the war, the Turks had asserted their independence of German direction; all such moves pointed to an ultimate result of Turkey for the Turks. This goal was made more attainable by the fact that war had stripped away the Arab provinces from Turkish control, leaving only the far more homogeneous territory of Anatolia and a European enclave around Istanbul. This was still the Ottoman state, but it came more frequently to be called *Türkiye*, a name officially adopted only with the later creation of the republic.

Like all wars, the Great War speeded up the process of social and cultural change. Since the start of the Young Turk period in 1908 the ruling elite had been broadened by new infusions of army officers, civil servants, and professional men, many of whom contributed to the Turkish revival after the 1918 defeat. This broadening process continued during the war as educational opportunities were expanded. Women, even more than during the Balkan wars, found greater freedom to attend schools and to work in offices and shops. In Istanbul, many had discarded the veil by 1918, substituting so diaphanous a covering as to be only a token. A daring few wore hats and cut their hair. Some restrictions on polygamy were written into law, and a few mixed social gatherings began to take place. Though Islam was still a pervasive influence, various other secularist trends appeared also: religious courts were put under the secular ministry of justice; medreses were put under the ministry of education. In both instances the Sheikh-ul-Islam's powers waned.

In the moment of defeat, however, such signs of change counted for far less than the dismal situation faced by the Turks. The economy had suffered acutely from wartime disruption and inflation. Many lives had been lost in the fighting that had been almost continuous since 1911. Allied forces were in control of Thrace, of the Straits, and of Istanbul, and the Ottoman government there was obliged to cooperate with the occupying powers. In 1919, British and then French troops occupied parts of south central Anatolia near the Syrian and Iraqi frontiers, Italians landed in southwestern Anatolia, and Greeks were in Izmir.

Meanwhile, the Allied victors were discussing at Paris, and at a subsequent series of conferences through 1919 and into the spring of 1920, the terms of peace to be imposed on the Turks. Secret wartime agreements among the Allies had laid down a scheme for partition of the Ottoman Empire—not only of its Arab areas, but also of Turkish Anatolia. The Turks were aware of these agreements, which had been revealed and repudiated by the new Bolshevik government in Russia. The Allied promise that Russia could control Istanbul, both shores of the

Straits, and northeastern Anatolia would of course not be carried out now. But the menace of a partition of Anatolia and of foreign control of the Straits remained. At Paris the representations of the government of Sultan Mehmed VI Vahideddin, who had succeeded to the throne in 1918, were brushed aside with harsh words. A number of leading Turks felt that their only hope lay in the Wilsonian doctrine of self-determination of peoples, and in the twelfth of Wilson's Fourteen Points, which said that "The Turkish portions of the . . . Ottoman Empire should be assured a secure sovereignty." But appeals to the principles of Wilson were also unavailing.

In May, 1920, the Ottoman government was handed the peace treaty. By its terms all European territory except a small area around Istanbul was cut away, the Straits were demilitarized and made open to all ships, at all times, under an international commission. The region of Izmir was given over to Greek administration. An independent Armenia and an autonomous Kurdistan were set up in eastern Anatolia. Portions of the rest of Anatolia left to the Turks were, by a separate agreement, assigned to France and Italy as spheres of economic influence. The capitulations were restored, and Turkish finances were put under Allied control. The treaty—this death warrant of Turkey—was perforce signed at Sèvres on August 10, 1920, by the government of Sultan Mehmed VI.

That government, however, exercised almost no authority by the time of Sèvres, nor did it represent the Turkish people. In the nearly two years between the armistice of Mudros and the Treaty of Sèvres there had sprung into existence a nationalist movement that successfully battled against partition and foreign control. The movement began, in the gloomy and dispirited days after the armistice, with a number of knots of local resistance in Thrace and Anatolia, called "Defence of Rights" associations. In 1919 and 1920 it became better organized and coordinated, and was transformed into a government in Anatolia. By 1923 this government had driven out the invader, overturned Sèvres for a new peace treaty, ended the sultanate, and proclaimed itself a republic. The movement had also found a leader. He was Mustafa Kemal.

At the time of the Mudros armistice Kemal was commanding general on the Syrian front. His whole career had been in the military service. As a young officer he had been involved in the Young Turk movement before the 1908 revolution. He had also been a member of the CUP, but stayed aloof from that organization after 1909. During the Great

War he was the most successful Ottoman field commander; the reputation he gained at Gallipoli was reaffirmed on other fronts. By 1917 he had foreseen Germany's coming defeat, and had learned to resent the German influence within his country. And he was on bad terms with Enver Pasha. Thus he emerged in 1918 untainted by close association with the CUP, its war-lord, or the Germans. He had energetically opposed some of their hare-brained offensive schemes, emphasizing instead the necessity for defense of the homeland and preservation of Turkish manpower. If he was not already a Turkish nationalist, it is probably fair to say that he was realistic enough and independent-minded enough to become one; later he expressed publicly his bitterness over the sacrifices the burden of the Ottoman Empire had placed on the Turks. He had also rejected pan-Turkism and pan-Islam as illusory. A convinced westernizer, he privately thought Islam to be in many ways a barrier to progress, and was more secular-minded than all his colleagues.

Now thirty-seven years old, Kemal came to Istanbul after the armistice looking for ways to revitalize the country and its government. He arrived there on November 13, 1918, the day when the Allied warships came to the Bosporus. "As they have come, so will they go," he is said to have remarked.[2] But in the capital his restless spirit found no opportunities. With the aid of some friends in the government, Kemal secured appointment as military inspector for Eastern Anatolia and embarked to aid in organizing national resistance to the invaders in the Anatolian homeland. On May 19, 1919, he landed at Samsun. May 19 is now celebrated in Turkey as Youth and Sports Day, a national holiday commemorating the start of the four-year struggle for national salvation. From there, Kemal went on to organize military resistance, to forge political cohesion among the Turks, and to gain diplomatic recognition for the nationalist movement.

A decisive spur to the movement was the ill-advised landing of Greek forces at Izmir which had taken place four days before Kemal reached Samsun. Ostensibly an Allied occupation under the armistice terms, it was in fact a Greek occupation, portending an effort to expand Greece across the Aegean in accord with the long-lived Greek dream of reconstituting the Byzantine empire. In the Izmir region lived many Greek Orthodox, although they were not a majority. Turkish resentment immediately flared up against this attack by a people whom they regarded as subjects, conquered in the early Ottoman days. And the

<hr>

[2] *Islâm Ansiklopedisi* (Istanbul, 1940–), s.v. "Atatürk," I, 730.

Greek landing seemed to complete a ring of enemies around the Turkish homeland—Allies at the Straits, Greeks at Izmir, Italians and British and French in the south, and a newly proclaimed independent Armenia in the east.

Human resources were available to Kemal, but they had to be welded into a movement. Nationalist guerrilla bands operated in several areas. On the eastern front there still existed a Turkish army, commanded by General Kâzim Karabekir who gave invaluable assistance. Other military men like Rauf [Orbay] and Ali Fuad [Cebesoy] did likewise. Civil officials throughout Anatolia were linked to the movement by telegraph. It soon became apparent to the Istanbul government that Kemal was acting on his own. His recall was ordered; when he refused, his arrest was ordered, but Kâzim Karabekir refused to carry it out. Instead, Kemal resigned his commission, to have a free hand.

The political leadership for the nationalist movement was forged in part by two congresses. The first, held in July, 1919, at Erzurum in eastern Anatolia, had representatives from the eastern provinces only. The second, held in September at Sivas, was more broadly representative of all Turkey. Each set up a Representative Committee, of which Kemal in each case was elected president. The Representative Committee of the Union for the Defense of Rights of Anatolia and Rumelia, set up at Sivas, began to function as a de facto government in Anatolia. Its program, worked out at the two congresses, became the basis for a National Pact: the integrity of all Ottoman-Muslim territory within the armistice lines, complete independence, no legal or financial servitudes. There was a strong Islamic cast to the nationalist movement —Turkishness was not yet the popular criterion. The Sultan-Calif was recognized as rightful ruler. Kemal, who already harbored ideas of a secular republic, was careful not to offend the people's sentiments of loyalty to the Sultan-Calif. But the Sultan was declared to be under Allied control. Until the Istanbul government could be truly representative of the nation, the Representative Committee would act as spokesman of the national will.

Pressure exerted by telegraph on the Istanbul government led it to call for new parliamentary elections in the fall of 1919. A large nationalist majority was returned. Most of the deputies gathered in Ankara, to which Kemal had moved his headquarters, and affirmed the National Pact before going on to the chamber meeting in Istanbul. Kemal, because of the danger to him, remained in Ankara. The new chamber duly voted the National Pact in January, 1920. This became the non-negotiable minimum on which the Kemalists would accept peace. The western powers were alarmed, and their alarm grew as nationalist troops drove French forces from Marash. On March 16, 1920, the British therefore imposed a tighter military control on Istanbul. They arrested and deported to Malta some two score deputies. The British military occupation, like the earlier Greek landing, was a new spur to the nationalists. It transformed their movement into an effective separate government. Those deputies who could, escaped to Ankara. There, on April 23, 1920—this day too is a national holiday, Children's and National Sovereignty Day—they voted to create the Government of the Grand National Assembly. They did not declare the sultan deposed, but maintained that while he was an Allied captive they alone represented the nation. Mustafa Kemal was the next day elected president of the Assembly, and presided over a council of ministers. This organization was elaborated in a constitutional law of January, 1921, which stated that sovereignty belonged unconditionally to the nation. The country was also now officially, for the first time, called "Turkey" (*Türkiye*).

Sultan Mehmed VI's reply to these acts of nationalist independence was bitter. His Sheikh-ul-Islam issued a *fetva* encouraging the killing of rebels as a religious duty. A court martial in Istanbul condemned Kemal and other nationalist leaders to death, in absentia. Irregular troops, the "Army of the Caliphate," were organized to fight the nationalists. Such moves made any reconciliation between the government in Ankara and the sultan in Istanbul almost impossible. When, finally, in August of 1920, the Istanbul government signed the humiliating treaty of Sèvres, Ankara absolutely refused to accept it. If the nationalists needed any further spur to decisive action, the sultan's government had provided it. They could rely now on themselves.

The task confronting Kemal and his associates was extraordinarily difficult. Even to maintain internal cohesion was hard. Kemal was no dictator, no all-powerful leader, despite his energy and magnetism. He was confronted by dissident personalities and groups within the Assembly, the armed forces, and the movement as a whole. He had to reason, argue, cajole, threaten. There were many Turks who held back at first from committing themselves to the cause. There were also dissident guerrilla bands to be curbed or absorbed; at least one had strong communist tendencies. Supplies for the armed forces had to be scrounged, stolen, captured, or brought from abroad. Ankara, a backwater provincial capital, could provide almost nothing; it had telegraphic connection to the outside, a railway running to Istanbul, but only one restaurant and no adequate space for a government. Improvisation was the order of the day.

Yet between 1920 and 1922, the Government of the Grand National Assembly managed to break the ring of enemies surrounding its territory. Success came not only through armed resistance, but also through the growing dissension among the great powers. Soviet Russia, at odds with all other powers and especially with Britain, was willing to supply the Kemalists with war material and gold bullion. The Communist propaganda that came along with this was rejected. Kemal even formed his own "official" Communist party to deflate the small one that had germinated in Turkey. Turks and Russians competed for the territory of the independent Armenian state, which by the end of 1920 was destroyed and partitioned between them. In 1921 Moscow and Ankara signed a treaty of friendship, by which the Ankara government was given full recognition. French and Italian occupation forces withdrew in the same year from southern Anatolia. Both nations were becoming more disillusioned with British opposition to the Kemalists, and decidedly unenthusiastic over the Greek occupation in western Anatolia.

It was the Greek occupation that posed the most serious threat to the Ankara government. The Greeks had expanded their area of control in a series of attacks, starting in the summer of 1920. In that year and the next they drove the Turks back. Twice, early in 1921, Ismet Pasha checked the Greek advance at Inönü, a little west of Eskishehir. But a renewed Greek offensive in July caused Kemal himself to order a strategic retreat, bartering space for time, until the invaders were on the Sakarya river, only some fifty miles from Ankara. The military crisis threatened to become political, as the Assembly berated Kemal for the disaster. But he persuaded the Assembly to vote him full powers as commander-in-chief. In a three-week battle on the Sakarya in the late summer of 1921 Kemal threw back the Greeks. The Assembly, overjoyed, bestowed on him the title of Gazi, warrior and victor for the faith—the appellation once proudly borne by the earliest Ottoman sultans. The Greeks had dug in on new lines, but Kemal prepared a renewed attack that was launched on August 26, 1922. The Greeks broke and fled to the sea, their commanding general was captured, and on September 9 the Turkish nationalists entered Izmir in triumph.

There were still, however, Greek forces in Thrace, across the Straits, and guarding the Straits were a small number of British troops backed by naval units. Kemal's forces now advanced into the Straits zone, up to the British lines. At this point both sides wisely held their fire and agreed to negotiate: the British, to cut their losses; Kemal, to safeguard what had been won. By the armistice of Mudanya, signed on October 11, the Allied powers agreed to restore Turkish control in Istanbul, Thrace, and the Straits. It was also agreed to convene a peace conference. The treaty of Sèvres was now utterly demolished; a new treaty had to be made.

When the Allies issued formal invitations to the peace conference to be held at Lausanne, in Switzerland, they included both Turkish governments—Ankara and Istanbul. Divided counsels could only injure Turkish prospects at the forthcoming negotiations. The Allied invitations precipitated Kemal's decision to abolish the sultanate by separating it from the califate. He faced opposition from close collaborators and Assembly deputies, many of them members of the ulema; their loyalty to the traditional institutions was deeply ingrained. After hours of argument in a committee of the Assembly, Kemal jumped on a bench and said loudly, "Gentlemen, sovereignty and sultanate are not given by anyone to anyone at the dictate of scholarship; or through discussion or debate. Sovereignty and sultanate are taken by strength, by power, by force." [3] The nation, he continued, had taken sovereignty into its own hands, and the one question remaining was how to give expression to the fact. The committee yielded to his forceful presentation, as did the Assembly. On November 1, 1922, the Assembly declared the sultanate had ceased to exist as of the date of the British military occupation of Istanbul over two years before. The Assembly also resolved that the calif was to be chosen, from the Ottoman line, by them. On November 17 the last sultan, Mehmed VI, fled his palace in a British ambulance and his capital on a British warship. Not even a constitutional monarch, such as some of Kemal's colleagues wished for, was left. So passed into history, after six centuries, the Ottoman ruler. Only a shadowy calif elected by the Assembly, Abdülmejid, was left— a member of the house of Osman, but not girded with his sword.

When the Lausanne conference met in November, 1922, therefore, the Ankara government alone represented Turkey. At the head of the

[3] Kemal Atatürk, *Nutuk Gazi Mustafa Kemal Tarafından* (Istanbul, 1938), p. 495.

delegation was Ismet Pasha, taken from military command by Kemal and made foreign minister for this purpose. Ismet displayed at the conference a stubborn ability to get almost all of the National Pact's demands. It was a long, drawn-out process, and Ismet's intransigence in early February, 1923, broke up the negotiations for two months. He insisted on absolute sovereignty for the new Turkey. All the Turkish bitterness deriving from years of experience with great power intervention, foreign financial and judicial privileges under the capitulations, and revolt by minorities was reflected in his arguments.

The treaty of Lausanne was finally signed on July 24, 1923. Under its terms the capitulations were abolished. Although some financial burdens and tariff restrictions remained for Turkey, there were no reparations to pay. There was no Armenia or Kurdistan in eastern Anatolia, no Greek zone in the west. There were no spheres of great power influence anywhere. The boundaries were essentially those demanded by the Turks, with one big exception. The British would not relinquish Mosul to Turkey, and finally, in 1926, the Turks had to accept a League of Nations award that gave Mosul to Iraq. The Hatay, the district around Iskenderun (Alexandretta) which Turkey also wanted, remained in Syria—a "Turkish Alsace-Lorraine" as one deputy called it. Nevertheless the boundaries were generally satisfactory to the Turks. Turkey's sovereignty in the Straits region was recognized, but she had to accept the creation of a demilitarized zone and an international commission to supervise the freedom of transit. Yet even this was an accomplishment, since Soviet Russian demands that the Black Sea states and Turkey should alone control the Straits were avoided by Ismet; Turkey had accepted help from Russia, but would not become dependent on her.

The contrast with the treaty of Sèvres of three years before was striking. Lausanne was negotiated among equals, not imposed. It met the essential Turkish demands. In these facts lies the explanation of why Turkey alone of the five countries defeated in 1918 was not later a revisionist, but bent her energies to internal development instead of external aggrandizement. One other problem was solved at Lausanne, in drastic fashion, with a Greek-Turkish agreement to a population exchange to get rid of troublesome minority questions. Only the Greeks of Istanbul and the Turks of Greek-held western Thrace were excepted. The large-scale transfers which followed caused much human misery. Not only were these peoples being uprooted from their native place, but they often did not speak the language of their new homeland.

Many of the Greeks, while Greek Orthodox in religion, spoke Turkish only; many of the Turks, while Muslim, knew Greek far better than Turkish. But the exchange did, within a few years, make good relations between Turkey and Greece much easier.

The conclusion of a genuine peace, following the military victory, gave the nationalist government sufficient prestige and stability to take two other steps. Each was a practical move. On October 13, 1923, Ankara was officially named the capital of Turkey. On October 29 the Turkish Republic was proclaimed by the Assembly, which then elected Mustafa Kemal, who had prodded it to take the step, as its first president. Ismet became the prime minister. Each move also symbolized the further cutting of ties with the Ottoman past and its cosmopolitan capital on the Golden Horn. The republic, with its new capital secure in the Anatolian homeland, now set out to make a new Turkey for the Turks, and new Turks for the new Turkey.

8

The Turkey of Atatürk, 1923-1938

Younger Turks of today, who know the Kemalist era only at second hand and as heirs of its lasting results, have an impression of mass, of a period packed with changes, bunched together, that pointed Turkey in a new direction. Older Turks, who lived through the period themselves, have an impression of immediacy and of speed: one change following another, under pressure, almost faster than could easily be absorbed. Both impressions are correct. The first fifteen years of the republic, dominated by Mustafa Kemal, brought rapid innovation in many fields.

Innovation was easier once the old shackles of the Ottoman Empire and its burden of extra territory had been thrown off. Innovation was easier also because the Ottoman Empire had established a trend toward westernization of institutions, of thought, of customs—in that order. The older practices, beliefs, and habits of the Ottoman and Islamic civilization had not disappeared, of course. Some had been modified, more had simply been challenged. They remained in contest with the new, causing anguish of soul. At the same time, the republic had inherited a capable elite of bureaucrats, officers, and professional men to guide its destiny, together with experience in parliamentary forms, a complete system of local government, the beginnings of a new educational system and of westernized law, and much else. Unlike most of the developing nations of today, Turkey had never entirely lost its independence; the traditions and experiences of ruling and decision-making were there to draw on. The republic had a great advantage over the empire in that it was at peace through the whole course of its development. It also had the driving leadership of Mustafa Kemal.

Kemal's efforts during the first four years of the republic were devoted essentially to shaping the government, to consolidating his control over it, and to secularization designed to bring Turkey closer to western civilization. This process began while the republic was still in gestation. In the spring of 1923, Kemal, to strengthen his own hand domestically and to strengthen Ismet's bargaining position at Lausanne, formed the party which became the Republican People's Party. It was the only political party. At first it spanned a highly heterogeneous collection of viewpoints, yet it served as a vehicle for Kemal's reform plans. Within the party caucus there was often freer discussion than when the members sat as deputies in the Grand National Assembly. The proclamation of the republic on October 29, 1923, had again been Kemal's work: he had deliberately provoked a ministerial crisis to bring this about. The result was not only formal recognition of the fact that sovereignty belonged to the people, but also an increase in Kemal's power as elected president of the republic.

One potential rival to the republic remained—the califate. The calif Abdülmejid might serve as a focal point for opponents of the republic, of innovation, of secularization, of Kemal. Abdülmejid might try to expand his religious role into a political one; at one point he spoke of a "califal treasury." When two Indian Muslims, the Agha Khan and Ameer Ali, wrote a letter to Ismet Pasha late in 1923 asking that the califate be placed on a basis that would command the esteem of Muslims everywhere, and when this letter was published in Istanbul papers, Kemal decided to seize the opportunity. He prepared the ground by reaching an agreement with some of his chief supporters, and by persuading influential newspaper editors to campaign against the califate as a bar to progress. On March 3, 1924, the Grand National Assembly duly voted to depose Abdülmejid, to abolish the califate, and to banish from the country all members of the house of Osman.

This secular triumph, which weakened the traditional Islamic complexion of the government, was accompanied by others. The office of Sheikh ul Islam was abolished. The religious schools, the *medreses* and *mektebs,* were also abolished, and all schools put under the Ministry of Public Instruction. The ministry of the *evkaf*, which administered the pious foundations, was terminated and its functions transferred to an office directly under the prime minister. Soon after, all religious courts were closed, leaving to the secular courts the application of religious law in appropriate cases. Government and religion were not entirely divorced by these moves, but obviously governmental control over religious institutions was drastically increased while the importance of those institutions was downgraded, if not altogether eliminated.

The essence of the political changes of 1923 and 1924 was summed up in a new constitution which the Grand National Assembly adopted on April 20, 1924. It proclaimed that Turkey was a republic, its capital Ankara, its religion Islam. Sovereignty belonged to the nation—a male nation for the moment, since only men were allowed the vote—which exercised it through the Assembly, where both legislative and executive authority resided. The Assembly elected the president, who was the chief executive. The president chose the cabinet. In a one-party state this meant that if Kemal could control the party, he could also control the Assembly, and his power as president would be unobstructed.

Kemal was not, however, unopposed. Many Turks were shocked at the abolition of the califate, and at the accompanying blows to Islamic institutions. Some of these men, along with others who were quite western-minded, were also concerned about the uninhibited power that Kemal was gathering into his own hands. Among them were several of his stanchest supporters from the early days of the Nationalist movement—men like Rauf [Orbay], Ali Fuad [Cebesoy] Kâzim Karabekir, and Dr. Adnan [Adivar] who were honest opponents of one-man rule. When Kemal insisted that army officers who were elected to Assembly seats would have to choose between a military or a political career, Ali Fuad and Kâzim Karabekir resigned their military commands. As deputies, they also resigned from Kemal's Republican People's Party and late in 1924 formed the Progressive Republican Party, which emphasized democratic practices, the separation of powers, and civil liberties. For the moment Kemal bent slightly to their wishes by removing his devoted supporter Ismet Pasha, against whom they had grievances, from the premiership and appointing the conciliatory Fethi Bey in his place.

A different form of opposition burst forth in February, 1925. In the Kurdish regions of eastern Anatolia a revolt led by Sheikh Said of Palu, head of the Nakshbendi order of dervishes, was fed by Kurdish nationalism, but even more by Islamic sentiment. The army had sufficient strength to quell the revolt, yet Ismet and others of the People's Party wanted sterner measures in order to curb opposition generally. With Kemal's support, Ismet was restored to the premiership, and the Assembly passed the drastic Law for the Maintenance of Order, giving exceptional powers to the government. Special courts, known as Independence Tribunals, condemned Sheikh Said and more than forty other rebels to be hanged. Dervish convents in the east were shut. Using its new powers, the government took the occasion to close down a number of Istanbul newspapers, to arrest journalists, and to suppress the Progressive Party. The one-party dominion was confirmed.

While the government still had broad powers conferred by the special law, Kemal initiated other secularizing and westernizing measures. The most dramatic of these, and deservedly the best known, was the banning of the fez. That cylindrical red headcovering had been introduced as a reform measure by Mahmud II only a century before, but it had by now become the symbol of the Islamic-Ottoman Empire, even though Ottoman Christians and Jews also wore the fez. The armed forces had introduced variants, even new caps with vizors, but in general the fez was still the headdress of the Turks. Kemal began to criticize it, and was joined by some of the press in comments about "civilized headgear," or "head cover with a brim." The word "hat" (*shapka*) was at first avoided, since it connoted infidel custom. But in August, 1925, Kemal appeared in a Panama hat in some of the more conservative towns of Anatolia, and then used the word *shapka* itself. His officials hastened to conform by donning European hats. Civilized men, said Kemal, must wear civilized headgear. In November, the wearing of the fez was made a criminal offense by law. This touched off a number of riots and demonstrations in the east, which were sternly suppressed by the Independence Tribunals, with some hangings. Obviously Kemal was administering shock treatment to tear people away from traditional ways. The European hat was more than a symbol, it was a psychological tool—perhaps the head under a western hat would think western thoughts. All kinds of new and second-hand European headgear found a sudden market in Turkey. One of the popular items was a vizored cap, which could be turned backward so the wearer, still covered, could touch his forehead to the ground during prayer.

At the same time as he inveighed against the fez, Kemal lashed out at religious vestments in general, at dervish orders, dervish convents, and worship at the tombs of popular saints. By law the orders were dissolved, and the convents and tombs closed. The veil was too delicate a matter for legislation. Kemal discouraged it, but left its disappearance to the law called "fashion," which of course operated much faster in the cities than in the provincial towns and villages. All this was done in 1925. With the start of the year 1926, the Gregorian calendar used in the West was officially adopted in place of the Muslim calendar and Ottoman governmental variants of it.

Less dramatic but more fundamental were the new law codes. Some portions of western law had been introduced in the Tanzimat and the Young Turk periods. The process was brought to a sudden climax in 1926 with the adoption of the Swiss civil code, of a penal code modeled on the Italian, and of a commercial code modeled on the German and Italian example. While Ottoman penal and commercial law were already heavily influenced by western precedent, the civil law—even when partially recodified in the nineteenth century—continued to be the *sheriat*. Now the religious basis was removed.

Speaking at the inauguration of the new law faculty at Ankara in the fall of 1925 Kemal had unmercifully criticized the old law and its practitioners as obstacles to progress:

This nation has accepted as an immutable truth the principle that the knowledge and means to create vitality and strength in the arena of the general international struggle can be found only in contemporary civilization. In short, gentlemen, the nation . . . esteems as a condition of its very existence the principle that its general administration and all of its laws be inspired solely by temporal necessities . . . and a secular administrative mentality. . . .[1]

The new civil code put this view into practice in the most intimate sphere of life, that of family relationships. Under this code polygamy was illegal, and marriage became a civil contract (although a religious ceremony might be added if so desired). The husband's advantage under Islamic law in securing divorce was swept away. This was a major step in ensuring the legal equality not only of the sexes, but also of the sects. It sounded the death-knell for the millet system. The Jewish, Armenian, and Greek communities in Turkey gave up their

[1] Türk Devrim Tarih Enstitüsü, *Cümhurbaşkanlari, Başbakanlar ve Millî Eğitim Bakanlarinin Millî Eğitimle ilgili Söylev ve Demeçleri* (Ankara, 1946), I, 28.

remaining right to their own communal law; all citizens of Turkey were to be under one code.

Of course such measures did nothing to diminish Muslim opposition, and in fact, the civil code was not uniformly observed in all corners of the country. Also, there was still opposition to Kemal personally. In 1926, a plot to assassinate him during a visit to Izmir was discovered. The organizer was a former deputy who had opposed the abolition of the califate, and who also nourished a personal grudge against Kemal. The independence tribunal again swung into action, and a broad range of Kemal's political opponents were haled before it. Fifteen were hanged, including Javid, the financier of CUP days. Others, including Rauf [Orbay] were condemned to exile. Some of the Progressive Party leaders were tried and acquitted; they were respected military men like Ali Fuad [Cebesoy] and Kâzim Karabekir. Opposition was effectively broken, and the dominion of Kemal and his party again confirmed. This was Kemal's only purge; he did not snuff out lives like the European dictators of the interwar period.

By 1926 the major measures of secularization had been carried out. Others followed, from time to time, at a slower pace. In 1928, the clause that proclaimed Islam the religion of the Turkish state was stricken from the constitution. Some of the cultural reforms of later years also had a secular connotation. In 1935, the weekly day of rest, itself an innovation in 1924, was changed from Friday to the European-style weekend of Saturday noon to Monday morning. This was actually more a measure of convenience for business and government, and a measure of westernization, than of secularization. Friday had not traditionally been a Muslim day of rest, but rather a market day and the day of the congregational worship with preaching in the mosque.

A turning point appeared to have been reached by 1927. It was symbolized by three events of that year. One was Kemal's visit to Istanbul—the first time he had seen the cosmopolitan city since his precipitate departure in 1919 to organize the nationalist movement in Anatolia. The visit marked the end of a period of exile. Kemal was greeted enthusiastically. He now felt more secure. The Law for the Maintenance of Order was prolonged to 1929, but the independence tribunals were eliminated. The second event was Kemal's prodigious six-day speech, from October 15 to 20, to the second congress of the People's Party. Full of documentation, the speech was his summing up of the nationalist movement since he disembarked at Samsun on May 19,

1919. It was a justification of his views and actions, and a vigorous indictment of those who had opposed him. It also looked to the future, ending with an exhortation to Turkish youth to defend national independence and the Turkish republic. This passage has since been memorized by countless Turkish students and inscribed on public buildings and monuments.

The third event of 1927 was the republic's first systematic census, taken on October 28 under the direction of a Belgian expert in statistics. All people, excepting those in essential services, were obliged to stay home for the day to be counted. The results, certainly not absolutely accurate but reliable enough for use, gave a population of 13,648,270. The census also revealed some of the republic's immediate needs. Well over four million adults were engaged in agricultural pursuits, but only about 300,000 worked in industrial enterprises of any sort, and about 257,000 in commerce. The population over seven years of age numbered 10,483,529, but of these only about ten per cent were literate. There were over 1,346,000 children between seven and twelve years of age, and over 2,076,000 between thirteen and nineteen, but of these only a fraction above one seventh were in schools of any sort. Increases in literacy, education, and industry were the tasks to be faced. Efforts along these lines had already been started, but after 1928 they were pursued more vigorously. Educational and cultural reforms were given particular attention in the years 1928 to 1933.

As striking as the hat reform, but more far-reaching in its effects, was the alphabet change in 1928. Arabic characters, although providing a kind of short-hand still preferred today by many Turks whose schooling pre-dates 1928, are unsuited to represent Turkish sounds, and are anything but phonetic. Because of their variations in form according to positioning in a word, the characters are difficult to learn. All proposals since the Tanzimat period to change to Latin characters had fallen into a conservative void. Now Kemal forced the pace. First the "international" numerals were introduced in 1928, to replace the type of Arabic numerals common in Muslim countries. Then Kemal prodded the commission working on a phonetic modern alphabet to complete its task. On August 9, at a gathering in a park in Istanbul, Kemal announced the alphabet reform. He then set out on a trip around the country, teaching the new alphabet himself in schoolhouses and public squares.

The entire nation literally went to school, for adults were obliged to learn the new writing as well as schoolchildren. On November 3, the Assembly made the new alphabet obligatory for public use in the coming year. It was again a shock treatment. Literacy rose, since the new characters were easier to learn than the old. Newspapers, books, and magazines increased in number after the initial difficulties of change-over, and their circulation mounted with lowered printing costs. But the alphabet reform, like the hat law, was also psychological in intent—it cut another tie to the past, and to the Islamic East, and pushed the nation toward the future and the West. Children educated in the new characters could not read what their ancestors had written, unless it were transcribed or republished in the new alphabet. It is rare today to find a Turk under fifty who can read the Arabic alphabet. There was also a nationalist element in the change—the new letters were not called Latin, but rather "Turkish," in contrast to the old Arabic script.

Other educational and cultural measures that followed also exhibited a strong nationalist purpose, as well as, in varying degrees, a westernizing and a secularizing purpose. The effort to promote a deeper sense of national identity, to make new Turks conscious of and devoted to the new Turkey, led Kemal to ventures in linguistics and in history, both in the year 1932. On his initiative, the Turkish Linguistic Society was founded and held its first congress to discuss ways of simplifying and purifying the language. Kemal himself attended. Those present said they felt his eyes boring into them. Thereafter, Arabic and Persian grammatical forms were attacked and discouraged, and Arabic and Persian words long used by educated Ottomans—in many cases by ordinary Turks as well—were replaced by substitutes culled from ancient Turkish texts or other Turkic languages. New words were coined from Turkish roots, or from western words.

But the purifying process went too far, as was recognized in two or three years, and a halt was called to extremist measures. The presence of common Arabic and Persian words in Turkish was "legitimized" by the concoction of a "sun-language theory." It claimed that all languages could be etymologized back to an initial sound emitted when the first man, a Turk, looked at the sun and registered his vocal reaction. Thus Turkish was the father of languages. The theory never gained much support, and was soon quietly buried. What remained was a slower process of simplifying and Turkifying the language; it continues to this day. Some of the new words have gained popular acceptance, some have official currency only, but the modern language is decidedly simpler and more Turkish than before. The change has been so marked that passages in Kemal's six-day speech of 1927 are incomprehensible to the Turkish student who reads it today unless he has a gloss.

Kemal had also caused the Turkish Historical Society to be founded. Its first congress was held in 1932. A "history thesis" was developed to demonstrate that, as in language, Turks had an honored place in the development of civilization. In new textbooks, the Turks were portrayed as the earliest civilized people, the ancestors of many civilizations in the world, including the Sumerian and the Hittite in the Near East. In Ottoman days, the history taught in schools was largely the history of the Ottoman dynasty and of the earlier Islamic califate. Interest in Turkish history, as such, had grown among some writers and scholars since the later Tanzimat period, but only under Kemal was the Turkish past made central to historical study. The first two volumes of the new official four-volume history, which by regulation every teacher had to own and every secondary-school student had to study, were devoted to pre-Ottoman times. In addition to contributing, like the language reform, to a sense of Turkishness and of national identity, the history reform had two further effects. One was to show that Islam entered into Turkish development only after there was already a Turkish civilization; Islam was a non-Turkish import. The other was to emphasize the connection between the people and the Anatolian homeland, a relationship that went back to the Hittite period. The extreme elements of the history theory were also discarded with the years, but its purpose was achieved. Interest in pre-Islamic Turkish history, in Hittite archaeology, and in other aspects of pre-Turkish Anatolian history, continues.

The new Turkish alphabet, the purified Turkish language, and the Turk-centered history were taught in an increasing number of schools to an ever greater percentage of Turkish youth. Illiteracy was under attack, though its conquest was still years away. In 1923, when the republic was established, approximately 358,000 students were enrolled in educational institutions of all sorts, from primary school through the university. The 1927 census had shown a commendable increase to 497,000 students. By 1932 there were 624,000, and the number thereafter grew yearly. In 1933, the primary-school students began reciting a creed that opened with "I am a Turk, honest and diligent," and pledged to protect the weak, respect their elders, to aim at progress, and to serve their country. Literacy, moral character, and nationalism marched hand in hand.

Formal education was supplemented by popular education, principally through the People's Houses (*Halkevleri*) estabished, from 1932 on, in all cities and chief towns. Evolved from a merger of the Turkish Hearths of the CUP period with the Republican People's Party, the Houses served as community centers to promote lectures, exhibitions, dramas, film-showings, and sports events. They emphasized various aspects of folk-culture for the westernized elite, and aspects of western culture for others. Like the schools, the Houses were vehicles for nationalism. They also served a political purpose, under the People's Party direction, of inculcating the principles of the republican revolution—not only nationalism and Turkish solidarity, but secularism and westernization.

Other measures of the early 1930s also fostered such principles. Western forms of painting and sculpture, poetry and prose, drama, architecture, and music were encouraged by exhibitions, prizes, academies, and conservatories. For a time, beginning in 1935, oriental music was even banned from public concerts and radio broadcasts. The metric system of weights and measurements, supposedly introduced in 1869, was rigorously enforced after 1934, replacing the chaos of traditional units. Aya Sofya, the great Byzantine church which since 1453 had been a mosque, was secularized as a museum in 1933, and the process of uncovering the medieval mosaics was begun. A greater blow to tradition came in 1932, with the inauguration of the call to prayer from the minarets in Turkish, instead of Arabic. Despite some popular demonstrations in Anatolian cities against the innovation, it was made obligatory the next year. The Koran was also publicly read in Turkish translation for the first time at services in Istanbul early in 1932. On the second such occasion ten thousand worshippers in the mosque heard thirty reciters sing portions of the Koran in Turkish, while another thirty thousand listened outside to loudspeakers. Of course this innovation too caused conservatives to grumble.

Traditional usages again suffered with the adoption, in 1934, of a law requiring all people to take surnames. Until that time, only a few Turks of distinguished lineage had family names. Most had one given name, supplemented either by another acquired when young, or by the father's given name, or by an adjective indicating place of birth or a physical characteristic. "Ahmed from Bursa" or "Lame Mehmed" might be sufficient in small communities, but the confusion among Ahmeds and Mehmeds in school, tax, and census records in an increasingly literate and mobile society can be imagined. In 1934 then, there ensued a popular hunt for family names. Mustafa Kemal was given the name Atatürk (Father-Turk) by the Assembly. Ismet became Ismet Inönü, after the site of one of his victories. At the same time, the old honorific titles like Bey, Efendi, Hanim (Lady) were abolished in favor of a simple Bay (Mr.) or Bayan (Mrs. or Miss) preceding the surname. But custom dies hard. Official usage follows the new rules. In popular usage however, even today Bay Mehmed Bulut is called Mehmed Bey instead of Bay Bulut, and it is likely that some of his close acquaintances will not even know Mehmed's surname or how to look him up in the telephone book.

Many of the cultural and educational changes affected the status of women. Increasing numbers were getting an education, finding employment, and taking part in public life. Atatürk vigorously preached the virtues of European social graces to women, and embarrassed many at first by urging them to participate in mixed public dancing. In the major cities, social emancipation proceeded rapidly. Even beauty contests, unthinkable a few years before, were introduced; a Turkish beauty queen was chosen Miss Europe as early as 1932. In the small towns and the countryside, women often kept the psychology of the veil, and sometimes the veil itself. Yet the seclusion of women and the traditional separation of the sexes were undeniably on the wane. By 1933, thirteen women held judgeships. By 1934, one of the last vestiges of formal separation in the cities, the reservation for women of the first two benches in tramcars, was disappearing. A logical sequel to such social change was the extension, in two stages, of the franchise to women. In 1930, they were given the vote for elections to municipal councils, and in 1934 for elections to the National Assembly. They could also be candidates. The elections of 1935 produced seventeen women deputies.

During the period of concentration on educational, cultural, and social change, there was also an experiment in organizing an opposition political party. The Free Republican Party was formed in August, 1930, by Fethi [Okyar], who had been one of Kemal's early supporters and, most recently, was ambassador to France. The move was made after consultation with Kemal, and probably at Kemal's own suggestion. Kemal's ultimate intention, however, is not certain: whether he meant to foster a true two-party system, or meant to allow an opposition party simply as an escape valve for grievances that were already being aired.

Some grievances were economic—a growing discontent with government restrictions, burdensome taxation, and lack of freedom for private enterprise. Poor harvest years and the first effects of the international depression augmented the discontent. Other grievances were political—protest against the authoritarian, one-party rule. Resentment was voiced most often against the prime minister, Ismet, and the People's Party, though Kemal himself may have been less popular than earlier, and somewhat out of touch with the people. The experiment released a jinni from the bottle. As Fethi began campaigning in September he attracted more enthusiastic support than had been anticipated, not only from liberals, but also from religious reactionaries and other malcontents. There was some rioting against People's Party organs. Kemal evidently was persuaded by Ismet and others of his party that the experiment was too dangerous. Fethi Bey, unwilling to lead a campaign which might turn into an attack on the Gazi Kemal as an individual, dissolved the party in November.

How violent the religious reactionaries might become was made even clearer the following month. At Menemen, near Izmir, a crowd was being harangued by a dervish leader who denounced the irreligious republican regime. A young officer named Kubilay protested. He was knocked down and his head hacked off. Troops had to be called to restore order. After the Free Party experiment and the Kubilay incident, the People's Party control over government and elections was strengthened. These events, which revealed such deep divisions in Turkish society, helped spur the efforts to promote national solidarity implicit in the language and history reforms above-mentioned, as well as the creation of the People's Houses to teach the principles of the republican revolution. The general discontent with the economic situation also led the People's Party to give greater attention to developing the Turkish economy.

In April of 1931, Mustafa Kemal set forth six principles which he proclaimed as fundamental. They were shortly adopted by a People's Party congress and, in 1937, were written into the constitution of the republic. The "six arrows," as People's Party symbolism depicts them, were republicanism, nationalism, populism, étatism, secularism, and reformism. The meaning of republicanism, nationalism, and secularism was already clear from previous acts and pronouncements of the regime. Reformism, which can also be rendered as revolutionism, was also clear —rapid, continuing, but non-violent change. Populism too, referred to well-known concepts: the doctrine that the people were sovereign, and also that the people were one, without class distinctions. The *new* arrow was étatism, or statism, meaning active governmental direction of, and participation in, economic development. In the 1930s, and especially from 1933 on, this program absorbed increasing amounts of money and thought.

In the first decade of the republic, not much had been done to improve the economy of the country, although Kemal, early in 1923, had promoted an economic conference at Izmir and had spoken vigorously then and later of the need for development. One of his recurring themes was that the plowshare was mightier than the sword. The burdensome tithe—actually a 12½ per cent tax—on agricultural produce was removed. But Kemal, Ismet, and the People's Party generally were more concerned with political, social, and cultural questions than with economic ones. The principal economic theme of the 1920's was to avoid any kind of foreign economic domination or influence such as had existed in the days of the empire. Much of the business skill available was gone with the loss of the non-Muslim minorities who had been so active in this field, but politically this was not a matter for regret. The doctrine of self-sufficiency led the young republic to avoid borrowing foreign capital, to buy up foreign-owned railroads in Turkey as fast as possible, and to develop agriculture, mining, and industry with indigenous capital—of which there was very little—administered through government agencies and development banks.

As soon as complete control over tariffs was regained in 1929, customs barriers were raised to protect native industry. But such industry remained at a very low level. Most of the population was engaged in agricultural pursuits. Only 155 industrial establishments employed more than 100 workers by the tally of the 1927 census. Agriculture too was largely undeveloped, traditional primitive methods continuing as before. The same census counted the nation's "agricultural instruments," almost all of which proved to be the old-style wooden plows. Even as late as 1937 there were fewer than a thousand tractors in the whole country.

The world depression caused Turkey to tighten import and currency controls. A favorable balance of trade was achieved by 1930 only through drastic cuts in needed imports, since exports also fell. Campaigns to "buy Turkish" were instituted; mosques and minarets in the sacred month of Ramazan were lighted with signs saying "Waste is sin! Buy home products!" It was in this difficult situation, rendered more urgent by the evidence of popular discontent, that étatism was inaugurated. The program had elements of state socialism, but it was not socialist or dogmatic; it was pragmatic. "State capitalism" is as good a term for it as any. A five-year plan, developed in 1933, was inaugurated the next year. A loan and technical advice were accepted from Russia to construct a textile manufacturing complex at Kayseri. On April 1, 1937, Ismet Inönü laid the cornerstone of a great steel works at Karabük. Light industries—paper, glass, cement—were built. Imports of machinery and metals were kept up even when other imports were drastically cut. These were the most obvious results of étatism. Agriculture improved very slowly; in 1934, for the first time, there was a small exportable surplus of wheat.

Without question there was some progress under the étatism of the 1930s, but development measures were often inefficient, tangled in bureaucratic regulations, without proper attention to distribution and marketing of what was produced. Private enterprise got little encouragement; the dissatisfaction of independent businessmen was to be an important element in the future. So also would be the results of insufficient attention to agriculture. When they later found a chance the peasant majority would manifest politically their objections to a continued low standard of living. But the state did recognize potential industrial labor problems. A labor law of 1936 prohibited strikes, set up arbitration procedures, and inaugurated a program of government insurance for old age, accident, unemployment, and death.

Throughout the entire republican period from 1923 to 1938, Turkey enjoyed one advantage that no previous regime had—genuinely peaceful foreign relations, uncomplicated by the intervention of any great power. "Peace at home, peace abroad," was Atatürk's prescription. Relations with Greece, naturally bitter at the end of the war in 1923, improved to the point of reasonable cordiality after a treaty of 1930. Longstanding border differences with Iran were finally resolved. Friendly relations with Russia were promoted by a treaty in 1925 that was later renewed and extended. Ankara had made the treaty with Moscow partly as a mark of dissatisfaction with the award of Mosul to British-mandated Iraq, but by 1926 Ankara had accepted the situation and relations with Britain improved. In 1932 Turkey became a member of the League of Nations.

The rise of Hitler, and Mussolini's aggressive tendencies, in the

1930s, disturbed Atatürk, and he took several steps to preserve the status quo and improve the Turkish position. One was the Balkan Pact of 1934, made between Turkey, Greece, Yugoslavia, and Rumania to guarantee the status quo; it was really a safeguard against Bulgarian revisionism. The somewhat weaker Saadabad pact of non-aggression, concluded in 1937, linked Turkey to Iraq, Iran, and Afghanistan. Turkey's request to the powers to be allowed to fortify the Straits zone, which under the terms of Lausanne had been demilitarized, was prompted by Mussolini's aggression in Ethiopia. At a conference at Montreux, in 1936, the request was approved. By her peaceful methods of negotiation, as compared to Italy's belligerence, Turkey gained considerable international stature. Turkey's good foreign relations were a consequence of Atatürk's unyielding resistance to any revival of Ottomanist, pan-Turanian, or pan-Islamic expansionism. The national state in its national frontiers was not revisionist.

To this rule, after the Mosul question was settled, one exception existed. Turks wanted the Hatay, the district around Iskenderun (Alexandretta) and Antakya (Antioch) which had been given to France as part of her Syrian mandate. Many Turks lived there. When in 1936 France took steps to give Syria, including the Hatay, independence, Atatürk was much exercised. By negotiation with France in 1937, he arranged for the Hatay to be a separate region, linked to Syria only in economic and foreign policy matters. Turkish would be an official language in the Hatay. Local disorders led Atatürk to assume a threatening attitude, and in 1938 France agreed that French and Turkish troops would supervise the elections there. As a consequence of Turkish pressures, the republic of Hatay in 1938 had a majority of Turks in its ruling assembly.

The negotiation over the Hatay was essentially Atatürk's last public act. He had been ill since late in 1937. In the summer of 1938, he went to the cooler shores of the Bosporus but failed to improve, and on November 10, 1938, he died in the palace of Dolma Bahche, once the summer residence of sultans. At the news of his death the outpouring of grief in the nation was overwhelming. Lighted on its journey to Ankara by the torches of peasants, the train carrying the body of the great man who had become a father-figure to his people crossed Anatolia, back into the Turkish heartland.

A recent biography of Atatürk is entitled *Tek Adam*—"Unique

Man."[2] There was certainly none other like him. The word *tek* also means solitary, alone. This he was also. Atatürk had, by his single-minded, driving energy, carried through changes which had seemed impossible, at least at such a rapid pace. He had defied and dominated both opponents and supporters. Under his leadership the republic and the nation had without question been firmly established. Independence and national sovereignty were facts. Foreign relations were on a sound basis. Westernization had made great strides. Şecularism had made parallel advances, though whether all of them would be permanent was still problematic. Islamic polity had been firmly rejected; Islam was somewhat Turkified, but many felt that religious and moral values had been lost or weakened in the secularizing process. Economic progress had been minimal; étatism still had to prove itself. And although republican doctrine envisioned a Turkey without economic class distinctions, seeds of possible division were present.

Undoubtedly the revolution which Atatürk had led, in all phases of life, had been most effective in the city. The gap between educated urbanities and uneducated villagers, inherited from the Ottoman Empire, had not been much narrowed—in fact, in some ways it had increased. For the westernizing reforms had only slowly and sporadically begun to touch the countryside. They could not all be locally enforced, and indeed, the inefficiency of government bureaucracy may have been a safety valve; if all reforms had been applied as vigorously as the hat law, there might have been peasant revolt. It was the urban elite which had been most affected by Atatürk's revolution. He had captivated, reinvigorated, and reshaped military men, government officials, and professional men and women. They would supply the leadership now that he was gone, and deal with problems he had only begun to confront.

[2] Sevket Süreyya Aydemir, *Tek Adam*, 3 vols. (Istanbul, 1963–1965).

9

Turkey After Atatürk
1939-1967

There was, fortunately for the Turkish Republic, a natural successor to Atatürk. This was Ismet Inönü, who had fought with Atatürk against the Greeks during the war of independence, who had represented Turkey at the ensuing peace conference, and who had been until 1937 the prime minister under Atatürk. Whatever differences may have arisen between the two in the last year of Atatürk's life, it was agreed in the Grand National Assembly that Inönü was the logical successor. He was unanimously elected president on November 11, 1938. Inönü also assumed the leadership of the Republican People's Party, thus gaining—though without the charisma of Atatürk's magnetic and impetuous personality—the same machinery of direction that the founder of the republic had been able to use.

Inönü was at once confronted with a dangerous international situation. He took office on the eve of the second World War, after Munich. Hitler's push to the East implied a menace to the Balkan states and thus to Turkey. Mussolini's aggressiveness in the Mediterranean and his seizure of Albania were of even more immediate concern. Turkey thought it wise to seek a closer relationship with the Western democracies, in defense of the status quo. With Britain, Turkey joined in a declaration of mutual guarantee in May, 1939. With France, Turkey concluded a non-aggression pact in the following month. Rapprochement with France was made possible by the French agreement to outright Turkish annexation of the Hatay, the thumb of territory which Atatürk had been so anxious to control. This done, despite Syrian protests, the path to eventual alliance with the Western powers became much easier.

There was, however, the Soviet Union to be considered also. The Nazi-Soviet pact of August 23, 1939, indicating that Russia had abandoned Britain and France, the status quo powers, posed a delicate problem for the Turks. When Hitler launched the war by attacking Poland on September 1, and when the Soviets openly revealed their complicity by occupying eastern Poland later that month, the Turkish search for security was rendered even more difficult. From this point on the Turks were caught between two blocs. Remembering the disaster of their entry into war in 1914, hoping for both neutrality and security, they sought a treaty arrangement with Russia. But the trip of the Turkish foreign minister to Moscow proved fruitless, when it became clear that the main Nazi-Soviet aim was simply to prevent Turkish alignment with Britain and France. No Soviet guarantees were forthcoming. Disillusioned, the Turks signed on October 19, 1939, a mutual defensive alliance with the Western powers. Under it, Turkey would give aid if war came to the Mediterranean area. A special provision stipulated that Turkey would not be obligated to fight against Russia. The Italian attack on France in June, 1940, did actually bring war to the western Mediterranean. But the Turkish government, convinced that belligerency would be useless, tried to steer a course of neutrality between the two blocs.

The Axis victories, with the swift fall of France, became more and more impressive to the Turks. The victories became also more dangerous in the spring of 1941 as German forces, following Mussolini's debacle in attacking Greece, poured through Yugoslavia into Greece and occupied Aegean islands near the Turkish coast. Nazi troops were also in Bulgaria, not far from Istanbul. In part surrounded, Turkey yielded to German pressure and signed a non-aggression pact in June, 1941, though stipulating at the same time that the Anglo-French alliance with Turkey remain intact. Then came the rapid Nazi advance into Russia after the June 22 attack. German pressures proved even harder to resist. In the fall of 1941 Turkey signed an agreement to sell chrome ore, vital to the making of very hard steel, to Germany, while still honoring her earlier commitment to sell chrome to Britain as well. German demands for political collaboration were resisted, although the fact that Germany was now, as in the first World War, fighting Turkey's historic enemy to the north made her more popular.

In late 1942 the tide of war turned. With the British victory at el Alamein in Egypt, the Russian defense of Stalingrad, and the American landings in French North Africa, the slow Axis retreat began. The three allies, each with its own viewpoint, began to seek Turkish assistance. Britain and America hoped to use Turkish air bases. A series of meetings with Turkish statesmen, culminating in Roosevelt's and Churchill's talk with Inönü in Cairo in December, 1943, secured Turkish agreement in principle to provide military facilities. But the Turks would do so only if sufficient arms were supplied them. Naturally they feared retaliatory German bombing or invasion. And if they were liberated from German invasion by the Russians, could they escape the hug of the bear? Turkish neutrality was therefore maintained. Controversy over whether Turkey should have entered the war still continues. American and British criticism of Turkish neutrality is counterbalanced by evidence indicating that allied leaders, except for Churchill, did not really want Turkey to abandon neutrality. To open a new Turkish front and to risk Nazi invasion would require the diversion of arms, materiel, and shipping from other fronts where the Allies desperately needed all they could muster. They had made no plans for such a new front. From the standpoint of Turkish national self-interest, and even from the standpoint of British and American interest, therefore, the Turkish policy was probably right. The Turkish declaration of war against Germany on February 23, 1945, was anticlimactic. It came at that point so that Turkey might be represented at the conference on the United Nations organization about to meet at San Francisco.

The war had profound effects on Turkey's domestic political and economic situation. The government, like many others in wartime, had become more authoritarian. In part, this was a result of the economic situation and the necessity of governmental controls. Though chrome exports brought a high price, and many farmers also made profits, the international trade of Turkey fell, the cost of living index rose to over three times its 1938 level by 1943, and some articles such as shoes were over five times more expensive. Merchants and black marketeers often made great profits; those on fixed incomes suffered. The state was faced with greatly increased military expenditures despite its neutrality. In this situation, and because of inadequate tax revenues, a capital levy (*varlik vergisi*) was imposed in late 1942. Assessed in varying ways on different groups, the tax was applied in confiscatory fashion to members of the non-Muslim minorities—especially the wealthier Greek, Armenian, and Jewish merchants—and defaulters were subjected to property seizure, arrest, and deportation to forced labor. What might have been a legitimate emergency measure had become a vehicle for discrimination against minorities who in legal theory suffered no disabilities as citizens of the Turkish Republic. Abandoned by stages after mid-1943, and now recognized by the Turks as a shameful episode, the application of the *varlik vergisi* remains one of the isolated examples of an exceptional nationalist or xenophobic feeling which occurs during periods of crisis.

As the war in Europe ended, Turkey was again faced with a threat from her neighbor to the north. Some of Russia's desires the Turks had got wind of during the war, and Nazi documents captured after the war proved that Stalin had demanded of Hitler in November, 1940, as a price for further Nazi-Soviet cooperation, that Russia have effective military control over the Bosporus and the Dardanelles. In the spring of 1945 Russia denounced her treaty of neutrality and non-aggression with Turkey that had been signed in 1925. At the same time a potential Russian pincers movement directed against Turkey became evident. Russian troops had occupied Bulgaria, on Turkey's western frontier, in the fall of 1944; Communist guerrillas threatened to take over Greece; to the east, Russian troops were in occupation of northern Iran. Not only was their departure illegally delayed well into 1946, but late in 1945 a Soviet satellite state, Azerbaijan, was carved out of the Turkish-speaking northwestern area of Iran. Russian claims to territory on the trans-Caucasus frontier lost to Turkey in 1918 were advanced. To climax these moves, on August 7, 1946, Russia demanded of Turkey that the international convention governing the Straits be revised to provide that the Black Sea powers alone (in effect, Russia, her satellites, and Turkey) control the Straits, and that the military defense of the Straits be a joint Russo-Turkish undertaking. İnönü's government, vigorously supported by the United States and Britain, rejected the Soviet proposition as "not compatible with the inalienable rights of sovereignty of Turkey."

Though the debate over the Straits continued sporadically for some years, it remained in the realm of diplomatic notes. The Russian moves, however, had revealed the potential danger to Turkey. The British were financially unable to assume the burden of continuing aid to

Turkey and Greece. In 1947, therefore, the United States began, under the so-called "Truman Doctrine," to bolster Turkey further with military and economic aid. Active American assistance programs in support of Turkish independence and development have continued since.

At the same time that the Russian threat was building up externally, economic and political pressures within Turkey produced the beginnings of a dramatic political change which, within a few years, brought an end to the one-party system. Wartime economic restrictions and price rises had occasioned much discontent with the government. Businessmen sought more freedom for their activities. Peasants sought escape from compulsory crop contributions. There was also a strong intellectual dissatisfaction with the one-party domination at a time when Turkey, along with other democracies, was ratifying the United Nations charter. Why should Turks not also enjoy a more complete political democracy? In the summer of 1945, four deputies to the National Assembly—Jelal Bayar, Adnan Menderes, Refik Koraltan, and Fuad Köprülü—asked for reforms to bring a truer democracy to Turkey. Upon taking their case to the press, they were expelled from the Republican People's Party. President Inönü, breaking with the more authoritarian views of some of his party, proposed lifting the restrictions on political discussion so that an opposition party might function. In January, 1946, the Democratic Party was founded by the four dissenters, and began to work in preparation for the new elections to be held in 1947.

An exciting period of debate followed, politically freer than any other time modern Turkey had known. As it became clear that the new opposition would attract many votes, the People's Party government changed the election date to July 21, 1946. The Democrats, though crying "unfair," continued vigorous work on their organization down to the village level. The election gave them 65 out of 465 Assembly seats. Their greatest strength was in the cities. Without question the Democrats would have won more seats had there been no pressure on voters from local government officials and had there been a fair public tally of the ballots. There now existed, however, a vocal opposition in the National Assembly. The opposition set out to see to it that a fair count would be strictly observed in the future—Bayar at one point hinted at more drastic measures if this were not done. Debate was acrimonious.

At first the People's Party government tried to stifle the opposition. But President Inönü, in statesmanlike fashion, took a position above party, declaring in the summer of 1947 that a multi-party state demanded that both parties have the same privileges, conduct themselves responsibly, and respect the opposition's rights when in power. From that time the attitude of the People's Party government began to change gradually. There were changes in the premiership—first Rejep Peker, then Hasan Saka, then Shemseddin Günaltay. Whether a desire to please democratic America had any influence on the Turks is problematic; nonetheless, by 1947 American diplomatic support was reinforced by economic assistance, and in any case the People's Party could not help but recognize the trend of opinion within Turkey. In particular, it recognized the widespread desire for more open Islamic observances and a relaxation of some of the secular requirements for which the party had long stood. This was to have an effect on the next elections, since much of the now less inhibited religious leadership seems to have swung to the support of the Democrats in reaction to the period of secularization.

In 1950 the National Assembly passed a new electoral law which both parties approved. It stipulated supervision of elections by the judiciary, as well as the secret ballot and the open count. Both major parties tried hard to woo the voters in the energetic campaign that followed. The Democrats had greater success because they naturally appealed to those seeking a change of regime, for whatever reason. On May 14, 1950, nearly 90 per cent of the country's eligible voters cast ballots. The election was orderly, the counting fair. As one Turk said of his village, in the 1946 election tellers had been instructed to let no one else see the ballot and to make sure that the right party won; in 1950 the ballots were publicly shown and counted, so that this one for Ahmed and that one for Mehmed went in the correct pile. The Democrats' victory, although predicted by many, was unexpected in its sweep. They rolled up an absolute majority, about 53 per cent of the total vote; the People's Party won about 39 per cent. Because the system provided that in each province the voters elect a slate or single list of deputies for the entire province, who were usually of one party only, the disproportion in Assembly seats was great. The Democrats won 396 seats, the People's Party only 68.

The political revolution of 1950, for such in reality it was, gave expression to changes taking place in Turkish society. The Democrats had appealed to a broad spectrum of discontent, to which the People's Party had only belatedly paid attention. In many rural areas the Democrats ran strong—the villager had found a sympathetic ear. Among the deputies in the new assembly there was a greater percentage than heretofore of professional men, especially lawyers, and of businessmen. Conversely, the percentage of deputies with official backgrounds, bureaucratic or military, was smaller. The revolution was consummated when the People's Party peacefully turned over the government to the Democrats. There was no military intervention. Inönü stepped down to become leader of the opposition. Bayar was elected president, and Menderes prime minister, in the new government. Nothing like it had been seen in Turkey before. So began a Democratic period of government that was to endure for ten years.

There had been no real difference between the two parties on foreign policy before 1950, and this continued to be so after the Democrats' victory. Essentially, the national policy was friendship with America and the Western powers, coolness toward Russia and the Communist bloc. Turkey responded at once to the United Nations' call for troops in Korea in 1950. The Turkish brigade which fought there distinguished itself for its bravery. Turks, who value military qualities highly, felt in this common action a real partnership with the West, and were therefore the more aggrieved that their concurrent bid for membership in NATO was turned down. But the NATO powers reconsidered, and in 1952 Turkey, along with Greece, became a full member of the alliance. The Turkish port of Izmir became the headquarters of NATO's South-East Europe command. During the mid-fifties Turkey also negotiated defensive military alliances with countries on both sides of her. A Turkish-Greek-Yugoslav alliance was signed in 1954. In the same year a Turkish-Pakistani treaty paved the way for the so-called "Northern Tier" system of defense against Russia. The key to the new combination was a Turkish alliance of 1955 with Iraq; this Baghdad Pact was shortly after joined by Britain, Pakistan, and Iran. The United States, which had strongly encouraged the arrangement, failed to join, though later it became a member of the committees (including the military committee) of the Pact organization.

These treaties may be interpreted in part as Turkish following of the American and British lead in the "pactomania" of the day. But they exhibited nonetheless three fundamental aspects of Turkish policy. One was the Turkish desire to preserve the status quo and to remain at peace. It is worth remarking that since 1922, except for the Korean action under the United Nations, the Turks have fought no war. Such a stretch of unbroken peace is without precedent since the beginning of the Ottoman dynasty. Another fundamental aspect of the treaties, with roots going back two centuries, was the recognition that Russia—not Communism as such, for Yugoslavia was Communist—represented the greatest potential threat to Turkish security. The third aspect, contributing of course to the other two, was the desire to cultivate good relations with neighbors wherever possible.

With some neighbors this proved a difficult task. Syrian-Turkish relations were never good, and most Arab governments—excepting Iraq's—tended to disapprove of Turkey, in part because it had recognized Israel. The disapproval was particularly strong in the case of Nasser's Egypt. Turks, for their part, generally held no high opinion of the Arabs, whom they had known for four centuries as subjects of the Ottoman Empire. When a revolution in Baghdad in 1958 overthrew the pro-Turkish Iraqi regime, the Baghdad Pact lost its only Arab member. The organization, renamed CENTO (Central Treaty Organization), removed its headquarters from Baghdad to Ankara.

Turkey's friendly relationship with Greece also was soon disturbed—in this case by the Cyprus question. The terrorism of Greek Cypriotes against British rule there alarmed the Turks; it was not only a concern for the safety of the Turkish minority, one fifth of the island's population, which aroused the Turks, but even more so it was the potential threat to their own security. If Cyprus, only 50 miles from the Turkish coast, were to be joined to Greece, then Greek possessions, including the Aegean islands, would half-encircle Turkey. Should British rule on Cyprus end, Turkey wanted partition of the island. In this situation, an incident in September, 1955, was sufficient to set off major anti-Greek riots in Istanbul. There may have been government toleration of the demonstrations; in any event, the disturbances got out of hand, wrecking considerable Greek-owned property in the city. The Cyprus problem and the riots seriously weakened Turkish ties with Greece and Yugoslavia under the Balkan Pact. Not until the London agreement of 1959 were good Greek-Turkish relations restored. Under this agreement, to which Britain was a party as well as Turkey and Greece, Cyprus became independent in 1960 with a Greek president, a Turkish vice-president, and a proportion of seven Greeks to three Turks in the island government. Military units from Greece and Turkey were stationed on the island, and Britain retained her bases there.

Economic questions were even more troublesome than foreign affairs during the Democratic regime. There had been genuine differences between the two major parties on economic policy. The People's Party favored étatism, while the Democratic Party stood for a relaxation of government controls, more opportunity for private initiative, and greater concentration on agricultural development. In the first half of the Democratic decade, until 1954 or 1955, Turkey's economy seemed to develop rapidly. There was an apparent prosperity, aided by good weather and bumper grain crops. This was not, however, entirely the result of the announced Democratic policies of private initiative, etc. The new regime, in fact, continued and even increased government expenditure upon economic development, industrial as well as agricultural. It was willing to incur annual financial deficits and an unfavorable balance of trade, as imports consistently exceeded exports. Much of this was made possible by economic aid from the United States, as well as by American military aid which helped support one large portion of the Turkish budget.

Later criticism has pointed out that much of the development, which did bring real advantages, was too costly, uncoordinated in plan, and in some cases uneconomic. New industry was sometimes located for political or strategic reasons rather than for strictly economic ones. That symbol of agricultural modernization, the tractor, was imported in large quantities; not only did this use valuable foreign exchange, but so many tractors could not rationally be employed unless farms were bigger. Further, maintenance and repair posed real problems. New desires for consumer goods were awakened in city and farming village alike, helping along a process of price inflation. In the later 1950s the economic situation became more serious, with mounting deficits and a larger trade gap. By 1957 the fact of economic crisis was recognized. The Democrats, who had won much of the peasant vote and granted agricultural subsidies, were unwilling to tax agricultural income as a remedy. A considerable foreign loan in 1958 eased the situation, but more stringent monetary controls had to be applied, imports curbed, and some necessities such as coffee disappeared from the market.

In the election campaign of 1950, the Democrats had appealed not only to those who wanted economic liberalism, but also to those who wanted a greater freedom for traditional religious practices. The first action of the Democrat-controlled National Assembly was to restore the right of giving the call to prayer in the traditional Arabic, instead of in Turkish as had been required since 1933. The decision, taken just as the holy month of fasting, Ramazan, was to begin, was telegraphed to provincial officials and welcomed by the people. A slightly larger place was made for religious instruction in primary education, schools to train Muslim prayer leaders were started, and more foreign exchange was made available to those who wished to make the pilgrimage to Mecca. Such rather cautious acts of government were accompanied by an increase in mosque attendance, by the publication of an increasing number of Islamic tracts and books, and by the repair of many mosques and the building of many new ones. Some of the religious upsurge represented a reactionary tendency. This was particularly true of the rather sudden growth in activity of a religious order, the Tijani, whose members smashed a few statues of Atatürk in their campaign against "idolatry." But the government, still committed to the secular republic, kept careful watch and imprisoned a number of Tijani leaders.

The question debated in the 1950s, and still argued to some extent today, is whether the expression of Muslim feeling represented political and religious reaction, or a true rivival of religion, or simply an open reappearance of the religious sentiment that had existed all along and had been repressed under the stern secularism of the People's Party. Probably the latter view is closest to the truth, although it is also clear that some Turks who had led secular lives began to feel the need for worship and a religious base for morality; for them it may have been a revival. The bulk of Turkey's population was still in the villages, however, and these had been far less touched by Atatürk's secularism than had the cities, so that after 1950 they simply continued, perhaps more openly, in their beliefs and practices.

The political atmosphere also underwent a decided change during the Democratic decade. Just after the 1950 election and the transfer of power from the one party to the other, there was a political "honeymoon." For a few years the regime was as liberal as any Turkey had known. But soon enough there were signs that the Democrats, no less than the People's Party, regarded opposition to the government in power as reprehensible. Considerable amounts of the People's Party property was confiscated on the grounds, perhaps in part true, that it had been illegally acquired through use of public funds during the one-party era. Their local party headquarters were shut down. A new press law was passed by the Democrat-controlled Assembly which imposed heavy penalties for publishing inaccurate information which might endanger Turkey's stability. There is no doubt, however, that the Democrats were still by far the most popular party, especially during the prosperity of the early 1950s. The elections of 1954, completely free and fairly counted, increased their majority of the popular vote to 58 per cent, yielding them 503 Assembly seats, while the People's Party garnered only 35 per cent of the votes and 31 seats.

The increased majority, coupled with the worsening economic situation, seemed to push the Democrats toward more authoritarian government, even though there were objections from within the party. Twenty-eight Democrats in the Assembly broke away to form the Freedom Party. Still another press law of 1956 increased governmental controls. The Democrats became sensitive, even hypersensitive, to criticism. That the criticism mounted anyway is evident from the 1957 election results. The voting figures were never officially released by the government, but their previous popular majority was reduced to a plurality of about 48 per cent, though they retained an overwhelming 424 seats under the single-list electoral system. The People's Party increased its share of the vote to 41 per cent, and its seats to 178. The voting was fair, but opposition parties charged the authorities with unfair counting and reporting in some instances. The increasingly authoritarian tendencies of the government, and the curbing of the opposition, raised fundamental questions. Was the role of a political opposition really acceptable in Turkey? Would a majority party inevitably disregard minority rights and consider itself the only legitimate spokesman of national interest?

By 1959 the internal situation of Turkey was quite unstable, even though it was clear that the Democrats, and Menderes in particular, still enjoyed a marked popularity among the villagers. But discontent because of economic difficulties and political repression, and, in certain intellectual quarters, because of a fear that the increase in religiosity could bring reaction which might undo much of Atatürk's work, resulted in increased criticism of the regime.

Among those affected were army officers. Inflation meant that their fixed salaries bought less. As members of the intelligentsia—and since World War II many had enjoyed foreign training or quite western contacts in the American-aided armed forces—they feared reaction against the secular progress of the Turkish republic. The officer class had, of course, been instrumental in creating that republic with Atatürk, and many looked upon themselves as the guardians of the Atatürk tradition. In earlier times, further, the army had intervened at crucial moments in political affairs. During the life of the republic the military had gradually been separated from political life; by 1950 it was unquestionable that they were subordinate to the civilian regime. Atatürk in his day had vigorously promoted the separation. Yet the officers retained a political consciousness. Some may have been hurt by the realization that a new Turkish middle class was eclipsing them in terms of national importance.

It seems to have been in 1954 that small officer cliques began to form —first in İstanbul, then in Ankara—to discuss the political situation. By 1957 some were considering a political coup. An approach to İnönü as a potential leader was rebuffed by him. But Jemal Gürsel, commander of the ground forces, joined with some of the colonels and other officers to provide the necessary high-level leadership. They felt that the violence accompanying political argument in the spring of 1959 meant possible civil war unless the Democrats were removed from office, and planned a coup if there were not honest elections in 1960; they had, however, reached no consensus on the future conduct of government if the coup were successful.

Much is still not clear about the origins and motives of the bloodless revolution which actually did occur in 1960. But the tensions in the spring of that year were obvious. No election date had been set, yet both Menderes and İnönü were travelling and making, in effect, campaign speeches. The Democrats tried to curb the opposition on several occasions. On April 2 troops were sent to stop İnönü's train near Kayseri. They did so, but the Pasha, as he was still known from his generalship of forty years before, walked up to the troops, who parted before him and saluted. It was an error for Menderes to believe that he could call on the army for this sort of political duty, and he should have taken more serious warning. In the same month the Democrat-controlled Assembly, after violent partisan debates that ended in fisticuffs, set up a special committee to investigate the activities of the People's Party. The committee was endowed with extraordinary powers to prohibit political activity, seize documents, suspend newspapers, and imprison violators of these and other rules. This move touched off a series of student demonstrations in the universities of Ankara and Istanbul, followed on May 21 by a spontaneous anti-government demonstration by the cadets at the Ankara military school.

In this tense situation the plotters could no longer defer action. Before dawn on May 27 the armed forces secured control of Istanbul and

Ankara, arresting Bayar, Menderes, and other officials. What Menderes and his colleagues and the investigating commission knew of the plans for a coup or of alleged revolutionary tendencies by the People's Party is still debatable. The investigating committee's report was never made public, although it was declared complete on May 25. The armed forces had, at least at that moment, the confidence of the people of Istanbul and Ankara, who believed that things would be set right quickly. Scenes of wild rejoicing in these cities followed the news of the government's overthrow. May 27 has now been added to the roster of national holidays.

It is always easier for the military to take power than to abdicate it. General Gürsel wanted to turn the government over to a constitutional civilian regime after a very brief interval. This was not to be. He became head of state, chief of government, and chief of the general staff. Power resided with him and 37 other officers—most of them under 40 years of age, "Young Turks" in a new setting—who controlled an interim government and a nonpolitical cabinet of technicians. It soon became apparent that the Committee of Nation Unity, as the 38 were called, were not of one mind on all questions. Fourteen, mostly younger, of whom Colonel Alparslan Türkesh became the most prominent, were purged from the Committee in November, 1960. In general they seemed more radical than the others, more inclined to maintain a longer period of authoritarian military control over the government in order to proceed rapidly with economic and social reforms on the Atatürk model. Several of the Fourteen are again active in Turkish politics.

Meanwhile all party activity had been stopped. The Democratic Party was dissolved, and the Democratic deputies as well as cabinet ministers were arrested and put on trial for violations of the constitution of 1924. A new constitution to remedy the defects of the old—in particular to prevent any recurrence of authoritarian rule by an elected parliamentary majority—was drafted by a committee of lawyers that had been flown in from Istanbul University just a few hours after the revolution; other lawyers were added later. The draft was thoroughly reworked by a constituent assembly that met in Ankara from January to May, 1961. The final text was very detailed. It set up a Senate, and an Assembly whose membership was to be based on proportional representation, where formerly there had been only one chamber; it provided a constitutional court to review legislation; it contained a strong section on individual rights; and it confirmed the essential secularizing reforms of the Atatürk period. All but the last-mentioned were innovations. On July 9, 1961, the constitution was submitted to a national referendum. Sixty-two per cent of the voters approved, 38 per cent voted against. Thus it became the fifth in the series of Turkey's written constitutions since 1876.

The referendum results were, however, disappointing to the Committee of National Unity. The issue before the voters was in effect political rather than constitutional: were they for or against what the interim military regime had done, or, put in the reverse, were they against or for the previous Menderes regime? Nearly two-fifths, at least, of the voters evidently were pro-Menderes still. There was now no Democratic Party. The trial of its leaders on Yassiada, an island in the Sea of Marmara, was still going on. But party activity had again been allowed; and while the People's Party urged a "yes" vote in the referendum on the constitution, the new Justice Party, which inherited the bulk of the former Democrats, did not. The trial of 592 Democratic defendants helped to discredit them with some of the educated elite, but obviously did not have that effect on the villager. After nearly a year, the special court on Yassiada handed down its decisions in September, 1961: 15 death sentences, 433 varying terms of imprisonment. Twelve of the death sentences, including that of former President Bayar, were commuted to life imprisonment. But three ministers were hanged, including Menderes. Both the legality and the wisdom of the trials and sentences are still debated. Very possibly the size of the anti-constitution vote persuaded the National Unity Committee not to commute Menderes' sentence also. Given his popularity, he would be dangerous. Many superstitious villagers already thought him almost divine, after he had earlier walked away unscathed from an airplane accident that killed fifteen other Turkish officials travelling with him to London. If he again escaped death . . . ?

Seventeen months after the May 27 revolution, elections at last were held for Senate and Assembly. The balloting on October 15, 1961, gave no party a majority. Fourteen parties were in the field, but only four were of major importance. Under the new proportional representation system, which accurately reflected the popular vote, the People's Party won 173 Assembly seats, the Justice Party 158, the New Turkey Party 65, and the Republican Peasants' Nation Party 54. In the Senate, whose members were still elected by majority vote of a province for a provincial slate, the People's Party captured only 36 seats to the Justice

Party's 70, while the other two obtained 28 and 16 respectively. An absolute People's Party majority, for which some of the ardent supporters of May 27 had hoped, did not materialize. Instead, the election returns meant coalition government.

From 1961 to 1965 Turkey lived under coalitions of varying degrees of instability, a new and rather unsettling experience for a republic that had known only majority party government for nearly four decades. The two chambers elected General Gürsel president, almost a necessity for national unity at that point. He resigned from the army and took office. It was harder to form a cabinet. Military pressure was needed to bring the People's Party and the Justice Party into a coalition in November under Inönü as prime minister. But because the Justice Party insisted on amnesty for the convicted Democrat politicians, little could be accomplished, and the coalition broke apart in 1962. Two successor coalitions, both under Inönü, combined the People's Party with smaller parties or independents. Neither coalition proved cohesive.

Although the interlude of army-dominated government had lasted nearly a year and a half, power was in fact returned to the civilians as had been promised. This stands in sharp contrast to the course of events in most other developing countries where there has been a military coup. Turkey had shown that its choice was democratic and civilian government, freely elected. Yet the revolution of May 27 raised several troublesome questions about the future. One was whether the armed forces would again feel they had to intervene in an emergency. Many officers, still regarding themselves as the guardians of a regime of progress, were discontented with the eternal bickerings of the politicians, and with the slow pace of economic and social advance. In February, 1962, there was an attempted coup by young officers of such mind. There was another abortive attempt in May, 1963. The chief of staff, General Jevdet Sunay, late in 1964 publicly warned political parties not to be a divisive element and not to turn the people against the army. The army, then, still waited in the wings. A second question was whether political stability could be attained under coalition government. Political pluralism was by now a fact in Turkish public life, but hard to manage. A good deal of popular cynicism, not confined to army officers, attached to the maneuverings and party-switching of the politicians. The third was whether the promise of rapid economic and social progress implicit in the aims of the revolution of 1960 could be fulfilled. During its short period in power, the Committee of National Unity made a start in this direction. It set up an economic planning organization, which was also embodied in the 1961 constitution. It restored some taxation on agricultural income and succeeded in attracting considerable foreign credits for Turkey. But it returned power to the civilians without seizing the chance afforded by the hiatus in partisan politics to press ahead in radical fashion.

Both Turkey's domestic political stability and her foreign relations were affected by a renewed crisis over Cyprus that began late in 1963. President Makarios had throughout that year been trying to alter the Cypriote constitution—agreed on in 1959 by Turkey, Greece, and Britain—in order to diminish the political rights of the Cypriote Turks and thus ease his problems of governing. In December fighting erupted between the two communities on the island, threatening to bring the intervention of Turkey and Greece and perhaps to provoke even larger-scale conflict. Published accounts do not yet make it possible to say whether Inönü's government was actually on the point of intervening militarily to protect the Turkish Cypriote minority from the violence of the Greek islanders, or exactly what role American representations had in urging Ankara to keep the peace. There was, in any event, no Turkish intervention, but instead a surge of diplomatic efforts to end the fighting. Makarios wanted only the United Nations to take up the question, and to eliminate the treaty right of Turkey and Greece to intervene. Turkey preferred to settle the question within the NATO alliance, or by direct negotiation with the Greek government, with which it could deal on equal terms; the small Turkish community in Cyprus certainly could not deal with the Greek majority there on equal terms. Again the spectre of the union of Cyprus and Greece rose; though Makarios did not press this point, he spoke of it from time to time as an objective. Turkey again spoke of the partition of Cyprus as the only acceptable solution, perhaps with a federation of the two parts.

By March, 1964, all parties had accepted a United Nations peace force on the island for three months; its term was thereafter periodically extended. The UN force guarded a neutral zone along the truce line in the capital of Nicosia and helped to reduce (though it could not prevent) outbursts of fighting in other areas. Under the United Nations resolution the integrity of Cyprus was recognized, but so were the treaty rights (including intervention) of Greece, Turkey, and Britain.

Turkey periodically reaffirmed this right, and on occasion threatened to use it to prevent what her foreign minister had called "genocide" on the island. Greece replied by saying that a Turkish invasion would demand a Greek defense of Cyprus. While the basic problem remained unsolved, fighting died down, only to flare up again at intervals. In June, 1964, President Johnson warned both Greece and Turkey to refrain from military moves. His letter to Inönü became an issue in Turkish domestic politics when it was revealed in January, 1966.

So long as Turkey did not intervene, the Cypriote Turkish minority was certain to come under increasing Greek pressure. Opinion in Turkey was naturally aroused. Inönü's Cyprus policy barely survived a 200-to-194 vote of confidence in the Assembly in June, 1964. Relations with Turkey's NATO partner Greece were of course badly strained, the more so after Ankara felt it had to expel Greek citizens resident in Istanbul as a retaliatory measure. Such expulsions began in the spring of 1964, and continued into 1965. From Greece, meanwhile, soldiers and volunteers clandestinely reinforced the armed Greek Cypriote forces who kept up pressure on the Turkish community there.

A new acute stage was reached in August, 1964, when Turkish planes strafed the northern coast of Cyprus where the Turkish Cypriotes were hardest pressed. The UN achieved a cease fire, but periodically Makarios clamped an economic blockade on this or that Turkish quarter, until UN representations forced cessation. Economic and military aid came to Makarios from Russia via Egypt. By the fall of 1964 fighting on the island had again died down, but no solution for the basic question was in sight. Turkey rejected in 1965 the view of the UN mediator, Galo Plaza, that such a solution was to be sought directly between Greek and Turkish Cypriotes; Turkey still insisted on direct negotiation with Greece. In November, 1967, new Greek Cypriote attacks on Turkish Cypriotes caused another threat of invasion from Turkey. It was averted only by American and United Nations mediation that led Athens to promise withdrawal of the many illegal Greek troops on the island, and Ankara to promise similar withdrawal of the few illegal Turkish soldiers. But in Cyprus itself the situation remained unstable in 1968.

While keeping the public aroused, the Cyprus question markedly affected Turkey's relations with countries other than Greece. Anti-Americanism sprang up in several cities, particularly among some of the more radical student groups. A number of anti-American demonstrations occurred in the summer of 1964 and sporadically in the years following.[1] Most Turks continued to remain friendly to America, but saddened and puzzled. Why, they asked, should America not support a struggle for freedom and human rights in Cyprus as it did in Korea and Vietnam? Why in particular should it not support the country that had fought with it in Korea? Would not America have backed Turkey if Kennedy were still president? The Cyprus issue triggered the questions and demonstrations, but they were symptomatic of a general reaction against too pervasive an American influence in Turkey. The American economic aid had been vital, but should Turkey become so dependent on one source of help, and on one foreign source of technical advice about what was good for Turkey? The American presence —especially the military presence with its NATO contingents, bases, and advisory groups—was too obvious. The 1960 census had counted 16,000 American nationals living in Turkey. Leftist voices were raised against American business firms, especially oil companies, operating in Turkey. Partly in appeasement of the protestors, partly as a gesture to Russia, the last Turkish contingent was pulled out of Korea in 1966.

The Ankara government, while maintaining the NATO alliance and close military and economic connections with America, had begun to follow a somewhat more independent line in foreign policy. It was more responsive to Soviet overtures—which now took a soft rather than a hard line—than at any time since the 1930s. In 1964 a Turkish parliamentary delegation visited Russia; the visit was returned by Russian parliamentarians in 1965. A Russo-Turkish trade agreement was worked out in 1964, supplemented in 1965 and 1967. Russian loans, and advice on some industrial projects, were accepted. In the fall of 1964 the Turkish foreign minister, Feridun Jemal Erkin, visited Moscow—the first such visit since the ill-fated trip of 1939. Foreign minister Gromyko returned the visit in 1965. In that year also the Turkish prime minister, Urgüplü, who had succeeded Inönü, visited Moscow; the Russian premier, Kosygin, visited Ankara in 1966; then Prime Minister Demirel visited Moscow in 1967. From these exchanges the Turks gained modest Russian diplomatic support for their stand on Cyprus: Gromyko and others assured Ankara that they favored protecting the rights of the two communities in an independent Cyprus. None of this meant that Turkey was turning her back on the West. She still knew that Soviet

[1] It should also be remarked that there were anti-American demonstrations in Athens and Cyprus too, as each side accused the United States of insufficient sympathy and aid.

bloc arms went to Makarios. She still wanted American friendship and support. She was glad to be received into the European Economic Community at the end of 1964. But her foreign policy was being given a healthy re-examination.

Meanwhile a new government had ousted the People's Party-dominated coalitions of prime minister Inönü. Early in 1965 his third coalition was upset on a budget vote in the Assembly. The Justice Party, under its newly elected leader Süleyman Demirel, had been chiefly instrumental in the move. A new coalition of the Justice Party and three minor parties, in which Demirel served as deputy premier, was formed under the non-partisan leader, Suat Hayri Ürgüplü. Inönü and the People's Party were for the first time since 1961 in opposition, as new elections were prepared. Six parties competed in the campaign. The People's Party, as before, appealed largely to the older elite of bureaucrats, officers, urban intellectuals, provincial notables and large landowners. The Justice Party appealed to the rising elements in Turkish society: landowning peasants, the growing commercial and industrial middle class, urban labor, the villagers recently migrated to cities.

During the campaign there was real discussion of such issues as land reform, economic development, foreign policy, and even capitalism and socialism. In addition to the Nation Party (representing religious and social conservatism), and the radical rightist Republican Peasants' Nation Party (favoring authoritarian government to speed development and reform), there was now also the Turkish Labor Party. This avowedly Marxist group, also authoritarian in tendency, was led by urban intellectuals, but hoped to capture the labor vote and even a peasant following. Its existence and its arguments affected other parties. The People's Party was pushed a bit left—"left of center" as Inönü said. The Justice Party was obliged to defend free enterprise and foreign investment in Turkey.

In the elections of October, 1965, a Justice Party plurality was expected, although not a majority because of the six-party field. The result, however, was an absolute majority for the Justice Party—53 per cent of the total vote, comparable to the Democratic Party sweep in 1950. The Republican People's Party did much less well than expected, with 29 per cent. Only three per cent of the votes went to the Labor Party, a poor showing that also confounded the prophets. The Justice Party had proved itself a real grass-roots party, with strong local organization. It had inherited not only the mantle but also the substance of the outlawed Democratic Party. Under the new proportional representation system, the Justice Party won 240 seats in the Assembly, the People's Party 134. Labor came in only fifth, with 15 seats. Now for the first time, however, an organized socialist voice was heard in the parliament.

Coalition government then disappeared as the new prime minister, Demirel, formed a Justice Party cabinet. He was a new style of politician —not only in that he had risen from modest origins, for such men as Âli Pasha of the Tanzimat period and Talât Pasha of the Young Turks had risen from similar circumstances to the grand vezirate. But Demirel was an engineer-administrator, with some private business experience and a brief period of study in the United States. He was young, earthy, and a moderate in his party.

Demirel's first task was to prove that the Justice Party could rule responsibly. This he did, winning at least the neutrality if not the approval of the army leaders, so that they ceased to fear that the Justice Party would wreak vengeance on them for the overthrow of the Menderes regime in 1960.[2] He was accepted by President Gürsel, the ex-general. Demirel curbed his right-wingers, maintained a western orientation while pursuing the detente with Russia, and gave the government a stability that helped to improve the economic climate. When Gürsel became so ill that he could not fulfill the duties of the presidency, his successor as Chief of Staff, General Jevdet Sunay, was elected in his place. Sunay, like Gürsel, was an experienced and moderate soldier of the First World War and War of Independence generation. He resigned his army command to take a senate seat, from which he was elected to the presidency in March, 1966. In 1964 and 1965 most of the Democrats who had been condemned to prison by the special tribunal in 1961 had been pardoned. Sunay shortly pardoned the aging Democratic ex-president, Bayar. Sunay in the presidency was one more sign of stability—the army was guardian of the republic, but held itself aloof from ordinary politics.

Some questions about future stability were, nevertheless, posed by the 1965 elections. One was the role that socialism might play. To some of the intellectuals, a planned socialist economy offered more hope

[2] That the ghost of Menderes still lived strongly in popular imagination was demonstrated in November, 1967, when plans were made to rebury his remains at the Eyüb mosque. The ceremonies threatened to produce a large-scale demonstration which might in effect have been a denunciation of the revolution of 1960. An embarrassed Justice Party administration forbade the reburial.

for the nation than the mixed, often inefficient, economy heretofore attempted. They regarded socialism also as a more constructive ideology than the cultural nationalism of Atatürk's day, or the liberalism of the early Menderes regime. The Labor Party had so far been the creature of intellectuals, and had failed to attract the city worker. Would it grow in the future, particularly if the nation failed to make faster economic progress? Another question concerned majoritarian autocracy—would the Justice Party, after its resounding victory, be tempted to curb political opposition and individual liberties like the Menderes regime? In 1966 and 1967 it cracked down on some leftist writers, and proposed measures to curb the extremist publications of both right and left. Would the Justice Party be able to reach accommodation with those intellectuals who feared it would sacrifice genuine westernizing progress by catering to the material, sometimes obscurantist, desires of the small town and village majority of the country? These questions gained added importance in the spring of 1967 when the People's Party split. İnönü and a majority, basing their stand on Atatürkist precedents, took a more leftist position. About a quarter of the People's Party deputies thereupon broke from the party to form their own, reducing further, at least for the moment, the size of the one major opposition party. But the Justice Party government in 1968 continued to avoid authoritarianism.

In the late 1960s, then, Turkey remained a forward-looking nation with a potentially bright future. In comparison to other developing countries of the Middle East she was well advanced. She also had many problems, of which Turks themselves were only too keenly aware. Perhaps the principal problem was how to get the economy moving. The question of political stability was closely tied to economic development. Could the government satisfy popular expectations? Could it propel Turkey forward?

Here was a country of nearly 300,000 square miles, approximately the size of Great Britain and France together. Its immediate primary resource was the land—agriculture and timber. Nearly three-fourths of the population, scattered across the country in villages and in towns of less than 10,000 inhabitants, were still engaged in agricultural pursuits. The agricultural product had grown in recent years, but much of this gain was negated by population increase. The 1927 census reported 13,648,000 people. The 1960 census counted 27,755,000, and in 1965 there were 31,391,000. From 1950 to 1960 the population growth rate was nearly three per cent a year. Fortunately thereafter it slowed a little. Even so, the government embarked in 1966 on a wide-ranging birth control program.

As in other developing countries, the importation of industrial products needed to satisfy both rising expectations and the requirements for further development necessitated an increase in exports. The existing balance of trade was unfavorable; foreign debt alone absorbed over one-third of the income from exports. An increase in exports would have to come in large measure from agriculture, which required more modern methods and education in their use, extension of new irrigation techniques, and the planting of forests to combat soil erosion. Tobacco and cotton were the largest earners of foreign exchange, but Turkey needed to become less dependent on these two crops. Turkey was not so hard pressed for agricultural land as many Middle Eastern countries, but fluctuating rainfall on the central plateau meant that new methods had to be used to avoid barren years after bumper years of grain harvests. Landless farmers and sharecroppers needed their own farms, and fragmentation into uneconomic units had to be avoided—the whole question of land reform and redistribution had made slow headway and was being debated anew in the later 1960s. There was also a problem of rural underemployment, which had been chronic over centuries, but was aggravated by partial mechanization of farming. There was a need for provincially located industry to use this labor to increase the national product.

Since the end of the second World War, many villagers had migrated with their families to shantytown squatters' settlements on the edges of the great cities, seeking employment there, frequently disappointed, and creating a social as well as an economic problem. Many of them, together with other Turks, found employment at good wages in western Europe, especially in West Germany, where in 1965 some 135,000 Turks were working. From Germany they brought back tape recorders, cars, sometimes tractors, and new material desires—as well as an occasional German wife. Their earnings, remitted home, helped considerably to narrow the Turkish balance of payments deficit.

Industrialization, despite progress under the republic, was still in its beginning stages. Turkey had some valuable mineral resources, only partially exploited. Oil wells in the east were producing in modest commercial quantities, as yet, however, insufficient for domestic needs. The five-year development plan begun in 1963 had brought reasonably good results, and great hopes rested on the second five-year plan start-ing in 1968. But government financing of industrial development needed to be paralleled by increased private investment in industry. Such in-vestment did increase in the 1960s. Yet many of the new Turkish middle class, diffident about the long-run economic future, preferred to put their capital into commerce, apartment houses, or other traditional ventures promising a quick return, rather than into industry and manu-facture.

The emergence of this Turkish middle class was one of the significant marks of social change within Turkey. In Ottoman days the Turks had been government officials, soldiers, learned men of Islam, peasants, craftsmen, but had largely left commerce, banking, and industrial management to the Christian and Jewish minorities or to foreigners. Under the republic this had changed, more rapidly since the second World War. Now there was a growing Turkish merchant and entre-preneurial class. Some of them had striking business successes. Their interests were often different from those of the traditional ruling group of officials and army officers.

There was also a small but growing industrial labor force which, when permitted to organize, began to do so. After the 1960 revolution the right to strike was recognized by law. By the mid-1960s it was not uncommon to see picket lines and strike placards; in 1964, for instance, there were 87 small strikes, revealing some abysmally low wage-levels. The new Turkish Labor Party had not, however, yet attracted mass support from these workers.

At the base of society, as always, remained the peasantry. Radio and highway brought the villager into closer contact with the towns and cities. Military service showed the peasant sons a different world, and helped them on to literacy. Those who managed to complete a lycée education could move up into a new social stratum. But the intellec-tual and psychological gulf between city and country remained. Since the peasants had discovered the power of the ballot by 1950, the gulf had political importance. In one sense the 1960 revolution was a pro-test of the traditional elite against the Democratic regime that had favored and enhanced this peasant power. Whether the intellectual gap between cities, on the one side, and small towns and villages, on the other, could be successfully bridged was one of the major Turkish prob-lems. More and better schools would help in the solution. According to the 1965 census about 50 per cent of Turks aged seven and over were still illiterate. Most of these were in the villages.

One index of the difference between city and countryside was the attitude toward religion. The city was more secular, despite its heritage of great mosques and libraries of Islamic learning. The countryside was more religious, though the religion was often a combination of orthodox Islam, mere religiosity, and folk-religion. The support that the Democratic Party got in the 1950s was a sign that Atatürk's secularization had never thoroughly penetrated the villages. Some of the urban intellectuals feared that religious reaction would arise, and as it gained political force would endanger the progressive reforms of the republic. They even spoke of the possibility—it had happened elsewhere—that religious reaction, which they called the "black power," might combine politically with the "red power," which was political radicalism or Communism, to undermine the republic. Communism had few devotees in Turkey, though some of the socialists might be attracted to it. But the black power was still a potential force.

One incident in 1965—exceptional, it must be said—gave food for thought, recalling the Kubilay incident of 1930. In a village in the region of Ismir some school teachers, members of the new educated elite, were attacked by a group of inhabitants because the teachers had sponsored a soccer match among their pupils. It was during the holy month of Ramazan. The villagers had been incited in the mosque by a preacher whom they had brought in for the occasion; he declared to them that the soccer match was ungodly. One of the teachers was almost killed. Gendarmes and troops had to be summoned when administrative officials failed to quell the disturbance and were in turn roughed up. The event, widely reported in the press, caused a soul-searching among Turks: how could such a problem arise in 1965, under the republic?

Yet Turkey had solved many of its problems. It had come a long way since Atatürk's death, a longer way since he had established the new state. National sovereignty was unquestioned. The republic was a fact. The Turks seemed to be determined to make multi-party democracy work. Westernization continued apace. Religion was not dead, nor would it become so, but obscurantism had decreased despite occasional episodes like the soccer incident. Secular law and secular education had come to stay. And a Turkish nationality had been created to fill the new Turkey. True, the Turk fundamentally still believed that

Muslim and Turk were two sides of one coin. It was almost impossible for him to conceive of a non-Muslim Turk, even though he would concede that non-Muslims could be citizens of the Turkish republic. But the Turkish people, as a whole, knew who they were.

In the half-century since the first World War had shattered the Ottoman Empire, the Turkish people had recovered a sense of identity and purpose. From the massive broken trunk there had sprung a new and sturdy tree with the potential for further growth. Growth meant continuing problems—sustaining economic development, reshaping society, educating individual minds, and trying to solve problems without abandoning democratic procedures and partisan politics. The Turkish nation, under the republic, had embarked on its own course and was in charge of its own destiny. It could not grow into a copy of some other country, but would develop in its own way. As Atatürk put it, "We resemble ourselves."

10

Turkey in the
1970s and 1980s

The major political problem to arise since 1965 has been that just indicated, namely, "how to solve problems without abandoning democratic procedures and partisan politics." An important step in the direction of providing a firmer economic and social foundation for partisan politics was the historic move to the middle left made by the Republican People's Party in 1965. With this shift İsmet İnönü hoped to deflect the new and powerful leftist current of opinion, which had appeared in society in the early 1960s, away from the Turkish Worker's Party founded in 1961. In 1965 this new stance did not appeal to the electorate, as indicated earlier. Not surprisingly the Party then lost a quarter of its less socialist Republican deputies of the old guard to a new and more central Reliance Party, led by the late Professor Turhan Feyzioğlu. The socialist, but liberal, Bülent Ecevit then became Secretary-General of the People's Party, and eventually displaced İnönü from power in 1972.

In the 1969 elections the Justice Party again won a majority of seats but was much less secure than it seemed. In 1970 it too then lost deputies (16%) who left to found a more right wing party, the Democratic Party. These developments occurred against a background of mounting political violence initiated by armed leftist groups operating at first from the universities. They were frustrated by the electoral failure of the new socialist Turkish Workers' party and were generally hostile to the "bourgeois" regime. Among their targets was "American imperialism", which led them to burn the American Ambassador's car and protest violently against a visit by the American Sixth fleet to Istanbul. But before long their main struggle was against armed rightist groups, which had emerged expressly to oppose them. When the major political parties showed they were unable to combine in order to suppress this violence the military intervened, on 12 March 1971, in what has become known as "the coup by memorandum". The government was forced to resign.

The military brought thousands to trial. They were accused principally of violence or of fomenting class conflict. A series of "above-party" governments was then appointed by the military. The first of these lasted eight months. It was partly technocratic in composition, and reformist in policy. Its program proposed land reform, a tax on agricultural wealth, stricter control of foreign investment, state-led development, and more "social justice". Faced with serious opposition in the Assembly, which was still allowed to remain in being, it resigned. Three decreasingly radical governments followed until new elections were held in 1973. At this point the major political parties jointly rejected a candidate sponsored by the military for President - a surprising degree of accord which unfortunately did not persist. Having done better than its principal rival at the polls, Ecevit's Republican People's Party, the heir to Atatürkist secularism, joined in an unlikely and stormy coalition with the new religious National Salvation Party led by Necmettin Erbakan. In 1974 Ecevit became immensely popular at home for authorizing the invasion of northern Cyprus to protect the Turkish-speaking minority there. But in 1975 Demirel was back in power again. Through coalitions with the National Salvation Party and the new, small, near-fascist Nationalist Action Party, or with the help of the independents, he remained in power until 1980 - save for just over a year in 1978/79, when Ecevit held office again in what was always a finely balanced parliament.

Firm government was badly needed, but was not provided. Although the freedoms of the 1961 Constitution had been somewhat curtailed after military intervention, Demirel's governments always complained that governmental power was still crippled. Certainly no government proved able to halt the new rise in violence which occurred, and which had no doubt been encouraged by the release of 4000 of those tried and convicted after the military intervened. Whilst at first the terrorist groups which emerged, or re-emerged, made targets of one another, rather than of the major political parties, or the institutions of the state, violence soon escalated and reached these areas. A good deal of latent social violence became manifest as a consequence too. In December 1978, for instance, political instigation inflamed underlying hostilities between *Sunni* (orthodox) and *Alevi* (Shi'ite) communities in Kahramanmaraş. Some 3,500 persons are estimated to have died from acts of violence in 1980. Moreover, to add to the disruption, the labor unions were deeply divided politically. Benefiting from the right to strike restored after the end of military intervention, they caused widespread upheaval. Other organizations, like business associations, schools and universities (and their professional associations) were deeply politicized. So too were areas of the public bureaucracy, including the police. Meanwhile the factionally deadlocked Grand National Assembly repeatedly failed to elect a new President of the Republic.

The politics of the whole decade were enacted against a background of severe economic difficulty, in which the world-wide oil price rise of 1974 played a large part. Economic instability also arose from the determination of governments to maintain the investment drive (which produced remarkable growth rates). Also, during the latter part of the decade there were recurrent large trade deficits, as well as rising public sector deficits due in large measure to the losses made by the State Economic Enterprises. The financing of shortfalls by monetary expansion was a major factor in creating super-inflation, which in 1979 reached over 70 per cent and in 1980 climbed to over 100 per cent at one point. "By 1978, in fact, Turkey already had one of the world's highest inflation rates..." (Hale, *The Political and Economic Development of Modern Turkey*, p.162). In this environment demonstrations, strikes and shutdowns were almost inevitable, and there was no shortage of political activists to encourage them.

When in 1978 the economic situation became critical Ecevit had to have recourse to international loans and standby arrangements which included conditions requiring cuts in public spending, devaluation, and realistic pricing of the products of the public enterprises - measures always extremely difficult for a socialist government to accept.

As the violence increased and the two major parties did not find the will to combine to stop the drift into chaos, the military command intervened again in a bloodless coup on 12 September 1980 under the leadership of the Chief of the General Staff, General Kenan Evren. The two major parties could still not respond to the military's continued demand for a common front - so adversarial had politics become. Frustrated by this apparent lack of concern for the public weal, the military finally decided, more than a year after they had intervened, to abolish all political parties (October 1981). They also closed down both left wing and right wing labor unions leaving only one moderate union in restricted operation. The universities were brought under strict control; numbers of academics were dismissed, or transferred to less desirable universities. Severe measures were taken to depoliticize the public service. Martial law was extended to the whole country and terrorist groups were hunted out - with results immediately beneficial for public safety. A 160 member Consultative Assembly was then selected by the military from among some 11,000 applicants. All those who had belonged to the political parties which had been abolished were excluded, as they were also later to be excluded in a new Constitution, from participating in party activities and from running for office. A civilian government was chosen, but the real control lay with the National Security Council composed of senior military officers under the leadership of General Evren. The new regime was quickly accepted by the West; the new rulers reaffirmed Turkey's membership in NATO, and applied with vigor in the new more controlled environment those policies for tighter economic management which had been advocated by international monetary bodies. The military stayed in power until 1983, when new elections were held.

The new Constitution drafted by the Assembly, but closely monitored by the National Security Council, was submitted to a referendum. It was linked, however, with the nomination of the popular General Evren for the position of President - a conjunction which rather clouded the issue in the public mind. The Constitution strengthened the powers of the President, but did not create a presidential form of government. It restricted the scope of political freedoms in order, the military argued, to prevent their continued abuse by those who sought to undermine the foundations of a liberal and democratic state. The military were determined to restrict the influence of the politicians of the abolished parties. They found ways to prevent all but the Motherland Party, the Nationalist Democracy Party (which they clearly favored) and a new moderate left wing Populist Party from contesting the elections.

To the chagrin at first, it seemed, of the military, the moderate right wing Motherland Party won 45 per cent of the vote and, thanks to a new, less proportional system of representation, over half the seats in the Assembly. The Party was led by Turgut Özal, an engineer (but educated also in economics) who had been a deputy prime minister in the government set up by the military in 1980. Its popularity was confirmed in freer conditions in the local elections of 1984 when its most potent rival was allowed into the contest, namely the left wing Social Democratic Party, under Erdal İnönü (son of İsmet İnönü). Faring badly in these elections the Nationalist Democracy and Populist parties began to disintegrate. By 1986 the Assembly was still dominated by the Motherland Party, but another party on the moderate right had found a substantial place for itself - the True Path Party - guided, because it could not legally be led, by the former Prime Minister Süleyman Demirel. The other former Prime Minister, Bülent Ecevit, worked behind the scenes too, his wife leading a new quite leftist and small Democratic Left Party, which refused to unite with the moderate left. In by-elections in 1986 the Motherland Party lost some ground. However, anxious to show that it could win the vote, especially over Demirel, Özal's government proposed a referendum to determine whether former party leaders banned from politics by the Constitution could in fact thenceforth participate openly. By less than one per cent the electorate voted in their favor.

With confidence renewed after so marginal a victory for the opposition, the government advanced the general election to November 1987. The Motherland Party won just over 36 per cent of the votes, but a remarkable 65 per cent of the seats. The feared rival, Demirel's True Path Party, won 19.5 per cent of the votes, but earned only 13 per cent of the seats. The chief opposition party still therefore remained the Socialist Democratic Populist Party (as it had now become) under Erdal İnönü; it won 25 per cent of the votes and 22 per cent of the seats. Ecevit's party did not win a seat and he retired from politics. The party led by the former Islamic and nationalist party leaders also failed to achieve parliamentary representation. The new electoral system had achieved its object of depriving minor parties of the excessive influence they had been able to exert in the balanced parliament before 1980. The electoral system now favored is one that enhances the parliamentary representation of the party which wins most votes - a system which, ironically, was important in leading to excessive dominance by one party betwen 1950 and 1960, and to the 1960 military coup, whose self-justification was the curbing of the tyranny of the majority.

As has been mentioned, in the economic sphere a significant change in economic policy, which had been inaugurated under the governments in the late 1970s, was consolidated after military intervention in 1980. This was the move away from the import substitution policies of the previous two decades to the development of an economy exposed to market forces and international competition. Özal had been a leader in this move. To some degree import substitution policies had fulfilled their purpose in laying the foundations for industrial development, but at the expense of agriculture, and of the larger and more efficient industries hampered in their export efforts by the maintenance of an expensive lira. The new directions were maintained with enthusiasm by the government of the Motherland Party, and were reiterated in its economic program of 1984, which was informed by monetarist policies, and benefited from the improved industrial discipline which followed military intervention. It did not altogether work out as planned, however. Government spending proved difficult to contain, and the export successes of the early 1980s could barely be sustained, let alone augmented. There were balance of payments and current account deficits, with 1986 being a bad year for exports to Iran and Iraq. However, trade had been growing with the EEC countries, which in 1986 took almost 44 per cent of Turkey's exports, this proportion having steadily risen from 30.5 per cent in 1982. In 1987 exports recovered, with the result that the current account deficit was almost halved from the $1.5 billion at which it stood in 1986. On capital account, debt repayments constituted some 7 per cent of GNP. Debt service payments fell to 30.4 per cent of export earnings, a favorable reduction from the 36.1 per cent ratio of the previous year. Despite these strains the credit available created conditions for an ebullient economy, marked by average growth rates of some five to six per cent over the five year period up to 1987, and exceeded in that year. The most intractable and dangerous problem was that of inflation, which at the end of 1987 was over 50 per cent according to most estimates. The reasons for this were said to lie in the structure of the economy (in over-regulation and lack of competition, for example) as well as in economic policy; it has been suggested that "there may be an inflation threshold below which it may be very difficult to descend" (OECD Economic Surveys, Turkey, 1986-87, p.17). In the summer of 1988 very high inflation, the large foreign debt and declining exports were making serious inroads into the government's popularity. Strikes and instances of political violence were also reappearing in sufficient seriousness to remind some observers of the troubled conditions of the previous decade. In June 1988 Özal was shot at in an assassination attempt, and slightly wounded (by a rightist, it is reported) whilst addressing a party conference in Ankara.

It was against a more stable background that in April 1987 the government rather suddenly applied for full membership in the European Community, Turkey having been an associate member since January 1964. This would seem to be a long enough period for adjustment, but the experience of associate membership has by no means proved to be untroubled. The Association Agreement of 1963 principally required a customs union to be established in stages. In 1970 an Additional Protocol was signed, to become operative in 1973; it laid down the details of the move to a full customs union, which entailed immediate free entry for most Turkish industrial exports, but required a long period to achieve completely free entry for Community exports to Turkey. The free movement of workers was also to be realized gradually before 1986 an issue which causes considerable disquiet in Europe.

After the signing of the Additional Protocol a number of external and internal factors began to muddy the picture. Externally, the Community was enlarged from six to nine in 1973, and the prospect of the second enlargement (Spain, Portugal and Greece) appeared on the horizon as something of a threat to Turkey's position, not least to the acceptance for Turkey of the principle of the mobility of workers. (There are many workers from Spain, Portugal and Greece who work elsewhere in the Community and who will eventually expect to have the *right* to work there.) Moreover the Community began to develop a Global Mediterranean Policy, which was also seen to undermine the Turkish Association Agreement. So too were other arrangements made with Third World countries which in certain respects Turkey resembled. Further, the Additional Protocol contained its own ambiguities, like the lack of definition of the rights of Turkish workers in the Community. Nor did it serve to prevent certain states, including Britain, denying Turkish textile imports the access originally envisaged. Internally, the 1970s were years of upheaval in Turkish politics when anti-European sentiments found ready expression in some political and administrative quarters, notably on the left and on the Islamic and nationalist right. These attitudes, enhanced by the sheer economic difficulties which the oil price rise had helped create, largely negated attempts to negotiate in detail and so to implement the Association Agreement.

The accession to power of the Demirel government in 1979 provided an opportunity for new initiatives. Turkey now showed a determination to press on for full membership in the Community before the inclusion of Spain, Portugal and Greece might make accession much more difficult. The move to a freer economy also created a better atmosphere for negotiation. Consequently, before military intervention in 1980 there were signs of much closer collaboration between the Community and Turkey. The Community prepared proposals, which were accepted by the Association Council, for closer integration of the Turkish economy, including a financial protocol promising some $650 million in a loan to Turkey. This was held up in 1981 at the instance of the European Parliament, however, which was concerned about human and political rights in Turkey. It had still not been released in early 1988, thanks to blocking by Greece, and was a subject discussed with the Turkish government by the British Prime Minister, Mrs Thatcher, on her visit to Ankara in April of that year. When Turkey applied for membership, the general advice received from Community governments was the need first to develop the Turkish economy further, to allay doubts about political and human rights, and to come to some agreement with Greece. On her visit to Ankara Mrs Thatcher pointed to the need to develop the existing Association Agreement first.

Relations with Greece have certainly been to the forefront of Turkish foreign relations since 1964. Although there have been, and continue to be, heated disputes concerning sovereignty over the Aegean seabed and the use of Aegean airspace, the prime cause of dissension with Greece is Cyprus, which Greece clearly wishes to have linked to consideration of Turkey's request to join the European Community. The present crisis in relations over Cyprus goes back to the problems of 1963 noted earlier. In that year President Makarios had expressed his dissatisfaction with the 1960 Constitution. He claimed that it had been forced upon Cyprus and maintained that it should be overhauled to reduce the power, and particularly the veto power, of the Turkish Cypriot community, which constituted less than a fifth of the whole. Turkish Cypriot protests led to violence, the introduction of a UN peace-keeping force, and threats by Turkey to come to the aid of the Turkish Cypriots. American hostility to a threatened Turkish invasion made the United States very unpopular in Turkey. Then in 1974, after a *coup d'état* in Cyprus threatened to unite the island with Greece, the Turkish government did intervene militarily in Cyprus - and extended her action when her demands were not met at the London Conference. The United States Congress, in reaction to these events, placed an embargo on arms to Turkey; it was not raised until 1978, despite the understanding for Turkey's position shown by the American administration.

The Cyprus affair not only embittered relations with Greece, therefore, but also powerfully helped Turkey turn against the United States. Other factors played their part too. As early as 1962, at the time of the Cuban crisis, the United States withdrew Turkey-based missiles, without fully consulting the Turkish government, in return for the Soviet withdrawal of missiles from Cuba. Then again, American pressures on Turkey since the mid-1960s to restrict her profitable opium cultivation (from which 80 per cent of heroin on the American market was said to derive) were widely regarded in Turkey as unwarranted. It was not until 1974 that Turkey introduced measures to control poppy harvesting in order to eliminate the illegal drug trade. This estrangement inclined Turkey to be less accommodating to the United States and to modify her policies towards others. A softer line towards the Soviet Union was adopted and greater control was exercised over American military bases in Turkey.

Under the influence too of the oil price rise (and the economically serious American arms ban) Turkey also began to pay more sympathetic attention to the Middle East. Turkey became, somewhat guardedly, pro-Palestinian and has in recent years played an important part in the Islamic Conference, though her main interests are clearly economic. In the early 1980s nearly half of Turkey's exports went to the Middle Eastern countries. Since 1980 relations with the United States have been stabilized with the signing in that year of a new Defense and Economic Cooperation Agreement. Negotiations for its renewal in 1986 were held up over the level of aid for military modernization and trade issues, but in February 1988 Turkey ratified the extension of the Agreement for up until 1990. Nevertheless these events, and, of late years, the relative decline in American world power, have led to a diversification of Turkish foreign policy since the 1950s, including her Association Agreement with the European Community in 1963 and her application to become a full member in 1987. If Turkey does succeed in this application, which will take a number of years to decide, she will be satisfying one of Atatürk's ambitions, namely to see Turkey develop into a fully-fledged European state.

Atatürk clearly wished to lay history aside and concentrate on the future. The same cannot be said, however, for some sections of the world's Armenian community. Inflamed by the recollection of the massacre of Armenians in eastern Turkey in 1915, they have in recent years called for revenge and compensation, and even for the cession of territory. From the mid-1970s terrorist groups began to conduct a campaign of assassination of Turkish diplomats and attacks on the institutions and installations of those countries where Armenian terrorists had been apprehended and prosecuted. Accusations of French dilatoriness in bringing culprits to justice have led to a deterioration of Turco-French relations. With Syria and Lebanon, where Armenian terrorists were alleged to have been trained, relations have also been strained. In the United States the Senate called for awareness of the "documented" massacres of the Armenians and voted the designation of 24 April as a "national remembrance day of man's inhumanity to man". In 1987, however, the House of Representatives defeated such a resolution, believing it contrary to American interests and based on debatable interpretations of historical events. The Turkish Government has claimed that those Armenians who died during the war from whatever cause numbered some 300,000, not one and a half million, as sometimes asserted, and that the Armenians largely brought their misfortunes upon themselves through their participation in armed risings supporting a Russian invasion during the First World War.

A more pressing and more internal problem for the Turkish government in recent decades has been that of the Kurdish minority in Eastern Anatolia, the former rivals of the Armenians, some of whose lands they occupied in Eastern Turkey after the events of the First World War. They now probably constituite some eight to ten per cent (perhaps more) of the population of Turkey. They are orthodox *Sunni* Muslims, like the vast majority of Turks, but speak an Iranian language not recognized as official by the Turkish government. Kurdish leaders have not held back from participating in Turkish political and social life. The small New Turkey party formed after the restoration of democratic politics in 1961 had a good deal of Kurdish support, and in later years Kurds voted for a variety of parties, often those promoted by their own tribal and other traditional leaders. In one of the short-lived governments set up after the military intervention of 1971 a Kurd, Ferit Melen, became Prime Minister; in 1979 the Minister of Works, Serafettin Elçi, was criticized for employing too many Kurds in his department and thus favoring them over available Turkish employees. Social and economic integration has been furthered by the fact that many Kurds have sought work in other parts of the country with the rapid development of Turkey over the past few decades. However, it has been claimed that so many Kurds have worked in western Turkey, where they have lived together in their own communities, that they have developed a greater consciousness of their own identity. In the 1970s it seems that leaders began to emerge from these groups in the west of the country. It is not therefore surprising if these leaders were impressed by the problems of industrialized society and imparted a very leftist orientation to their Kurdish nationalism. The main focus of discontent after 1971 became the radical Kurdistan Workers' Party, often referred to as Apoists, after the name of their leader, Apo (Aptullah Öcalan), though there were other groups as well. The arrest and trial of members of the Kurdistan Workers' Party and others after military intervention in 1980 did not halt Kurdish guerrilla activity in the east. But this has taken the old accustomed form, since its revival in 1982, of incursions from the Kurdish areas of Iraq and Iran. Kurdish separatists have not only attacked Turkish soldiers, but also civilian Kurdish supporters of the government in Kurdish villages. From time to time Turkish government forces have carried the offensive to separatist guerrillas in Iraqi and Iranian territory with the agreement of the governments of those two states, and pressure has been brought on Syria for stricter frontier control. Although the evidence suggests that there is a significant separatist movement, the notion that in the 1980s the bulk of the Kurdish inhabitants of Turkey were seething under a Turkish yoke is one to be approached with the greatest caution.

The major trials of those accused of various anti-state offenses before and immediately after military intervention in 1980, including those of Kurdish separatists, were largely concluded by the end of 1987. One of the trials which attracted most attention outside Turkey was that of some 2000 members of the Confederation of Revolutionary Labor Unions *(DİSK)* which was banned after 1980. After proceedings lasting five years 264 former members of *DİSK* were sentenced by military court to terms of imprisonment for seeking to establish the superiority of one class of society over others. There was no significant evidence of engagement in violence or of plots to overthrow the state, though one defendant was found to have had connections with the notorious Revolutionary Path *(Dev Yol)* terrorist group. Those convicted were deprived of rights to participate in labor union and political party activities; many of those convicted were eligible for immediate release, having been held in custody for long periods awaiting trial.

Another trial which attracted criticism inside and outside Turkey was that of members of the Turkish Peace Association, who were accused of belonging to an organization which sought to overthrow the state. At the conclusion of the trial in 1987 twelve prison sentences were handed down, including a four year sentence given a former Turkish ambassador to India, Mahmut Dikerdem. Only two of the accused faced further imprisonment. In 1986 and 1987 the trials of former members of the near-fascist Nationalist Action Party resulted in eight death penalties, fifteen sentences of life imprisonment, and 255 other, sometimes long, prison sentences. The far right thus did not escape lightly, but the majority of those found guilty were of the extreme left.

After the military take-over the leader of the small but influential National Salvation Party, Necmettin Erbakan, was accused of attempting to create an Islamic state in Turkey. At first found guilty, he was acquitted later in 1985. In fact official treatment of the religious right was not at all severe. That party was not involved in promoting violence, yet fear of the revival of Islam was one of the most important factors impelling the military to intervene. However, the Prime Minister, Turgut Özal, liberal and secularist though he is, was once a member of the National Salvation Party and there is a strong religious wing to the Motherland Party.

This situation in the Party reflects and encourages the marked revival of religious belief and popular practise evident in society. There has been an increase in the activity of dervish orders, despite their official proscription. Turks continue to be attracted to the *hajj,* the pilgrimage to Mecca, which the Prime Minister has himself recently made. There are said to be instances still of polygamy, which is against the law: one marriage may be through official process, but another may take place through a religious ceremony only. Children born about the same time to different wives may apparently be found registered as "twins" born to the same woman; in this way civic appearances are maintained at least. Many among the less educated women wear head scarves; but in recent years some of the students have started to wear them in university classrooms. Yet in 1982 and 1984 European beauty contests Turkish girls won the Miss Europe title. Completely westernized women continue to be prominent in the professions, in offices, and in shops. Iran has beamed broadcasts to Turkey to persuade Turks that Turkish democracy is not compatible with true Islam, and may have sent in agents primed with the same message. But the warning that comes across from the thousands of Iranian refugees who have been given temporary asylum in Turkey is to beware of the example of Khomeini.

Apart from the production of a voluminous popular literature, the greatest success of the revival of Islam in Turkey would appear to be its enhanced influence in educational institutions. In recent years there has been a marked increase in the teaching hours allotted in schools at all levels to Islamic culture and ethics. And the numbers of teachers of these subjects has shown a corresponding increase. In addition, there are now many high schools *(lises)* established for the purpose of training prayer leaders and preachers, constituting about one in three of all high schools. Almost one third of Turkish universities also now have faculties of theology. There has been something of a tussle between the President (reflecting still powerful secularist attitudes) and the government over its permissiveness when dealing with issues like the wearing by women students of traditional Islamic head coverings. In his new year address in 1987 President Evren specifically warned the nation against anti-secularism, and the military has shown concern about the growth of religious education in the schools. Yet the military's position is not without ambiguity, because it has come some way to accepting a common view that traditional Islam is a prophylactic against communism, and also perhaps against the new ideological religious fundamentalism itself.

Clearly the Motherland Party has provided a means for the reconciliation of religion and secularism at the level of practical politics. The Islamic wing of the Motherland Party influences, but does not dominate, the government. In the country generally religious awareness has revived, but does not seek exclusive political expression. In the 1987 general election the vote for the specifically religious Welfare Party led by Erbakan - less than seven per cent - suggested little support among the electorate for anything like a rigorously Islamic regime. Nor do the central secular institutions of the state appear to be significantly penetrated by those who would promote a full fundamentalist Islamic revival.

In the late 1980s Turkey was still a rapidly growing and changing country. By mid-1988 its population was about 54 millions, the product of a growth rate of almost 2.5 per cent per year. This rate of increase adds over a million new Turks annually to an already formidable total. The population continues to be very young; over half are below twenty years of age. Turkey can feed all these people, and can feed an increasing population for some time to come, but rapid population growth does nothing to alleviate the considerable unemployment (estimated at about 16 per cent) and underemployment that have existed in recent years. Urbanization has speeded up. By the time of the 1985 census thirty-five cities had over 100,000 inhabitants each; together these cities contain a third of the country's population. The same census showed that, counting the smaller cities too, Turkey's population had become predominantly urban for the first time in the country's history. Turkey also continues to have large numbers of workers abroad - in 1987 there were 1,800,000 Turks in European Community countries alone, West Germany having the largest contingent.

The number of Turkish children who attend school has been constantly increasing. According to the 1980 census 68 per cent of the population over five years old could read and write; among males literacy was 80 per cent, among females 55 per cent. Today these percentages should be higher. Education continues to expand at the top too. There has been almost an orgy of university founding. By 1986 twenty-seven universities were conferring degrees, some possessing only a few faculties, others with as many as ten or eleven. Under the impact of educational development the vocabulary of the Turkish language still shows a capacity to expand, with new words being cultivated from Turkish roots in a continuing effort, that has not relaxed since Atatürk's times, to replace words of Arabic and Persian origin. But the vocabulary of older Turks does not often keep pace with the general expansion of vocabulary, whilst younger Turks generally do not know many of the older Arabic and Persian words. This trend is encouraged by the wide use of neologisms in the vigorous and diverse newspaper press, especially in its more radical sections. In fact, a person's political complexion can often be deduced from the words he or she chooses to use. In the press there is wide reporting of events and opinions, both national and foreign. But reporters and editors practice self-restraint on some sensitive matters so as not to transgress the limits on press freedom, which are laid down in the Constitution - where the principle of the freedom of the press is itself asserted, however.

Despite urbanization, in 1986 nearly nine million Turks, or about 58 per cent of the work force over fifteen years of age, were officially estimated to be still engaged in farming, forestry, fishing and related pursuits. By 1987, however, nearly three fourths of all Turkish exports were manufactured products. Industry is growing apace. By 1986 the Turkish Murat, basically a Fiat, had outdistanced the Anadol and the Turkish-built Renault; there were 338 thousand of them on the roads in that year. The vehicle population in Turkey is probably increasing faster than the human; in 1986 the number of cars and trucks on the roads in Turkey reached nearly 1.7 million. It was estimated that over a thousand new vehicles were licensed every week in Istanbul alone, while few old cars were retired from service. Starting in 1983, in four years Turkey built an aircraft factory from the ground up and went into production. In this and other manufacturing and commercial ventures foreign companies have increasingly participated. By 1986 over six hundred of them had invested 1.8 million dollars in Turkey. The establishment in the 1980s of free trade zones, without customs duties and corporate tax, favors foreign business. The old fear of foreign capital seems to have disappeared now that there are no more capitulatory privileges such as existed in Ottoman days, and now that the Turkish government stresses the importance of foreign investment for development. Turkey is still at the low end of the scale of industrializing countries, but at the top of late developing countries with an estimated per capita income of $1250 a year.

Some large-scale projects symbolize Turkey's growth. The pipeline of the 1970s that carries Iraqi oil through Turkey to the Mediterranean is one. The huge GAP project (*Güneydoğu Anadolu Projesi*, or Southeast Anatolia Project) for damming Euphrates water and taking it in tunnels to distribute over an area of some 75,000 square kilometers in eastern Anatolia was well under way in the later 1980s, and was to double the reclaimed agricultural land of Anatolia. A proposal to build a pipeline from rivers in south central Turkey to the Arabian peninsula for the supply of fresh water there was being studied in 1988.

Contacts with other countries have grown apace, not only with the expansion of business and with the comings and goings of Turkish workers abroad, but also with the upsurge in tourism. Throngs of European tourists, and a good many Japanese and Americans, have now discovered Turkish beaches, harbors, and antiquities. New hotels and motels have sprouted into being. The Turkish authorities have been working hard at the restoration and preservation of historic monuments. The Mayor of Istanbul, Bedrettin Dalan, has led a campaign that has not only cleaned up the industrial shore of the polluted Golden Horn, transforming it into parkland, but is also tackling the problem of the polluted water itself with marked effect. Other plans, including the construction of high rise buildings, are more controversial. Istanbul has increasingly become a chosen center for international conferences of all kinds. The first bridge across the Bosporus, opened in 1973 to connect Europe to Asia by road, has been enormously successful in carrying Turkish daily commuters, foreign tourists, and the never-ending procession of double-trailer trucks bound from western Europe to Anatolia, Iran, and other points beyond. In July 1988 a second parallel bridge was officially opened when the Prime Minister drove his car across - followed by a hundred buses bearing pilgrims on the start of their journey to Mecca.

To conclude, since the mid-1960s Turkish history has shown a number of developments. In the first place, it is clear that the revivalist force of Islam, so powerful elsewhere in the Middle East, has been contained, though Islam has become more conspicuous in private and public life. Its fundamentalist version has not gained electoral support and the Islamic revival has had to live with, rather than seek to overthrow, the secular norms strongly embedded in Turkish society by Atatürk, and by some of his reforming predecessors. Secondly liberal democracy, if now more restricted in some important respects, has survived, after being rescued from mounting chaos by the military, who have certainly been at pains to preserve the framework of a liberal and democratic state. In the process they have asserted what is often forgotten, namely that liberal democracy cannot be a free-for-all, but is a form of *government* located within a *state*. The adversarial character of Turkish politics, the politicization of social and economic institutions (including the machinery of the state itself) and the political disruption caused by small groups and parties opposed to the system, were the major dangers to Turkish democracy in the decade before 1980. Some of them could arise again. Thirdly, the last decade has seen a revolution in economic policy in the direction of international economic competition, the greater encouragement of private enterprise in Turkey, and a steadily growing national product. This has been accompanied by a more disciplined labor force, which was fast becoming unruly before

1980. Finally, the last twenty years have witnessed some variation in Turkish foreign policy, in which the Cyprus question and very uneasy relations with Greece have played a major part. In the first half of 1988 a Turco-Greek dialogue was established between the prime ministers of the two countries giving some hope of a settlement of differences. The Central Treaty Organisation (CENTO) has been dead since 1979 when events in Pakistan and Iran destroyed it. However, Turkey is now more involved in the Middle East, especially in economic relationships. Yet this has not weakened her adherence to NATO, and by her application for full membership of the European Community in 1987 Turkey has again signalled her intention to achieve acceptance as a fully European state. This is a large question not only for Turkey but also for the Community, which is fearful of being overwhelmed by the economic, social and cultural difficulties Turkey's entry might initially create; some of its members also realize, perhaps, that Turkey's size, population, and potential for development are likely in the longer term to earn a very large say in Community affairs for a country whose Europeanness is still not accorded universal credence.

Suggested Readings

A people with a long history naturally have a long bibliography. This selection omits almost entirely the voluminous work in Turkish and in languages other than English. Focused on modern history, it omits also many out-of-print classics on the Ottoman Empire that are in English, and all works specifically on the non-Turkish peoples of that empire. Reliable guides to such books are the bibliographies cited at the end, and those in the books mentioned below.

A profile of modern Turkey, from various viewpoints, may be drawn from these: pictorially, Desmond Stewart and the Editors of *Life, Turkey* (New York, 1965) and also the books, brochures, and maps issued from time to time by the Turkish Ministry of Tourism and Information (formerly Press, Broadcasting and Tourism Department); geographically, William B. Fisher, *The Middle East*, 3rd ed. (New York, 1956); touristically, Hachette World Guides, *Turkey* (Paris, 1960); statistically the official *Türkiye Istatistik Yilliği* (Statistical Yearbook of Turkey) issued periodically in Ankara, which is easily understood since the numbers are arabic and the headings are in French as well as in Turkish. The best general introduction to modern Turkey is Geoffrey L. Lewis, *Turkey*, 3rd ed. (New York, 1965), written with a sensitive touch. Recent events and developments can best be followed in articles and chronologies in *The Middle East Journal* (Washington, 1947–), a quarterly.

An enticing glimpse of the many civilizations, from the stone age to the Ottoman Empire, which succeeded each other in the territory of present-day

187

Turkey is furnished by the illustrated catalogue of an exhibit of selected pieces from Turkey's museums: Smithsonian Institution, *Art Treasures of Turkey* (Washington, 1966).

There is no up to date and reasonably detailed general history of the Turks and of Turkey. Two very brief paperbacks reflect modern scholarly findings: Robert Mantran, *Histoire de la Turquie*, 2nd ed. (Paris, 1961) and Wayne S. Vucinich, *The Ottoman Empire* (Princeton, 1965). Vucinich adds a selection of readings. Somewhat more thorough as far as political detail is concerned are the sections on Ottoman and republican history by Kissling, Scheel, and Jäschke in *Handbuch der Orientalistik*, ed. Berthold Spuler (Leiden, 1959), VI, Part I, 3, 3–97. Two general texts are more complete: Sydney N. Fisher, *The Middle East: A History* (New York, 1959) and Leften S. Stavrianos, *The Balkans Since 1953* (New York, 1958). The latter, with a valuable bibliography, is excellent down to 1878, but veers away from Turkey thereafter and does not include material on the Turkish Republic, as Fisher does. The great histories of the Ottoman Empire, aside from recent works by Turkish scholars, are still Joseph von Hammer-Purgstall, *Geschichte des Osmanischen Reiches*, 10 vols. (Pest, 1827–1835), also translated as *Histoire de l'Empire Ottoman*, 18 vols. (Paris, 1835–1843); Johann W. Zinkeisen, *Geschichte des Osmanischen Reiches in Europa*, 8 vols. (Hamburg, 1840–1863); and Nicolae Iorga, *Geschichte des Osmanischen Reiches*, 5 vols. (Gotha, 1908–1913). The first two were reprinted in 1963 and subsequent years. There is as yet no replacement for them. Edward S. Creasy, *A History of the Ottoman Turks*, rev. ed. (London, 1877; Beirut, 1962) is essentially based on Hammer, as is George J. S. Eversley and Valentine Chirol, *The Turkish Empire* (London, 1923). Both are full of battles and sultans, and Eversley is rather Turcophobe. Better reading, though shorter and still old, is Stanley Lane-Poole, *The Story of Turkey* (London, 1888; Beirut, 1966); later editions are called simply *Turkey*.

Turkish history is inseparable from Islam. Hamilton A. R. Gibb, *Mohammedanism* [(London, 1949) and the later paperback editions] provides a good general introduction. More specifically Turkish aspects of Islam appear in John Kingsley Birge, *The Bektashi Order of Dervishes* (London, 1937) on the beliefs and practices of that Janissary-associated order; in Frederick W. Hasluck, *Christianity and Islam Under the Sultans*, 2 vols. (Oxford, 1929) on folk-religion and the interplay of the two faiths; and in Leon Ostrorog, *The Angora Reform* (London, 1927) on Ottoman Muslim law, reforms, and the republic's introduction of western codes.

Vasilii V. Barthold, *Histoire des Turcs d'Asie Centrale* (Paris, 1945) gives a concise account of the Turks before Islam. The Seljuk invasion and rule in Anatolia are now best recorded in a freshet of articles, most of them noted in the bibliographies. Claude Cahen, "The Turkish Invasion: The Selchükids," in A History of the Crusades, ed. Kenneth Setton (Philadelphia, 1955), I, 135–76, is easily accessible. Speros Vryonis, in "Seljuk Gulams and Ottoman Devshirmes," Der Islam, 41 (1965), 224–52, shows the continuity from Seljuk to Ottoman times of the slave-levy system for warriors and administrators.

Two significant monographs describe the emergence of the Ottoman state out of Seljuk Anatolia: Paul Wittek, The Rise of the Ottoman Empire (London, 1938) and Mehmed Fuad Köprülü, Les origines de l'Empire ottoman (Paris, 1935). Köprülü criticizes Herbert Adams Gibbons, The Foundation of the Ottoman Empire (Oxford, 1916), which still has value for its broad view. How the Ottoman sultans conquered and organized is succinctly described in Halil Inalcik, "Ottoman Methods of Conquest," Studia Islamica, 2 (1954), 103–29. The Fall of Constantinople, 1453 (Cambridge, 1965) by Steven Runciman, who is somewhat a Grecophile, now replaces Edwin Pears' work of 1903 on the same subject; Franz Babinger's useful (though much criticized for errors) biography of Mehmed the Conqueror exists in German, French, and Italian editions, but not in English. Barnette Miller, The Palace School of Muhammad the Conqueror (Cambridge, Mass., 1941) is a fascinating description of the training of slave administrators. Anthony D. Alderson, The Structure of the Ottoman Dynasty (Oxford, 1956) digests a great deal of interesting information on succession, marriage, harem, fratricide, etc.

The great age of Süleyman is described in Roger B. Merriman's semi-popular Suleiman the Magnificent (Cambridge, Mass., 1944), accenting the military campaigns. Merriman's chapter on government summarizes the classic description by Alfred H. Lybyer, The Government of the Ottoman Empire in the Time of Suleiman the Magnificent (Cambridge, Mass., 1913). The admiration of a westerner for that government appears in the very readable Turkish Letters of Ogier Ghiselin de Busbecq, trans. Edward S. Forster (Oxford, 1927). Europe's relations with the Ottoman Empire are carefully investigated in Dorothy M. Vaughan, Europe and the Turk . . . 1350–1700 (Liverpool, 1954).

Some idea of Ottoman culture, as well as government and society, may be obtained from Bernard Lewis' delightful Istanbul and the Civilization of the Ottoman Empire (Norman, Oklahoma, 1963). The first volume of Elias J. W. Gibb, A History of Ottoman Poetry, 6 vols. (London, 1900–1909) contains a good introduction to Ottoman literature, as does a chapter by him in S. Lane-Poole's Turkey, mentioned above. Ottoman architectural achievement is described and pictured in Behçet Ünsal, Turkish Islamic Architecture in Seljuk and Ottoman Times, 1071–1923 (London, 1959); see also Harrison G. Dwight's chatty Constantinople, Old and New

(New York, 1915) and its nearly identical second edition entitled *Constantinople: Settings and Traits* (New York, 1926) on both architecture and life. Martin Hürlimann, *Istanbul* (London, 1958), has some excellent photographs of buildings. The UNESCO folio volume, *Turkey: Ancient Miniatures* (New York, 1961), reveals in splendid color a little-known Ottoman art; a small paperback edition of the same, *Turkish Miniatures* (New York, 1965), has poorer color but is one-eighteenth as expensive. Both have perceptive introductions by Richard Ettinghausen. The famous *Letters* of Lady Mary Wortley Montagu, from the early 1700s, exhibit an appreciation of Ottoman culture in the age of political decline; available in many editions, the best is *The Complete Letters*, ed. Robert Halsband, vol. 1 (New York, 1966).

Almost exactly contemporary with Lady Mary was Mehmed Pasha, whose "book of counsel," an example of how Ottoman decline appeared to an administrator of the empire, is translated by Walter L. Wright, Jr. as *Ottoman Statecraft* (Princeton, 1935). Eighteenth-century government and society, with much emphasis on historical antecedents, are surveyed in detail in Hamilton A. R. Gibb and Harold Bowen, *Islamic Society and the West*, vol. 1, *Islamic Society in the Eighteenth Century*, 2 parts (London, 1950–1957). Norman Itzkowitz, "Eighteenth Century Ottoman Realities," *Studia Islamica*, 16 (1962), 73–94, suggests modification of some of Gibb and Bowen's views, as well as of Lybyer's.

For the period of westernization that began in the late eighteenth century, there is no better guide than Bernard Lewis, *The Emergence of Modern Turkey* (London, 1961); it reaches to 1950. Niyazi Berkes, *The Development of Secularism in Turkey* (Montreal, 1964), covering almost the same time span, is really an intellectual history. Robert E. Ward and Dankwart Rustow, eds., *Political Modernization in Japan and Turkey* (Princeton, 1964) contains essays on the army, education, press, etc. Stanford J. Shaw, "The Origins of Ottoman Military Reform," *Journal of Modern History*, 37 (1965), 291–306, describes the important new army venture of Selim III. Matthew S. Anderson, *The Eastern Question, 1774–1923* (London, 1966) provides sound coverage of diplomatic aspects, some of which can be back-stopped by documents in the handy collection by Jacob C. Hurewitz, *Diplomacy in the Near and Middle East*, 2 vols. (Princeton, 1956), running from 1535 to 1955. Harold Temperley, *England and the Near East: The Crimea* (London, 1936) describes Ottoman reforms but he is principally interested in diplomatic affairs from 1808 to 1854.

Internal developments from the mid-nineteenth century are discussed in Roderic H. Davison, *Reform in the Ottoman Empire, 1856–1876* (Princeton, 1963), mostly with a political and administrative slant; in

Serif Mardin, *The Genesis of Young Ottoman Thought* (Princeton, 1962), slanted toward political theory; and in Robert Devereux, *The First Ottoman Constitutional Period* (Baltimore, 1963), which examines the 1876 constitution and the parliament that followed. Odysseus (Charles Eliot), *Turkey in Europe* (London, 1900, 1966) is a classic critical view of the time of Abdülhamid II, and Ernest E. Ramsaur, Jr., *The Young Turks* (Princeton, 1957) uncovers the movement that overthrew Abdülhamid in 1908. The life and teachings of the most influential *philosophe* of the Young Turk era, Ziya Gökalp, are the subject of Uriel Heyd's *The Foundations of Turkish Nationalism* (London, 1950); many of Gökalp's articles are translated in *Turkish Nationalism and Western Civilization*, ed. Niyazi Berkes (New York, 1959).

World War I is best described militarily in Maurice Larcher, *La Guerre turque dans la Guerre Mondiale* (Paris, 1926); socially, politically, and economically in Ahmed Emin [Yalman], *Turkey in the World War* (New Haven, 1930); and, from the viewpoint of the Turkish-German alliance, with much new archival information, in Ulrich Trumpener, *Germany and the Ottoman Empire, 1914–1918* (Princeton, 1968). Harry N. Howard, *The Partition of Turkey· A Diplomatic History, 1913–1923* (Norman, Oklahoma, 1931; New York, 1966) has been superseded in spots, but still is a great compendium of information.

Well written personal views by participants in the changes in the last days of empire and the first days of the republic are *Memoirs* (New York, 1926) and *The Turkish Ordeal* (New York, 1928), both by Halide Edib [Adivar], Turkey's leading woman author, and *Turkey in My Time* (Norman, Oklahoma, 1956) by Ahmed Emin Yalman, a prominent newspaper editor. Lord Kinross's (Patrick Balfour), *Ataturk* (New York, 1965) is now the best biography of the republic's founder. Atatürk's own account of the struggle in 1919–1923 is his six-day speech: *A Speech Delivered by Ghazi Mustafa Kemal* (Leipzig, 1929), a not entirely accurate translation of the Turkish; it is often catalogued in American libraries under "Turkey, Reisicümhur." Elaine D. Smith draws on this and other Turkish sources in *Turkey: Origins of the Kemalist Movement . . . 1919–1923* (Washington, 1959). Gordon Craig and Felix Gilbert, eds., *The Diplomats, 1919–1939* (Princeton, 1953; New York, 1963) surveys the nationalists' successful diplomacy in Chapter 6, while Dankwart A. Rustow analyzes the vital military politics of the period in "The Army and the Founding of the Turkish Republic," *World Politics*, 11 (1959), 513–52.

Lewis V. Thomas has a well-informed interpretive essay on the republic under Atatürk and Inönü in Thomas and Richard N. Frye, *The United States and Turkey and Iran* (Cambridge, Mass., 1951). Richard D. Robinson, *The First Turkish Republic* (Cambridge, Mass., 1963) is best on economics, society, and foreign policy. Kemal H. Karpat focuses on political developments and the advent of the multi-party system after 1945 in *Turkey's Politics* (Princeton, 1959). A penetrating analysis of the nature of the ruling group in the republic, principally of deputies in the assemblies of 1920 to 1957, is Frederick W. Frey, *The Turkish Political Elite* (Cambridge, Mass., 1965). How the 1960 revolution came about, its results, and the new elections are analyzed by Walter F. Weiker in *The Turkish Revolution, 1960–1961* (Washington, 1963). Nuri Eren, a Turkish diplomat, examines the beginnings of the second republic against a historical background in *Turkey Today—And Tomorrow* (New York, 1963). The place of religion in the republic is the subject of essays by Howard A. Reed and Dankwart Rustow in Richard N. Frye, ed., *Islam and the West* (The Hague, 1957). Turkish villages, like Indian and African, are beginning to get their resident foreign anthropologists; one of the best studies is Paul Stirling's *Turkish Village* (London, 1965). See also Joseph S. Szyliowicz, *Political Change in Rural Turkey: Erdemli* (The Hague, 1966) and John F. Kolars, *Tradition, Season, and Change in a Turkish Village* (Chicago, 1963) for political and geographical viewpoints. For descriptions and analyses of the republic's economy, the best sources are International Bank for Reconstruction and Development, *The Economy of Turkey* (Baltimore, 1951) and Zvi Yehuda Hershlag, *Turkey, An Economy in Transition*, 2nd ed. (The Hague, 1966). A major question in Turkey's foreign policy is conveniently summarized with documents in a State Department publication, *The Problem of the Turkish Straits* (Washington, 1947), written by Harry N. Howard. George S. Harris, *The Origins of Communism in Turkey* (Stanford, 1967) analyzes on the basis of new evidence the abortive Soviet and Communist efforts to gain a foothold in Turkey, 1918 to 1925. The relationship of education to social transformation and westernization is discussed critically, with emphasis on the lycée, by Andreas M. Kazamias in *Education and the Quest for Modernity in Turkey* (Chicago, 1966).

Two books in this series, "The Modern Nations in Historical Perspective," provide historical and contemporary information on regions that fell away from Ottoman control: Charles and Barbara Jelavich, *The Balkans* (1965) and Robert O. Collins and Robert L. Tignor, *Egypt and the Sudan* (1967).

One of the best sources for concise information on institutions and individuals is the *Encyclopaedia of Islam*, 1st ed., 4 vols. and supplement (Leiden, 1913–1938), especially the second edition (Leiden, 1954–), by 1967 completed up to the letter *H*. The Turkish version, *Islâm Ansiklopedisi* (Istanbul, 1940–), by 1967 completed up to the letter *S*, is often better and fuller on Turkish subjects. Articles in these encyclopaedias include fine bibliographies. Other good bibliographical guides are: American Historical Association, *Guide to Historical Literature* (New York, 1961),

Sections M and S; Jean Sauvaget, *Introduction to the History of the Muslim East*, rev. by Claude Cahen (Berkeley, 1965), Chapters 19 and 23; Richard Ettinghausen, ed., *A Selected and Annotated Bibliography . . . Near and Middle East* (Washington, 1952; with 1954 *Supplement*); John Kingsley Birge, A *Guide to Turkish Area Study* (Washington, 1949). A valuable bibliography of articles is James D. Pearson, *Index Islamicus . . . 1906 to 1955* (Cambridge, 1958), and its *Supplement, 1956–1960* (Cambridge, 1962).

If bibliography palls, relief can be found in the writing that evokes the atmosphere of the old Turkey and the new. Harrison G. Dwight, *Stamboul Nights* (Garden City, 1916) is a collection of short stories on characters and situations of the late empire. Halide Edib [Adivar], *The Clown and His Daughter* (London, 1935), a novel, is set in the reign of Abdülhamid II, portraying humble types in a quarter of Istanbul and government types of the era. Irfan Orga, *Portrait of a Turkish Family* (New York, 1950), a somewhat fictionalized autobiography, is best on the last years of the empire, 1908–1918, and the transition to the republic. A novel by Ann Bridge, *The Dark Moment* (New York, 1952) interprets the atmosphere of the period of the war for independence, 1919–1923. The village peasantry is the subject of the stories—true life, not fiction—of Mahmut Makal, A *Village in Anatolia* (London, 1954). The villager and the landlord in the Taurus region are depicted in Yaşar Kemal, *Memed My Hawk* (New York, 1961). Selections of modern Turkish prose and poetry in English translation take up the whole Winter, 1960–1961, number of *The Literary Review* (Fairleigh Dickinson University, Teaneck, New Jersey).

Additional Suggested Readings

The years since 1967 have produced a spate of writing on Ottoman history and modern Turkey. Only a selection of the best works can be included here, and articles must unfortunately be omitted. The order of arrangement parallels the preceding Suggested Readings.

John C. Dewdney, *Turkey: An Introductory Geography* (London/New York, 1971) can be complemented for past centuries by Douglas E. Pitcher, *An Historical Geography of the Ottoman Empire* (Leiden, 1972). More general introductions to the country and its past are in the fourth edition of Geoffrey Lewis's *Turkey* (London/New York, 1974) and Andrew Mango's *Turkey* (London/New York, 1968). Three general Ottoman histories appeared almost simultaneously: Lord Kinross (Patrick Balfour), *The Ottoman Centuries* (London/New York, 1977), quite readable; Stanford J. Shaw and Ezel K. Shaw, *History of the Ottoman Empire and Modern Turkey* (2 vols.; Cambridge, 1976-77), full of information and sometimes requiring checking; Michael Cook, ed., *A History of the Ottoman Empire to 1730* (New York, 1976), made up of chapters from the *New Cambridge Modern History* and the *Cambridge History of Islam*.

The Turkish penetration of Anatolia is the focus of three scholarly works: Speros Vryonis, *The Decline of Medieval Hellenism in Asia Minor and the Process of Islamization* (Berkeley, 1971; reissue, 1986); Claude Cahen,

Pre-Ottoman Turkey ... 1071-1330 (London/New York, 1968); and Rudi P. Lindner, *Nomads and Ottomans in Medieval Anatolia* (Bloomington, 1983), which discusses the origins of the Ottoman state. So does Halil İnalcık, *The Ottoman Empire: The Classical Age, 1300-1600* (New York, 1973), the best short introduction to the Ottoman rise. It should be supplemented by essays by the same master, İnalcık's *The Ottoman Empire: Conquest, Organization, and Economy* (London, 1978). Norman Itzkowitz's *Ottoman Empire and Islamic Tradition* (New York, 1972) is an even briefer introduction. Metin Kunt gives insight into Ottoman provincial administration at the Empire's height in *The Sultan's Servants* (New York, 1983). *The Historian Mustafa Ali (1541-1600)* looks at the writings and the mind of one government functionary. Suraiya Faroqhi, *Towns and Townsmen of Ottoman Anatolia* (Cambridge, 1984) probes society and economy, as do the many essays in four languages in Osman Okyar and Halil İnalcık, eds., *Social and Economic History of Turkey (1079-1920)* (Ankara, 1980).

Various aspects of Ottoman culture are described in a number of works. Godfrey Goodwin, *A History of Ottoman Architecture* (London, 1971), a big work, spawned a little version, *Ottoman Turkey (Islamic Architecture Series)* (New Rochelle, 1978). Aptullah Kuran has topped off his *The Mosque in Early Ottoman Architecture* (Chicago, 1968) with a detailed study of *Sinan: The Grand Old Master of Ottoman Architecture* (Washington, D.C., 1987). Esin Atil, ed., *Turkish Art* (Washington, D.C., 1980) contains illustrated essays on ceramics, books, carpets, etc. Raphaela Lewis writes about family, festivals, religion, jobs, etc. in *Everyday Life in Ottoman Turkey* (London, 1971); one aspect of this occupies Ralph S. Hattox, *Coffee and Coffeehouses* (Seattle, 1985), on the origins of this Near Eastern social institution.

In the period of increasing western influence Charles Issawi provides a series of source readings with commentary concerning *The Economic History of Turkey, 1800-1914* (Chicago, 1980). Carter Findley examines the administrative personnel and organization in *Bureaucratic Reform in the Ottoman Empire: The Sublime Porte, 1789-1922* (Princeton, 1980). Stanford J. Shaw includes foreign relations as well as domestic aspects in *Between Old and New: The Ottoman Empire Under Sultan Selim III, 1789-1807* (Cambridge, MA, 1971). Kemal H. Karpat gives many figures in *Ottoman Population, 1830-1914* (Madison, WI, 1985), while Justin McCarthy probes in greater detail *Muslims and Minorities: The Population of Ottoman Anatolia at the End of the Empire* (New York, 1983). Ottoman society and economy before the Young Turk Revolution of 1908 are the subject of essays by Donald Quataert, *Social Disintegration and Popular Resistance in the Ottoman Empire, 1881-1908* (New York, 1983). Feroz Ahmad, *The Young Turks ... 1908-1914* (London, 1969) describes their period of rule, and Erik Zürcher, *The Unionist Factor ... 1905-1926* (Leiden, 1984) traces the Young Turk influence from pre-war years to the post-war nationalist movement. The foreign relations of that movement as it created the independent republic are the subject of Salahi Sonyel, *Turkish Diplomacy, 1919-1923* (Beverly Hills, CA/London 1975).

Mustafa Kemal Atatürk is explained, as the title indicates, by Vamık D. Volkan and Norman Itzkowitz in *The Immortal Atatürk: A Psychobiography* (Chicago, 1984); it covers his entire life, emphasizing early years.

Other works on the republican period include an excellent introduction to contemporary Turkey, George S. Harris, *Turkey: Coping with Crisis* (Boulder CO, 1985). A shorter introduction, but with useful detail, is David Barchard, *Turkey and the West* (London, 1985). See also the originally presented *Turkey: The Politics of Authority, Democracy, and Development* by Frank Tachau (New York, 1984) and D.A. Rustow, *Turkey, America's Forgotten Ally* (New York, 1987). A perceptive portrayal of Turkish affairs is by Andrew Mango, *Turkey: A Delicately Poised Ally* (Beverly Hills/London, 1975). A survey of mainly economic developments since the early republic is given by William Hale, *The Political and Economic Development of Modern Turkey* (London, 1981). Also useful for economic developments is *Turkey* by Anne O. Kruger (New York, 1974), as too is Edwin J. Cohn, *Turkish Economic, Social, and Political Change* (New York, 1970). For a recent authoritative analysis of the Turkish economy see Z.Y. Hershlag, *The Contemporary Turkish Economy* (London, 1988). A comprehensive analysis of Turkish political and social development is provided by Walter F. Weiker, *The Modernization of Turkey: From Atatürk to the Present Day* (New York, 1981). The detail of political history is contained in Feroz Ahmad, *The Turkish Experiment in Democracy, 1950-1975* (London, 1977), whilst problems of democracy in Turkey are discussed in *Democracy and Development in Turkey* (Beverley, England, 1979) and *The Crisis of Turkish Democracy* (Beverley, 1983), both by C.H. Dodd. See also his *Politics and Government in Turkey* (Manchester/California, 1969). For valuable contributions on a number of important topics sec William Hale, ed., *Aspects of Modern Turkey* (New York/London, 1976). A discussion of the role of the state in the republic is that by Metin Heper, *The State Tradition in Turkey* (Beverley, 1985). Valuable studies of aspects of Turkish history and politics in the republican period include Jacob M. Landau, *Radical Politics in Modern Turkey* (Leiden, 1974) and *Pan-Turkism in Turkey* (Leiden, 1981), Robert Bianchi, *Interest Groups and Political Development in Turkey* (Princeton, 1984), Ergun Özbudun, *Social Change and Political Participation in Turkey* (Princeton, 1984), Kemal H. Karpat, *Social Change and Politics in Turkey* (Leiden, 1973) and *The Gecekondu: Rural Migration in Turkey* (Cambridge, 1976), Nermin Abadan-Unat, *Turkish Workers in Europe, 1960-1975: A Socio-Economic Reappraisal* (Leiden, 1976) and *Women in Turkish Society* (Leiden, 1981). Other studies of social changes include Paul J. Magnarella, *Tradition and Change in a Turkish Town* (New York, 1974) and Çiğdem Kağıtçıbaşı, ed., *Sex Roles, Family, and Community in Turkey* (Bloomington, 1983). On the role of Islam in political change see Binnaz Toprak, *Islam and Political Development in Turkey* (Leiden, 1981). On developments in foreign affairs an interpretative survey is *Turkey's Foreign Policy in Transition, 1950-1974* (Leiden, 1975) by Kemal H. Karpat. For relations with the United States see George S. Harris, *Troubled Alliance: Turkish-American Problems in Historical Perspective, 1945-1971* (Washington, D.C. 1972).

A superb bibliographical reference work began publication in 1975 in Austria, *Türkologischer Anzeiger/ Turkology Annual* (Vienna, 1975-   ) with classified and indexed references to articles, books, reviews, and Festschrift chapters concerning all aspects of Turkish history, society, and culture, in every conceivable language, from earliest times to the present. *TA*'s annual volumes offer a rich resource. Meral Güçlü, *Turkey* (Santa Barbara CA, 1981) is a bibliography of selected but well annotated items, very useful for its descriptions. Abraham Bodurgil's works are unannotated, but contain articles as well as books: *Atatürk and Turkey ... 1919-1985* (Washington DC, 1974) and *Kemal Atatürk: A Centennial Bibliography* (Washington DC, 1984). The *Encyclopaedia of Islam*, 2nd edition, useful as ever, is now in the letter M, and *İslâm Ansiklopedisi* has come to the end of the alphabet.

A good deal of Turkish literature has been translated into English here and there. Among the good translations are Nermin Menemencioğlu and Fahir İz, eds., the *Penguin Book of Turkish Verse*

(London, 1978); Aziz Nesin, *Istanbul Boy* (2 vols.; Austin TX, 1977-79), a famous writer's delightful reminiscences of a 1920s childhood; Richard L. Chambers and Gunay Kut, eds., *Contemporary Turkish Short Stories* (Minneapolis, 1977), with work of well-known writers; and Talat S. Halman, *Modern Turkish Drama* (Minneapolis, 1976), four plays put into English by an expert.

Index

Turkish terms are defined on the pages indicated by bold-face numbers.

Index

To chapter 10

STATE AND POLITICS
IN THE USSR

19